P9-BJU-654

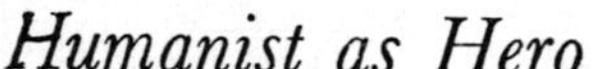

Humanist as Hero

HUMANIST AS HERO

The Life of Sir Thomas More

BY

THEODORE MAYNARD

(Facsimile of the 1947 edition)

HAFNER PUBLISHING COMPANY
NEW YORK
1971

Reprinted by arrangement with The Macmillan Company

Published By
HAFNER PUBLISHING COMPANY, INC.
866 Third Avenue
New York, N. Y. 10022

Library of Congress Catalog Number: 74-15380

Printed in the U. S. A.

To Robert McWilliams

JUDGE OF THE SUPERIOR COURT OF SAN FRANCISCO

The person of the greatest virtue this kingdom ever produced.

SWIFT
Concerning the Universal Hatred
Which Prevails Against the Clergy

He may come to be counted as the greatest Englishman, or at least the greatest historical character in English history.

G. K. CHESTERTON
The Fame of Blessed Thomas More

More was killed, but [his] principles must, in the end, triumph. If they do not, the civilization of Europe is doomed.

R. W. CHAMBERS
Thomas More

Foreword

In the writing of this book I have used the Early English Text Society editions of Roper and Harpsfield and Monsignor Hallett's translation of Stapleton. In the absence of Dr. Elsie Hitchcock's edition of "Ro.Ba," which is still in preparation, I had to fall back on what Christopher Wordsworth published in 1818 in the second volume of his *Ecclesiastical History.* The citations from More himself come from his *English Works,* of which two volumes have so far appeared, edited by W. E. Campbell and with valuable introductions and notes by the editor and Professor Chambers. These give in facsimile the great folio of 1557, along with a slightly modernized version. The *Apology* used is that edited by Dr. Taft and published by the Early English Text Society, and the versions of the *Utopia* and the *Dialogue of Comfort* are those included in Everyman's Library.

Of recent biographies by far the most valuable are those by Professor Chambers, Father Bridgett and Miss Routh. But those by Dean Hutton, the Abbé Bremond, Algernon Cecil, Christopher Hollis and Daniel Sargent have been of service, as is true of a number of other works alluded to in the text. Of special importance, because of their legal knowledge, are the studies by Lord Campbell and Sir James Mackintosh. The letters of Erasmus, as translated by F. M. Nichols and as edited by P. S. Allen and his successors, and the *Calendar of Letters and Papers of the Reign of Henry VIII,* as well as the lives of Henry VIII and Wolsey by A. F. Pollard, should also be mentioned. Unfortunately Elizabeth Frances Rogers' *Correspondence of Sir Thomas More* was published too late to be of service to me.

I have to thank the New York State Library for the loan of books. Further grateful acknowledgements must be made to other librarians—Father Matthew Hoehn of St. Mary's Abbey, Newark, N. J., Brother Thomas of Manhattan College, Mother Gertrude Buck of Manhattanville College, and Mother Marguerite of the College of New Rochelle. My wife compiled the index and helped with the proofs.

Contents

CHAPTER ONE

In the Cardinal's Household

THOMAS MORE, when towards the end of his life he composed an epitaph for the tomb he expected to occupy in Chelsea church, described himself as sprung from honest but not illustrious stock. The claim was characteristically modest. His father rose to be a judge and received knighthood. And though John More, like his father before him, had been butler to Lincoln's Inn, this was no menial position, but corresponded to clerk of the council, according to the *Encyclopedia Britannica;* and his father, like himself, was called to the bar. The Mores were in fact a distinguished legal family. The greatest of them was therefore saying no more than that they made no aristocratic pretensions.

February 6, 1478, is now fixed with virtual certainty as the date of Thomas More's birth at Milk Street off Cheapside in London.[1] More's mother, who was born Agnes Granger, a daughter of a Sheriff of London, died while he was a small child. Not of her do we have any impression but only of his nurse, Mother Maude, whom he recalled while writing his last completed book in the Tower as a great teller of animal fables. It would seem to be from her that he derived his fondness for these homely inventions. Almost all that we know of Agnes Granger is that she was married to John More at St. Giles, Cripplegate, in which church Oliver Cromwell was later married and Milton buried.

Stapleton, however, who published at Douai his life of Thomas More in his *Tres Thomae* tells that John Clement had heard old Sir John More relate that his first wife on the first night of her marriage had a dream in which she saw depicted upon her wedding

[1] The earlier biographers gave 1480 as the date, and though later investigators hesitated between 1476, 1477 and 1478, the matter seems to have been settled by Professor Chambers. See his *Thomas More,* p. 49. In his *Place of Thomas More in English Literature and History* he reproduces the entry made by John More in his copy (of course one in manuscript) of Geoffrey of Monmouth's *History.*

ring the faces of the children she was to bear. The face of one was hardly discernible—explained later when that child was still-born—but one of the others shone with splendor. It naturally came to be inferred that this was the celebrated Thomas.

Another "prodigy" is recorded by Stapleton. Once when his nurse—presumably Mother Maude—was crossing a ford she was nearly carried away by the current. To save the babe she threw him over the hedge that fringed the river, and when she managed to get safely to the bank, she was surprised to find him quite unhurt and smiling at her. "Such portents," added Stapleton gravely, "indicated that this child would one day become great and famous." As Stapleton indicated his belief that he was writing the life of a saint—though of one who had to wait four hundred years for canonization—marvels of this sort were of course proper to his concept of hagiography. Yet they need not be dismissed on that account, for they seem likely enough. Almost any family with a member more remarkable than the average commonly discovers incidents, unnoticed at the time, which in the light of subsequent events may be taken as pointing to future distinction.

One vivid childish memory of Thomas More's—a curious footnote to history—is of a day in April, 1483, when he was just over five. "The self night in which King Edward [IV] died," he was to write in his *Richard III*, "one Mistlebrook, long ere morning, came in great haste to the house of one Pottier, dwelling in Redcross Street without Cripplegate; and when he was with hasty rapping quickly letten in, he showed unto Pottier that King Edward was departed [dead]. 'By my troth, man,' quoth Pottier, 'then will my master the Duke of Gloucester be king.' " More went on to remark that what reason Pottier had for this comment it was hard to say, though of course he drew the inference that the servant, because of his close attendance on the future Richard III, already had some inkling of his dark intentions towards his nephews.

School came soon after this. And medieval school life was one of severity and sparseness, with Latin flogged in well at the nether parts, and few but rough games. Yet the school attended by this boy was the best in London, until Colet founded St. Paul's. Here, under Nicholas Holt in St. Anthony's on Threadneedle Street, the foundation of the famous scholarship was laid. The teachers, though no doubt adhering to the discipline then in vogue, must have made letters attractive; had it not been so there could never have been that love for learning which was to be one of the distinguishing marks of the little boy who was to be St. Anthony's most celebrated alumnus.

Amenities were all but absent, books few, and almost completely lacking was everything that we think of as class-room equipment. The master sat at his desk on a dais, the boys on stools or on the floor. The defects of such a system at least prodigiously developed the memory, and as More used to claim that his memory was exceptionally good, it must have been marvelous.

As to this we have plenty of evidence in his writings. The brains of people of today have largely been turned into paper and ink, but More's power of instantly recalling what he had learned and pigeonholed for use was really more efficient than the best of filing systems or several rows of reference books. It accounts in large part for the evident ease with which he drove his versatile talents in tandem under serene control. Because of this he was simultaneously a scholar of varied interests, the most prominent lawyer of his time, and a man immersed in public affairs. But of course phenomenal industry was also needed, however much he may have owed to his brilliant cleverness and his charming affability.

In the verses he was to write for some decorations for his father's house he expressed the point of view of the average schoolboy of the time rather than his own:

I am called Childhood, in play is all my mind
To cast a kite, a cocksteel and a ball.
A top can I set, and drive it in his kind.
But would to God those hateful bookès all
Were in a fire brent to powder small.
Then might I lead my life always in play:
Which life God send me to my dying day.

Certainly books were not hateful to this boy, and we may suppose that his games did not include the detestable one in which a cock was buried up to its neck, so that "steels" could be hurled at its head. It is surely safe enough to infer that much of the Utopian who so despised hunting as to relegate it, along with the necessary butchering of animals, to condemned malefactors. Though organized sports were in those days unknown—unless archery can be called one, and at that More's rather poor eyesight would have made proficiency unobtainable—there can be no doubt that one so perfectly normal, so high-spirited, and so healthy was not merely a book-worm but enjoyed a popularity among his fellows. More than that we do not know.

At home there was a father not so dried up by his profession as to be unable to enjoy the exercise of a sardonic wit. Some specimens of this have been preserved by his son, and if they are mostly slightly derogatory remarks on marriage, it was probably always understood that they were purely conventional. For John More married—apparently in every case happily, and the last time when nearly seventy—no less than four times.

One of these sayings of his was that a man who put his hand into a bag containing seven snakes and one eel had a better chance of getting hold of the eel than a man, dipping his hand into the lucky-bag of marriage, had of securing a good wife. Another was that when men blame their wives for being shrews, they are unjust; for there is only one shrew in the world—the woman to whom each man is married. Such obiter dicta did not deter his son from marrying twice. Thomas More described his father as "courteous, affable, innocent, gentle, merciful, just and uncorrupt;" and though it may seem that some less laudatory terms could be included in that list, his chief failing, after all, was a certain narrowness of outlook. This made him unable to understand his son and might have caused serious resentment had it not been for Thomas's sweetness of temper. But whatever strain there was soon passed, and Sir John spent some of his declining years in the Chelsea household. He is shown there in the Holbein picture of 1527, perhaps in the interval between his third and fourth matrimonial ventures.

Thus the boy grew up in his father's house until he was about twelve, sufficiently happy and very alert. He lived almost in the heart of the London of early Tudor times, a city much the largest in the whole kingdom, but one only about a mile wide each way and, since the Black Death, reduced to perhaps a hundred thousand inhabitants. The streets were narrow and crowded with life, but were also constantly threatened with pestilence because of the insanitary conditions that prevailed. Yet English wealth—and particularly the wealth of London—was already proverbial on the continent, and with it went movement and color and the first stirrings of the intellectual excitement of the Renaissance. Splendor and squalor were side by side, flaunted greed and hidden charity. The observant boy took it all in, and he never seemed to forget anything. London born and bred, he lived almost all his life in or near London. Though the green fields were not far away and the Thames still ran silver, his heart was in the streets full of bustling shops and noisy ale-houses, where lordly palaces and convents of friars and stores and brothels jostled one another. And over all the spired churches rose the lofty shaft of the cathedral of old St. Paul's.

Now there came what were for young Thomas a couple of years of the utmost importance for the development of his character and talents; he was placed as a page in the household of Archbishop Morton, Lord Chancellor but not yet Cardinal. And there he remained until he was fourteen, for him a series of delightful experiences upon which he drew freely in the writing of his later years.

Just how this came about has been a matter of conjecture, though Algernon Cecil believes (probably correctly) that conjecture can be pretty nearly removed if we remember that the boundary of an estate owned by John More at Gobions at Hertfordshire adjoined part of the appurtenance of the bishopric of Ely. This bishopric had been held by Morton until 1486, and it is as

Bishop of Ely that he figures in Shakespeare's play *Richard III*. Yet even aside from that likely association, there could have been a number of opportunities for Morton and John More to get to know one another. The lawyer was already eminent enough to have been autumn reader at Lincoln's Inn in 1489. What is probable is that somewhere the Archbishop encountered the boy in his father's company and was struck by his bright young face. The gruff old politician who had safely weathered many dangerous storms, had now at last come into his own and could afford to indulge the kindliness at the bottom of his nature. He invited Thomas More to join his princely household at Lambeth.

There was no very special favor involved. Great nobles—and Morton ranked above them all by virtue of the chancellorship—customarily kept a large number of retainers. And pages could be useful, especially those of intelligence. Parents of the smaller gentry were glad to send not only their adolescent sons but their adolescent daughters to some such place. The theory was that there they would find opportunities for advancement, though there is reason to believe that some caustic foreigners may have been near the mark when they suggested that this English practice was really designed to rid fathers and mothers of their responsibilities and to avoid the expense of bringing children up at home. Be that as it may, in Thomas More's case the system worked wonders in the way of giving him stimulation of mind and a polish of manners he may hitherto have lacked.

The Archbishop took a fancy to the boy, and the boy in his turn showed a grateful affection for the Archbishop when, sixteen years after the Cardinal's death, he described him in the *Utopia*. He was a man, More wrote there, "not more honourable for his authority, than for his prudence and virtue. He was of a mean [average] stature, and though stricken in age, yet bare he his body upright. In his face did shine such an amiable reverence, as was pleasant to behold, gentle in communication, yet earnest and sage. He had great delight many times with rough speech to his suitors, to prove, but without harm, what prompt wit and what bold spirit was in every man. In the which, as in a virtue much agreeing with his nature, so that therewith were not joined impudency, he took great delectation. And the same person, as apt and meet to have an administration in the weal public, he did lovingly embrace." Morton may be supposed to have tested his page from time to time in this fashion, and to have highly approved what he saw. Though he could not have imagined that the boy was one day to succeed him in the office of Lord Chancellor, he used to tell his visitors, who also were impressed by the quick-witted and charmingly mannered page, "This boy, those who live to see it, will see to become a notable man." If that was a kind of a prophecy, More made another unwittingly of himself when he said of Morton: "Even in the chief of his youth he was taken from school into the court, and there passed all his time in much trouble and business, being continually tumbled and tossed in the waves of divers misfortunes and adverities. And so by many and great dangers he learned the experience of the world, which so being learned can not easily be forgotten."

The political game Morton had played during the Wars of the Roses showed his skill as well as his courage, and it was he who had been largely instrumental in arranging a marriage between the rival houses of York and Lancaster and in bringing Henry VII to the throne. He had been rewarded with the archbishopric of Canterbury, and now he was Chancellor. So evidently was he the source of much of the information in More's *Richard III*—the strawberry incident, taken from More by Shakespeare is a case in point—that until recently it was often argued that Morton himself must be the author of that book.

The gardens of Lambeth Palace went down to the river, which was all day long astir with life, as it was far more swift and pleasant as a highway than the rough rutted roads. Gay barges—the larger of them gilded and with liveried rowers—flashed past, and at night—or sometimes even during the day—music came from them over the water. From the great windows of the palace or its lawns one could see the King's palace at Westminster and the already venerable grey mass of the Abbey.

Through the massive brick gatehouse—then abuilding and still standing as one of the noblest pieces of Tudor architecture, and the last portal to be crossed by Sir Thomas More forty-four years later as a free man—all kinds of distinguished people passed to be entertained by the Archbishop of Canterbury. Nobles and judges and military commanders and great ecclesiastics and scholars, sooner or later they were all there. And behind Morton's chair stood a slim, good-looking youth with quick gray eyes and attentive ears, missing no sparkle of wit, no casually thrown out bit of learning, no piece of court gossip—least of all any of the frequent suggestions for what would now be called social reform. It is not of course necessary, or even permissible, to hold that any of the conversations reported as taking place between Raphael Hythloday and the Cardinal in the *Utopia* actually occurred, for More was to show considerable inventive powers. On the other hand, such conversations must have been true to character, and More was a master at catching the very inflection of a speaker's voice. In these pages, like so many others in the *Utopia,* More uses the device of putting into other people's mouths things to which he did not want to commit himself. We may nevertheless be sure that conversations along the lines recorded must have been overheard by an attentive and eager boy who profitted enormously from them.

What specially aroused Morton's admiration—and that of those sitting with him—was the way the boy, when Christmas plays were being presented in the great hall would (to quote Roper): "Suddenly step in among the players, and, never studying for the matter, make a part of his own presently [instantly] among them, which made the onlookers more sport than the players beside." Roper may actually have seen his father-in-law do this very thing on the private stage maintained at the house of John Rastell, who married More's sister Elizabeth. But he says nothing as to this, and is in fact often tantalizingly meagre, thinking of himself as hardly doing more than make notes for other people to work up. What Professor A. W. Reed has shown, however, is that many of these early Tudor plays, when a brilliant improvisor like More could not be counted upon, had parts written for and learned by heart by those who ostensibly "stepped in" spontaneously. He reminds us that Henry Medwell was one of Morton's chaplains and claims for him the place of honor among the dramatists of the time[2]. Going further than this, he suggests that Medwell's *Fulgens and Lucres,* in providing a part for two boys, had in mind young More and Rastell. He generalizes his views by saying: "It is becoming apparent that the break with the tradition of the allegorical morality and the rise of the freer forms of imaginative drama are connected in a remarkable way with the circle of the Rastells, More and Heywood, and that it seems that the movement towards dramatic freedom began in the household in which More was brought up, the household of Cardinal Morton."[3] He does not hesitate to say in another book, "To many it will seem bold to give More a place in the development of this drama, but I am confident that my suggestion is not lightly to be set aside."[4]

I set down these fascinating conjectures without being altogether convinced of their soundness. I am even reluctant to build too much on what Erasmus wrote, in his famous letter to Ulrich von Hutten, that More in his adolescence wrote and acted in some small comedies now lost. There was surely a potential dramatist in him, evidenced by his wonderful command of dialogue; but it does not seem to me safe to stretch Roper and Erasmus too far, or to believe that if More did more than "ad lib" in the Christmas plays, this much exceeded the production of a skit or two that tickled the fancy of old Morton and his guests on a convivial afternoon during the holiday season.

What is at least certain is that More made a great hit with Morton, and that he, for his part, left Lambeth Palace with

[2] *Early Tudor Drama,* p. 95.
[3] *Ibid.,* p. 117.
[4] *The Beginnings of the English Secular and Romantic Drama,* p. 28.

Morton's mark laid indelibly on him. Also he had acquired there an aplomb that was never to desert him, not even on the scaffold that awaited him. With his natural talents—people were already beginning to speak of it as genius—so sharpened and heightened, and with his modesty and good humor, he already possessed, as Morton saw, what would carry him very far in the world.

CHAPTER TWO

Oxford

THAT Thomas More went at about fourteen to Oxford was due mainly to Morton's influence and advice. John More of course had to give his consent, but it would appear from subsequent events that he did so reluctantly and perhaps only because he could see no graceful way of rejecting the offers of so powerful a friend as the Lord Chancellor.

The student was young, but not much younger than many youths who began a course of studies that lasted seven years before a degree was given. And he entered Canterbury College, which was under the charge of the Benedictines of Morton's cathedral city of Canterbury. Since the time of William Tilly of Selling—who is often called just Selling of Canterbury—who had been their Prior, and who had brought back Greek manuscripts from Italy, the place had been one of the main centers of Greek studies in England. Though the college was to be absorbed by Wolsey's foundation of Christ Church, its name is still embalmed in Canterbury Gate. That Thomas More went there was one of the main determinants in his career.

Another determinant was that a few years after More's entry—which was also the date of the discovery of the New World by Columbus—the man who was to give his name to the Western hemisphere, Amerigo Vespucci, was about to set out on those voyages of his which, when More read of them, provided him with the suggestion of the *Utopia,* the book upon which his literary fame chiefly rests. But already the year 1492 was one of the exhilarating opening of vast vistas, especially to the English, a seafaring race and the allies of the Iberian explorers. This could not have been lost on one who all his life showed himself so sensitive in his response to the various intellectual currents in his world

It is likely that Archbishop Morton recommended that his protegé take orders in the Church as the surest and swiftest road of advancement for a youth of his special aptitudes. But as we know nothing definite about this, it is best to suppose that it was left an open question. Morton probably saw that John More had other designs for his son. And it may well be that the lawyer was brought to agree with the Oxford plan only on the understanding that the boy was not to waste all his time on the fripperies of philosophy and literature but to take some studies in law. Though neither of the English universities paid much attention to English Municipal law, Canon and Roman Civil law were regularly taught, and Canterbury College, when founded by Archbishop Islip in 1363, had been primarily intended for these studies. It may be supposed that this was a fact that Archbishop Morton stressed in wringing from John More a consent he had not been very enthusiastic to accord.

Thomas More appears to have had rooms at St. Mary's Hall, and there he lived in an austerity scarcely conceivable today in an Oxford that has become a preserve of the well-to-do. Instead of the suite of rooms provided for each undergraduate, often into one barely furnished and quite unheated room four hapless young students were squeezed. A penny a day was the allowance for their commons, and even if we multiply this by twenty-five to allow for the difference in money, this would mean that they lived on two shillings or fifty cents a day.[1] No doubt many of the students were sent a little money from home to supplement such fare, but this was not so with Thomas More. He records specifically, though without any trace of bitterness—rather with approval—that his father supplied him with no pocket-money, even for the mending of his shoes. "Thus it came to pass," he used to say, as

[1] Belloc in an appendix to his *Wolsey* (and elsewhere) argues in favour of this higher figure, though the majority of historians think a multiplication by twelve or fifteen sufficient. I would be inclined to accept these lower and more cautious figures, even in face of Belloc's prowess as a political economist, were it not that since his *Wolsey* (1930), it has come within everybody's experience that the real values of money, even in England, even in the United States, have vastly declined.

recorded by Stapleton, "that I indulged in no vice or vain pleasure, and that I did not spend my time in dangerous or idle pastimes, that I did not even know the meaning of extravagance or luxury, that I did not learn to put money to evil uses, that, in fine, I had no love, or even thought of anything beyond my studies." Nicholas Harpsfield, who was himself an Oxford man, slightly changing Roper's phrases, further records More's telling his family after his fall from office that, if the worst came to the worst, they could, "like poor scholars of Oxford, go a begging with [their] bags and wallets, and sing Salve Regina at rich men's doors, where for pity some good folk will give us their charity." Though that was said in jest, we do know that impoverished students were sometimes given license to beg under the Chancellor's seal. More while at Oxford was not reduced to such straits. Morton provided the bare necessities of life, and John More may be presumed to have sent his son money (when asked) for the mending of his shoes.

From a sermon preached by Thomas Lever at Paul's Cross in 1550 we have further details of English university life at a slightly later period. The students attended Mass at five, after which they studied until ten, when they had their dinner, their first meal of the day—except for those who had breakfasted on a crust of bread and a tankard of stale beer. This dinner of their's consisted of a piece of coarse corned beef and some broth or oatmeal—a rough but nourishing diet. Then we hear of their working again until nine or ten, though we may be sure a good many among them did not adhere very strictly to such a schedule. To end the day the students, "being without fire, are fain to walk or run up and down half an hour, to get a heat on their feet when they go to bed." In all probability the worthy Lever tended to lay his colors on rather thick, as many people still exaggerate—sometimes in a nostalgic mood—the rigors of their youth. Yet after all allowances have been made, the life of Oxford must be said to have been hard, and nothing much was done to alleviate its austerities for Thomas More.

For him, however, those two years at Oxford were a delightful experience. He was in love with learning, and walking upon air, and so hardly noticed whatever privations he suffered. In another sense, too, he was in love at the end of this period, for we have a Latin poem of his—written twenty-five years afterwards—which commemorates a love-affair when he was sixteen. He says, alas:

> Then the duenna and the guarded door
> Baffled the stars, and bade us meet no more.

Though the rest of the poem makes it perfectly clear that this little *tendresse* was completely innocent, it may account for John More's withdrawing his son from Oxford. Or rather, it may have been used as the pretext; for other more solid objections to Oxford had always been in his mind.

The chief of his objections was that the lad was getting much too fascinated with literature and especially with Greek studies. In that Oxford these were regarded as extra-curricular, though there were quarters in the University in which they were being pursued with enthusiasm. Yet how far Thomas More himself got at this time with Greek is open to question. Roper says merely that at Oxford his father-in-law was "both in the Greek and Latin tongue sufficiently instructed." And Stapleton goes no further than to point out that Grocyn had recently returned to England and was teaching at Oxford; he does not say that More studied under him there. All that we definitely know, and that is not much, comes from the letter More wrote to Dorpius in 1515, indicating that he did attend some of Linacre's lectures. In the case of both these men, however, More's close contact with them came about in London a few years later. Chambers therefore remarks that "a pretty and quite imaginary picture has been drawn of these dons all studying Greek together with young Thomas More, aged fifteen." Yet whatever reasonable doubts may be cast upon the more fanciful elements in the picture, it can hardly be open to question that it was at Oxford that Thomas More first became enamored of Greek, and so gave John More a reason for withdrawing him from the University.

Though in this John More's main motive was undoubtedly that of starting his son in the profession of the law, he had on his side almost the whole body of respectable opinion in distrusting the first flowering of the Renaissance. He was of the old school, as was probably almost every man of his acquaintance. The "New Learning" was looked upon with misgivings by all conservatives, who considered it as, at best, frivolous, and, at worst, dangerous to faith and morals. Thomas More did as much as any man in England to break down this attitude of mind; at this stage it proved a temporary check to the career he had just begun.

For his formal studies—those that led to a degree—More seems to have had little regard. Rashdell's *Universities of Europe in the Middle Ages* says somewhat acidly that these represented nothing but "the dreary routine of expiring scholasticism."[2] More himself described the syllogism-making into which scholasticism had degenerated as like one man milking a he-goat while another man held the sieve—the most scathing image of futility. From such barren employments he turned to Greek and French and geometry and every book of history upon which he could lay his hands. He also learned to play the viol and the flute and even sang, though, as Erasmus informs us, not very well. No wonder he found Oxford full of enchanted delights in spite of the severity of the regimen.

Neither can there be any wonder that his father was displeased. Latin was indispensable to a lawyer and to every educated man. And philosophy, because it sharpened the mind, was useful. But what possible value was there in Greek? As his son showed every disposition to become one of those feckless wandering scholars of which the world was already too full or, worse still, a poet, John More after having endured his misgivings for two years, found his patience suddenly exhausted and so ordered the boy home and set him to the sober and profitable study of the law.

[2] Vol. II, p. 246.

CHAPTER THREE

The Reluctant Lawyer

Lord Campbell, one of several eminent lawyers who have been More's biographers, after some rather sarcastic remarks about how, in his day, a sufficient knowledge of jurisprudence was supposed to be gained by the eating of a certain number of dinners in the hall of one of the Inns of Court, says that, in More's time, "the Inns of Court and Chancery presented the discipline of a well conducted university; and, through professors, under the name of 'readers', and exercises under the name of 'mootings', law was systematically taught, and efficient tests of proficiency were applied before the degree of barrister was conferred, entitling the aspirant to practice as an advocate." Campbell published his *Lives of the Lord Chancellors* in 1845; fourteen years earlier Sir James Mackintosh says much the same thing of these Inns in the sixteenth century. "It was not a metaphor to call them a university," he writes: "they had professors of law; they conferred the characters of barrister and serjeant, analogous to the degrees of bachelor, master and doctor, bestowed by universities; and every man, before he became a barrister, was subject to examinations, and obliged to defend a thesis." John More entered his son at the Inn of Chancery known as New Inn, where, as Roper puts it, "for his time he very well prospered." This I take to mean that he was, as compared with the hard life he had led at Oxford, very well off. John More, greatly relieved at having recovered his son from the deleterious delights of literature and set him in the straight paths of the law, was as indulgent a parent as it was possible for a man of his somewhat cold nature to be.

Thomas More must have worked very hard, because when he was transferred two years later to Lincoln's Inn he was "pardoned four vacations." Miss Routh says that this was through John

More's influence, but presents no evidence for the statement. To me it seems that the four vacations pardoned, which presumably were the equivalent of four terms' credit, was due to his having followed extra courses either during his two years at New Inn or while he was at Oxford.

In spite of this, and all the further proof Thomas gave, during the next few years, of industry and ability, his father was far from being satisfied. The law is proverbially an exacting mistress, and the fact that the son had so many interests unrelated to law was an offence. No consideration was given to his working probably harder than most other students at the law, or to the aptitude that he was showing for it. John More was so disgusted at his giving even a little of his time to anything else that he came close to disinheriting him. This would seem to have happened at the time of his admission to Lincoln's Inn in 1496, for Roper says that he went there "on very small allowance"—a time-honored means for the expression of parental disapproval.

Erasmus hints that More was more or less driven into the legal profession against his will, and this may actually be the case. But after all, no studies can be really distasteful to a man in which he excels, as More did in the law. Perhaps Erasmus is not the safest witness on this point, as his natural disposition, being egotistical, was to see everything through his own eyes. To him such studies would have been horrible; therefore he concluded that they must have been equally so to his friend. And indeed, it is not unlikely that Thomas More may have permitted himself passing growls at the fate that condemned him to be a lawyer. It is easy to understand that in the company of such a man as Erasmus—the scholar pure and simple—the law may have seemed dusty and dreary. But I do not recall that More in any of the autobiographical passages in his writings ever deplored the choice he finally made. What is remarkable is that he contrived to be a first-rate lawyer and to be equally first-rate at a number of other things.

His father, an able man in a plodding fashion, was altogether unable to understand his son's versatility. At this time he believed it would prevent him from making any headway in the one profession he cared about. And though he was eventually proved wrong on this point, perhaps he never came to value at its proper worth anything except his son's legal eminence. In the Holbein portrait the old gentleman is shown with a very quizzical and bored look as Margaret Giggs eagerly leans forward with a book pointing to a passage. However, by that time he may have been brought to a bewildered assent to the proposition that literature was evidently loved by those who loved it, and that it need not necessarily impede a man's progress in the world.

Thirty years earlier he could not see even as much as this. That his son had good parts was obvious to him. He recognized in him the making of a lawyer—providing he would apply himself. But he could not regard it as other than folly to fritter time away translating Greek and Latin authors, and writing English poetry, and playing the flute and the viol. His was just the tragic case of a man who happened to be the father of a genius. It may have been all the more tragic because he was, in his own dried-up and narrow way, distinctly clever. Relations for a while became strained, and had it not been for Thomas's sweetness of temper might have resulted in a breach between the two men. This was averted only because the son withdrew for several years from his father's house. In his quiet and respectful style he was very determined, as King Henry VIII was afterwards to discover. So while doggedly digging into the murky caverns of the law, he contrived to be at the same time a scholar and writer and theologian, and so emerged a fully rounded man.

The same thing was not true of any other of his humanist friends, unless we except Thomas Linacre, who combined (or alternated) a Greek professorship at Oxford with the practice of medicine, and was mainly instrumental in founding the Royal College of Physicians about the same time (1518) that he belatedly received priesthood. He was always ready to turn from his pestles and alembics to discourse on a Greek poet—a tradition that was continued afterwards in More's own household by his secretary John Clement, and his adopted daughter Margaret Giggs, and even to some extent by Margaret Roper and More himself. But Grocyn, who had taught Greek at Oxford, was a donnish man; and when he came to London as Rector of St. Lawrence Jewry's, he was following in the footsteps of many such scholars who ended their days comfortably in a good benefice. The importance of these two men to More was that under them he now more seriously applied himself to the study of Greek than had been possible until then.

John Colet was a rather different type. He was Vicar of Stepney and was soon to become the Dean of St. Paul's and the founder of St. Paul's School. He learned Greek late in life and probably never knew a great deal of it. His chief interest in the "New Learning" was what he hoped it might effect in the way of raising the standard of the clergy and so bringing about a much needed religious and moral reformation. His humanism was applied to a single practical end.

These men were all considerably older than More. Slightly older was William Lily, with whom More collaborated in translating some of the pieces in the *Greek Anthology* into Latin verse. Where Lily was unique in that group was in the fact of having gone on a pilgrimage to Jerusalem and stopping at Rhodes to master Greek and to bring back a vision of a Greek Christendom in actual being.

Only Richard Pace (another future Dean of St. Paul's) was younger than More. As the boy of the band he was filled with admiration at the facility of his friend. Of More he was to write in 1517: "No one ever lived who did not first ascertain the meaning of words, and from them gather the meaning of the sentences which they compose—no one, I say, with one single exception, and that is our Thomas More. For he is wont to gather the force of the words from the sentences in which they occur, especially in his study and translation of Greek. This is not contrary to grammar, but above it, and an instinct of genius." Though there is some point to the Abbé Bremond's comment, "It is also, we may add, characteristic of an amateur. In fact, More never had the time to become a professional scholar," the professional scholars of More's own time nevertheless completely accepted him as one of themselves and were not so very professional as to fail to recognize the refulgence of his gifts. They were all quite sure that he was the one genius among them.

One of these scholars, the greatest of them all, was to link his name so closely with that of More as to demand special mention at this point before we encounter him, as we shall, later on in More's life. This was of course Erasmus, already eminent at the time of his first visit to England in 1499 but with his highest achievements still ahead of him.

The story has often been told of how the two men met—More then only twenty-one and Erasmus about eleven years older—at a dinner given by the Lord Mayor. Somehow they had not been introduced when they sat down at table but they immediately recognized one another as kindred spirits. After the exchange of a few initial sallies, Erasmus exclaimed—in the Latin in which they always conversed—"Either you are More or you are nobody," to which came the retort, "Either you are Erasmus or you are the devil." But though that story is open to doubt, as we first hear of it from the not always reliable Cresacre More, Sir Thomas's great-grandson, it has this much plausibility: the distinguished foreign visitor would unquestionably have been told about the extraordinarily talented wit and scholar as soon as he arrived in England; he could have been sure that the country did not contain *two* youths of such brilliance and charm as the one who sat with gray smiling eyes besides him.

It is, however, safer to rely on Erasmus's own account of their early acquaintance. He had come to England at the invitation of William Blount, Lord Mountjoy, who had been his pupil in Paris and who was now in a position to play the patron to his former mentor. From Mountjoy's country house at Deptford the two of them, accompanied by More, so we read in a letter written by Erasmus, went for a walk to the adjoining village of Eltham. It was there that the royal children were being educated, except for Prince Arthur, Henry VII's eldest son. Mountjoy and More (who may have been in a little plot together) gave Erasmus no warning as to where they were going, but took him straight into the palace. There in the great hall, which still stands with its richly timbered roof, they were received. In the midst of the young Tudors stood the future Henry VIII, a boy of eight, with Princess Margaret, aged eleven, on his right hand and, on his left, Mary, a child of four. Edmund was carried by his nurse. More, who had come prepared, presented the Prince with something in writing, and poor Erasmus was embarrassed at having nothing to offer, especially as Henry during dinner sent him a note asking for one of his effusions. Erasmus understood very well that this was an occasion that had to be improved and that his friends had taken him there with an eye to his future benefit. So Erasmus, who was always quick to take advantage of such opportunities, concludes: "I went home, and though the Muses, from whom I had long been divorced, were unwilling, I finished the poem in three days." It was, as might be expected, a Latin laudation of the King and of his children and of England.

It was no more than the truth that Erasmus was greatly enjoying his English visit. To one of his friends he wrote: "The Erasmus you once knew has now almost become a sportsman, not the worst possible rider, a fairly skilful courtier; he can make a polite bow, smile gracefully, and all this in spite of himself . . . If you knew the charms of England you would wish for the wings of Daedalus." Among those charms Erasmus specially dwells—it was something to which he frequently reverted in his letters—upon the English custom of kissing. What is now thought of as a specially continental custom was in those days an English peculiarity. It never ceased to give Erasmus a kind of amused pleasure: "Wherever you go, you are received with kisses from everybody; when you leave you are dismissed with kisses. You go back, and your kisses are returned to you. People arrive: kisses; they depart: kisses; in fact whatever way you turn, everything is full of kisses."

But his main delight in England was in his contacts with its cordial scholars. He writes to tell Robert Fisher, a brother of the Bishop of Rochester, "I have met with so much learning, not hackneyed and trivial, but deep, exact, ancient, Latin and Greek, that I am not hankering so much after Italy"—which was where Fisher was at this time—"except just for seeing it. When I hear my Colet, I seem to be listening to Plato himself. In Grocyn, who does not wonder at that perfect compass of all knowledge? What is more accurate, more profound, more keen than the judgement of Linacre? What did nature ever create milder, sweeter or happier than the genius of Thomas More? . . . It is marvellous how widespread and how abundant is the harvest of ancient learning which is flourishing in this country." It is very significant that the stripling More should be included in this group, without the faintest trace of condescension, but rather in such a way as to indicate a belief that here was its crowning glory.

Other things are equally illuminating. Erasmus went off early in 1500 to Paris, though Colet, who was lecturing on the New Testament at Oxford, pressed him to join him there and lecture on Latin poetry or the Old Testament. Erasmus realized that he was not yet equal to that particular demand; for the same reason his edition of the New Testament waited until he had perfected his mastery of Greek. But the important fact to seize is the sober purpose instilled into this somewhat flippant and cynical mind through its friendship with the English humanists. The world now remembers Erasmus mainly as the author of *The Praise of Folly,* just as the world now remembers More mainly as the author of the *Utopia.* But we should misunderstand both men if we failed to perceive that the fundamental purpose of each was very serious.

It might also be noted that, though Erasmus's English friends valued him highly from the start, they—and especially More—had almost more influence upon him than he had upon them. And upon them all—though in varying degrees—another influence converged. It was that of Savonarola. In the case of Colet this was direct and avowed. But Linacre also had been touched by it during his visit to Italy. As for More, when he selected a model for himself, it was Savonarola's disciple, Pico della Mirandola, whose life he was to translate into English, his first extended piece of writing.

Further mention of this book of More's will be made later, in a more appropriate place. At this point it might be remarked that, though he was already producing occasional English and Latin poems, and continued to do so now and then, he undertook shortly after this visit of Erasmus, when he was only twenty-three a task that might have daunted the gravest theologian and the ripest scholar—public lectures in the Church of St. Lawrence Jewry, near the Guildhall, at Grocyn's invitation, on St. Augustine's *De Civitate Dei.* Concerning this, Harpsfield was to write: "Though it be a book very hard for a well learned man to understand, and cannot be profoundly and exactly understanded, and especially cannot be with commendation openly read, of any man that is not well and substantially furnished as well with divinity as profane knowledge; yet did Master More, being so young, being so distracted also and occupied in the study of the common law, openly read in the Church of St. Lawrence Jewry in London the books of the said St. Augustine de Civitate Dei, to his no small commendation, and to the great admiration of all his audience. His lesson was frequented and honoured by the presence and report, as well as that well learned and great cunning man, Master Grocyn . . . as well as with the chief and best learned men of the City of London."

If these lectures were nothing else, they were a triumph of audacity—perhaps too much so, in More's own mature opinion, as might appear from the fact that he did not preserve transscripts of them.[3] Dr. Grocyn himself, about the same time, had been lecturing in St. Paul's on the *Celestial Hierarchies of* Dionysius, another extremely abstruse book. It may have been because his lectures were a little too abstruse, or because he lacked

[3] It is possible, however, that they may have been among the papers which after his condemnation were seized by the authorities.

More's oratorical gifts, but whatever the reason, his audiences were much smaller than More's. Perhaps also the novelty of a young layman lecturing in a church—though this was something not unheard of at the time—itself proved a drawing-card. As for More himself, the fact that Grocyn invited him to give these lectures proves the estimation in which he was already held. And St. Augustine's great book is to be discerned as one of the sources from which he derived some of his Utopian ideas.

Such a performance at so early an age is really astounding, especially when we remember that in 1501 he was a busy lawyer. Yet the other and lighter side of More should never be forgotten. He had already produced a number of short poems in Latin and English, and continued to do so. His translation into Latin, in conjunction with Lily, of some specimens of the *Greek Anthology* has already been mentioned. But they, like the translation that he and Erasmus made a little later of Lucian, perhaps were no more than a sharpening of his pen. The same thing applies to the Latin epigrams which he was producing at this time, but which were not published until 1518. Now and then these throw some little light on his character, but they need not detain us in so brief a survey as this.

Some of his English poems, however, still have an interest. One of these is the elegy on the death of Elizabeth, the Queen of Henry VII, in 1503. It is perhaps the earliest of the adumbrations of the Spenserian stanza, in that More concludes the Chaucerian seven-line stanza, at that time called "balade or ballet," with a hexameter line. One sample of this may be given, both for this reason and because it mentions the future Henry VIII, then a boy of twelve, with whom his own fortunes were to be so closely entwined. The dead mother addresses various members of her family, and then comes to her children, starting with Henry, as Arthur was now dead:

> Adieu, Lord Henry, my loving son, adieu.
> Our Lord increase your honour and estate.
> Adieu, my daughter Mary bright of hue:

God make you virtuous and fortunate.
Adieu, sweet heart, my little daughter Kate:
Thou shalt, sweet babe, such is thy destiny,
Thy mother never know, for lo now here I lie.

That of course is not very good poetry, though it is perhaps the least stiff-jointed of all the stanzas. And it must be said that before long More reached the sensible conclusion that he did not have the poetic endowment. But he was at least enough of a poet to wish to write good verse, in English as well as in Latin, even if he achieved hardly more than his own pleasure and the entertainment of his friends.

There is one other early piece of his English verse that might be glanced at here. This is a humorous effort, and was used by the editor of the great folio of 1557, William Rastell, to open that volume. It tells a "merry jest," How a Serjeant Would Learn to Play the Friar. Though most of it would be unendurable to modern ears—at least it is to mine—it is very understandable that the audience for which it was composed relished it. In fact the line towards the end about commending the company to the Mayor probably convulsed everybody, for it would seem to indicate that the Lord Mayor of London was present when it was read. Dr. Reed conjectures that the piece was composed to be read aloud at the Serjeants' Feast of 1503, when we know that John More was one of those elected to that distinguished title. At these banquets it was customary for the Lord Mayor and the Sheriffs to be present. To those well dined and well wined it is easy to imagine that this light-hearted doggerel seemed delightfully amusing.

Nor would such an audience have failed to relish the fun Thomas More was poking at himself. They all knew into how many pies he had put his fingers, and that his versatility had been looked at dubiously by others besides his father. But now peace was restored between father and son. Two years previously Thomas had been called to the bar and was in successful practice, so he could afford to laugh at his own dangerous propensities. At the same time he was probably gracefully scoring off the newly made Serjeant went he wrote:

When a hatter
Will go smatter
In philosophy;
Or a peddler
Wax a meddler
In theology.
All that ensue
Such crafts new
They drive so far a cast,
That evermore
They do therefore
Beshrew themselves at last.

The fable is an illustration of this thesis. And the cream of the jest was that Thomas More, though not a Serjeant, had come close to playing the friar in his lectures on St. Augustine. For though these laid their main stress on the historical considerations suggested by that work, they could hardly avoid a good deal of philosophy and theology. Even if Dr. Reed is correct in his surmise about the circumstances under which the poem was recited, the poem does not for this reason become very good, but at all events it must be admitted that this may be a case when the circumstances would have given an edge to lines far worse. For by 1503, if that is the date of the poem, Thomas More was already recognized as being a rising lawyer. We may be sure that the most delighted person in the gathering was Mr. Serjeant More. Whatever the old gentleman's limitations, he had a keen sense of humor.

A very distinguished lawyer of our own time, Mr. Richard O'Sullivan, K.C., in an article contributed to the *Dublin Review* in 1936, has expressed some surprise that nobody who has written on More—and this would include the eminent lawyers Lord Campbell, Sir James Mackintosh and Mr. Edward Foss, has indicated the effect that More's legal training had on his mind.

Regarding this, no "layman" like myself is competent to say more than that I can see that Mr. O'Sullivan is making a good point. But I think it might be suggested that the very fact that so important an aspect of More has not been isolated for special consideration—even by the members of his own profession—shows how perfectly he succeeded in integrating all knowledge into the humanist completeness. Had Thomas More been content to be, as his father wished, nothing but a lawyer, he might still have risen to be Lord Chancellor. But in that event he would have been merely one of a long line of whom nothing much is to be said except that they were able and conscientious judges. As it is, we do of course remember that Sir Thomas More was Lord Chancellor of England, but we think of him as being much more than that—as wise and witty and learned, and a dabbler (or "meddler," as he put it) in almost everything from astronomy to medicine, from poetry to politics—but above all as one of the best examples there has ever been of the whole or the completely effectuated man.

CHAPTER FOUR

The Call of the Cloister

THE grouping of the matters treated in the preceding chapter called for the carrying of More's story down to 1503. But it must be said now that during that period there occurred a crisis in his life which needs special treatment at this point. He very nearly became a monk instead of a lawyer. For about four years he lived at the London Charterhouse, continuing his legal studies and his literary work, but all that time meditating joining the Carthusians himself. And after he had reached the conclusion that he had better abandon this idea, he thought for a while of the Franciscans until he reached the final decision that monasticism, or even the secular priesthood, was not his vocation.

It may seem very strange that a man so gregarious as More should even for a moment have entertained such a notion. For the Carthusians are an order of hermits, living in perpetual silence though in community. The Trappists, a seventeenth-century reform of the Cistercians, have an equally strict silence, but are in almost all other respects poles asunder from the Carthusians. For where the Trappists are not permitted individual cells, but sleep and work and eat together—always of course in silence—the Carthusians live each man in his own cell, which is really his own house, connected with the others only by the cloisters. And they never meet except in the Church for the office, taking even their meals alone. That the witty and talkative and friendly More should have been attracted to such a life seems astonishing. Such nevertheless is the fact, as it is also a fact that to his dying day he regretted that God did not call him to this life.

Just how More lived among the Carthusians is not very clear. But it would appear that he did more than reside in the Charterhouse as a paying guest. He could of course come and go as he pleased, yet he took part, so far as this was possible, in their spiritual exercises. Also he practiced great physical asceticism, sleeping on the ground with a block of wood for a pillow, rising at two in the morning after only four or five hours of rest, and beginning to wear at this time the hair shirt he never left off until the day before his execution in 1535.

The question arises as to whether he may not have had some such affiliation as exists between the Franciscans and Dominicans and their tertiaries, or between the Benedictines and their oblates. These are men and women living in the world, where they are indistinguishable (except, let us hope, by their piety) from the rest of ordinary Christians. They share in the merits of the Order, and when they die they have the right to be buried in its habit. It may interest my readers to know that at least three million such people exist today—most of them Franciscan tertiaries.

I do not know whether the Carthusians now have oblates, though presumably they did have at that time. Could this be the basis of the claim the Benedictines make that Thomas More is one of their saints? On the other hand, the Franciscans also list him among the saints of their Order. For neither claim have I been able to find any evidence, though I suspect that the Franciscan assertion may rest upon the misunderstanding of a letter More wrote to Erasmus in 1516, where he speaks of himself as wearing a Greyfriars cloak.[1] Such a reference, if not studied in its Utopian context, might easily send anybody astray.

[1] This seems to me to refer merely to the drab colors worn by his Utopians. He tells Erasmus, "My Utopians have made me their perpetual sovereign! I seem already to be marching along, crowned with a diadem of wheat, conspicuous in a Greyfriars cloak and carrying for a sceptre a few ears of corn." (The wheat and corn are, of course, the royal insignia of this republic.) He goes on to imagine himself surrounded by Amaurotians—Amaurote being the capital city of Utopia. A Franciscan friend, whom I consulted about More's alleged tertianship, supplied me with a number of references, especially the *Catalogus Hagiographicus Seraphicae Familiae* in *Acta Minorum* (*an.* xxviii, p. 203 *seq.*), which is an official list of all the Saints, Blessed and Venerable of the Orders of St. Francis, published in 1909. My Franciscan informant thinks that the appearance of St. Thomas More's name on p. 216 of this list settles the question. To me, however, it seems merely to prove that the claim has the sanction of the heads of the Franciscan Order. Father

Whatever may be the truth about this, there can be no question at all that More was Carthusian in spirit, and that he bore to the end the marks the Carthusians had put upon him. Not only that, but when the great sifting of souls came in the summer of 1535 the greatest number of martyrs (though still only a handful) were Carthusians, with whose names must be linked those of the Bridgettine Reynolds and one secular priest, John Hale. And among all the bishops of England, only one—John Fisher—stood firm. This initial protest against the Henrician tyranny was all but limited to the Carthusians[2] and their disciple, Thomas More.

There was another way in which the Carthusians influenced More, and this has been discussed in Professor Chambers' essay, "The Continuity of English Prose," contributed by him as the introduction to Dr. Elsie Hitchcock's Early English Text Society edition of Harpsfield, but published afterwards as a separate volume. Here attention is drawn to the fact that among the spiritual works mentioned with the highest approval by More is Walter Hilton's *Scale of Perfection*. Chambers further points out that the manuscript of this—or one of the manuscripts—in the British Museum, was copied with great care from the first edition, thus showing the anxiety of the brethren to have a correct text. On this

---

Cuthbert writes in the *Catholic Encyclopedia* (Vol. XIV, p. 645), "Blessed Thomas More is frequently spoken of as a tertiary of St. Francis, but there seems to be no historical evidence to support this statement." There is certainly not a word about this in any of the early—or for that matter—the later biographers. As for the Benedictine claim, a Benedictine friend I consulted was able to throw no light on the matter. And as this book goes to press Father Thomas Brogdon of the English Charterhouse writes to tell me that though the Carthusians did have men known as *Redditi*, and sometimes referred to as "oblates," attached to them until 1582, as these gave themselves completely to the service of the Order, More could hardly have been one of them.

[2] William Peto, provincial of the Grey Friars, however, had the courage, when preaching before the Court at Greenwich, to rebuke the King to his face. And all that Henry did was to leave the chapel. But that was before matters had proceeded very far. In 1533 Peto found it advisable to leave England, and he remained abroad until Mary's accession, when he was created a cardinal.

Professor Reed comments: "No one who is familiar with our earlier prose writers can fail to observe that More's prose style is like nothing that preceded it so much as the natural, lucid and easy prose of the school of Hilton . . . It may seem incongruous to associate More's hair-shirt with his prose style; but both, I believe, derived from his early days of prayer, reading, recollection and discipline beside the monks of the London Charterhouse." Chambers adds: "To read these manuscripts is to be brought very near to the most heroic episode in English history."

More spent, Roper tells us, about four years with the Carthusians, and the question arises as to when he went there and when he left. The period is usually assigned as about 1500 to 1504—that is, just prior to his marriage. I confess that I feel hesitant to accept these dates, as they suggest that the very moment More reached the conclusion he lacked the monastic vocation he rushed out to find a wife. This would make him a little too much like the Monk of Siberia of the limerick, who burst from his cell with a hell of a yell—which is not much in keeping with More's character. I would be inclined to suggest that his Carthusian period was from 1496, when he was all but disowned by his father, until 1500, when he was completing his legal studies. There is a difficulty here in the fact that Erasmus writes of him as living at Lincoln's Inn during the spring of 1500, but it may be that he had just left the Charterhouse to go there.[3] For Roper's "four years" in all likelihood was only an approximation of the length of time More was with the Carthusians.

Be this as it may, it is an admirable thing to record of More that he spent such a long time in deciding upon his vocation. Concerning his motives we have a letter written by Erasmus, of which the concluding sentence sometimes used to be seriously misinterpreted. The whole passage reads: "He applied his whole

[3] May this not even imply that More had not previously resided at the Inn? I am not wishing to press a conjecture too far, but it would seem from researches made on my behalf by Judge McWilliams, to whom this book is dedicated, that residence at the Inns of Court at this time, though the general rule, was not always insisted upon.

mind to exercises of piety, looking to and pondering on the priesthood in vigils, fasts, and prayers, and similar austerities. In which matter he proved himself far more prudent than most candidates who thrust themselves rashly into that arduous profession, without any previous trial of their powers. The one thing that prevented him from giving himself to that kind of life was that he could not shake off the desire of the married state. He chose, therefore, to be a chaste husband rather than an impure priest."

This has been taken by some of More's earlier Protestant biographers—though not, it should be noted, by the later ones, such as Professor Chambers and Miss Routh—as implying that all, or at least many, priests were impure. But a second reading of what Erasmus wrote will show that he meant nothing of the kind, for he has just pictured an ideal of monasticism of a very austere sort. Erasmus is saying only what any sensible novice-master would say—that if the obligation of celibacy seems too heavy *in a particular case* it should not be undertaken. If More had consulted, as he must be presumed to have done, any of the Carthusian Fathers, or Colet or Grocyn, they would have told him that a special grace is needed for the celibate life, and that he should not vow himself to celibacy unless he was sure he had the vocation for it. Is it not patent that if he had seen even the faintest signs of moral laxity among the monks with whom he lived for four years in such close proximity, he would not have stayed at the Charterhouse as long as four days? The whole point of the matter is that he greatly admired them and their mode of life, and that he never ceased to wish that it could have been for him, but that he regretfully reached the decision that he had better not attempt it. Though in later life, after having been twice married, he thought, as Stapleton tells us, that he had exaggerated the difficulties of celibacy, at the time he feared to accept them.

This of course is not to say that there was no immorality among the clergy of More's day. Erasmus, for instance, was the son of a priest, as no doubt he would have admitted to More in confidence, however disingenuous he was usually inclined to be about this circumstance. But it is worth noting that among the many charges that were brought against the English clergy by the first Protestant controversialists, though we hear much about their arrogance and laziness and covetousness, very seldom is the charge of immorality heard. More in his later controversial writings admits that among the clergy are men who are "naught," in other words, bad. But he maintained that the English priesthood was "far able to overmatch . . . the spirituality of any nation Christian." He pointed out that, if only canon law were observed as it should be, fewer priests would be ordained and none who did not have the title to a sufficient living or a patrimony of his own. Then the Church would be spared the scandal of tramp priests who lived as best they could by getting a "trental" (that is, thirty days' Masses) here and there, or as chaplains in private houses, or in other positions that were functionary rather than priestly.

But as none of this applied to More, there is no need to argue the point further. More came to believe that his own vocation was to be a lawyer and a married man and not a monk. And Harpsfield, after drawing attention to the commonplace of Catholic spirituality that the contemplative is superior to the active life, considered in itself, makes the self-evident concession that this is not necessarily true of the particular case. He goes on to say that More's marked preference for the cloister was overruled and that "God Himself seemeth to have chosen and appointed this man to another kind of life, to serve Him therein more acceptably to the divine honour, and more profitably for the wealth of the realm and his own soul also."

But though More decided against becoming a monk, he never ceased the ascetic practices begun while he was living with the Carthusians. It might be a source of edification to go to the Frick Museum in New York and look at the Lord Chancellor of England, as depicted in Holbein's masterpiece, and then reflect that, under the gorgeous robes of office, was a hair-shirt. More's piety was of as sweet and sunny a kind as can be imagined, but its gay and beautiful flowers sprang from the harsh and rocky soil of constant mortification.

Nobody will be able to read this book without perceiving my admiration for Professor Chambers. Yet here I must express my surprise that he should have lent the weight of his name to a suggestion that Thomas More's early life was not free from rather discreditable love affairs. The reason he gives for this strikes me as astounding. He says that it is a pity that Benvenuto Cellini never accepted Henry VII's invitation to go to England because "Cellini would have given us some interesting gossip, and perhaps even some scandal about Thomas More, which might have dissipated that atmosphere of blamelessness which is the greatest difficulty with which More's biographer has to cope."[4]

We are told not to be weary in well doing, and this should extend to the well doing of other men. It is not the atmosphere—blameless or otherwise—that the biographer wishes to exist but the atmosphere that really *does* exist which is the biographer's true concern. Here the Professor has been, in a weak moment, led astray by the late P.S. Allen who, immediately after having rather leeringly dilated on a Flemish noble who sired no less than thirty-six bastards, continues: "Thomas More as a young man was not blameless, but it is surprising that Erasmus in writing an appreciation of More in 1519, when he was already a judge of the King's Bench, stated the fact in quite explicit, though graceful, language; and further, that More took no exception to the statement, which was repeated in edition after edition."[5] Dr. Allen was an immensely learned man, but learned men do not always have much common sense, or even much feeling for logical or psychological probabilities. "Surprising" is what Dr. Allen calls this! It seems to me utterly incredible, if what Erasmus wrote can be understood in the sense our Doctor gives to it. The words are these: *Cum aetas ferret non abhorruit a puellarum amoribus, sed citra infamiam, et sic ut oblatis magis fruereteur quam captatis et*

[4] *Thomas More,* p. 104.

[5] *The Age of Erasmus,* p. 205.

animo mutuo caperetur potius quam coitu. Can it be imagined that Erasmus could have meant that More's relations with women in his youth were irregular, when he also said of him that his soul was purer than any snow? And is it not obvious that, if More had supposed that what Erasmus wrote could be taken in an objectionable sense, he would have promptly sought a correction of it? Of course all that Erasmus intended to convey was that More was an agreeable young man who was attractive to women and who was attracted by them.

There is one poem of More's—just one—that alludes to any kind of love affair, and it is a conclusive proof of how fresh and young was his middle-aged heart. For it was written when he was forty-one about a boyish attachment twenty-five years before. In the interval he had married twice, once very happily and once sufficiently happily. Yet he still remembers with tenderness the girl of fourteen he had loved, perhaps more than he ever loved any woman. I give the lines in Archdeacon Wrangham's translation:

> Scarce had I bid my sixteenth summer hail,
> And two in thine were wanting to the tale,
> When thy soft mien — ah, mien for ever fled! —
> On my tranced heart its guiltless influence shed.
> Then the duenna and the guarded door
> Baffled the stars and bade us meet no more.
> Crimeless, my heart you stole in life's soft prime,
> And still possess that heart without a crime;
> Pure was the love in which my youth prevailed,
> And age would keep it pure if honour failed.

Who that girl was we shall never know, nor does it matter. What does matter is that the silver is still untarnished, the bloom still on the peach.

CHAPTER FIVE

The Humanist

In the spring of 1505 More married. How he became acquainted with Jane Colt we do not know, or how long he had known her. Her father was a country squire, on a small but substantial scale, living at Netherhall near Roydon in Essex, and as he had a large number of children Jane's dowry could not have been opulent. From the worldly point of view, the marriage seems to have been an equal match.

More was rather older than men usually were in those days when they married. Not only that, he was already well-known and marked out for advancement in his profession. Had he been ambitious, it may be presumed that he might have married into a family richer and more influential than that of the Colts. Yet he chose a somewhat untutored country girl, and evidently he chose wisely.

Roper set in circulation a story which has often been repeated and rarely questioned. It is that More would have preferred Jane's younger sister—and Jane herself was only seventeen—but reflected that the elder might be hurt if she were passed over. Therefore, according to Roper, "he then of a certain pity framed his fancy towards her, and soon after married her."

Miss Routh casts doubt upon this anecdote, and so does Mr. Hollis, though of course there is nothing to set against what Roper says except general probabilities. But I do not think Mr. Hollis's comments can be improved upon. Once again common sense is a good guide. "No one," he writes, "could possibly have known, whatever they might have surmised, that More preferred the second to the eldest of Mr. Colt's daughters except by More's own confession. Now it is not very probable that More would have chosen his wife in this peculiar fashion, but had he been guilty of this strange chivalry, it is quite inconceivable that he would have told anybody about it. For by telling he would have destroyed any virtue, such as there was, in the act. He would merely have made everybody extremely uncomfortable.

"The fact then that More told this anecdote, as we must believe from Roper that he did, proves surely not that it was true but that it was untrue. If it was true, he certainly would not have told it. On the other hand he was an incorrigible *farceur*. Even his wife could never tell whether he was serious or not. He was certainly on most friendly terms with his sister-in-law, and there is no reason at all why he should not have had some private family joke with his children, the point of which was that he wished he had married their aunt—no reason at all, provided only that it was not in the least true. Roper, who had no very keen sense of humour, came later into the family, heard the story doubtless at second hand and a little stupidly missed the point of it."

We do not know a great deal about Jane More except that she bore her husband four children in rapid succession and then, in 1510, died. But as Chambers points out, the letter of Erasmus telling how More managed to interest his untutored wife in books and taught her music agrees very closely with the story of the Uneasy Wife in the *Colloquies* of Erasmus. We must be a little careful about asserting a perfect correspondence between factual circumstance and the use subsequently made of it fictionally. It is nevertheless true that writers of fiction do sometimes transfer raw slices of life into their imaginative productions. But the story Erasmus relates, however much embellished by him, or even embellished at the first telling by More, we may fairly safely suppose to have been heard at the Mores' table, with perhaps Jane laughing and in blushes declaring it all exaggerated but not denying its essential truth. As it appears in the *Colloquies,* it was of a man who had married a seventeen-year-old girl, who had lived all her life in the country and was quite uneducated. When her husband tried to "improve" her mind, even making her repeat the substance of the Sunday sermon, she used to cry and wish herself dead. Troubled by this, the husband told his father-in-law of the situation, and he replied, "Well, use your rights and give her a good beating." To this the husband answered, "I know what my rights are, but I would rather you used your authority," upon which the father pretended to be very angry with his daughter. So successful was this device that she fell at her husband's feet and asked his forgiveness.

Jane altogether lacked the pungency of her successor, who was as salty and as "English" a character as anybody would wish to encounter, but she was better liked by More's friends. Ammonius, the King's Latin secretary, who is very ungallant in at least one of his references to the second Mrs. More, mentions Jane in a letter to Erasmus as More's very kind wife. In the last year of his freedom her husband transferred her bones to the tomb he thought he would himself eventually occupy in Chelsea church, and in the long Latin epitaph he wrote for it he calls her "dear Jane, Thomas More's little wife." After more than twenty years his memory of her remained not only green but tender.

Her sweet but shadowy presence passes so briefly across a stage later to be often dominated by the redoubtable Dame Alice, that this might be the best place to introduce that lady. Though it disarranges strict chronology, I quote here what Father John Bouge, a former secular priest who had become a Carthusian, wrote to a lady shortly after More's execution. "He was," Father Bouge says, "my parishioner in London. I christened him two goodly children. I buried his first wife. And within a month after he came to me on a Sunday, at night, late, and there he brought me a dispensation to be married the next Monday, without any banns asking . . . This Mr. More was my ghostly child: in his confession to be so pure, so clean, with great study, deliberation, and devotion, I never heard many such." The many sentimentalists who have been shocked at a second marriage made so soon after the death of a first wife, had better ponder this letter. More was not of course acting romantically but sensibly for the benefit of a house full of young children. Alice Middleton was seven years his senior, which would make her thirty-nine, and she made an admirable housekeeper and step-mother. Once again More had chosen well. And though I am the last person in the world to suggest that "being in love" is not desirable in marriage, one has only to look around to see that it is no guarantee to its success. What *is* always needed for its success, that More gave—kindness and good humor and tact and faithfulness to the vow. There was happiness here and love, even if it is not of the kind that one celebrates in song.

There is nevertheless a kind of love song, and though it was probably written about 1505 (and certainly before 1510), it may, as a philosophical treatment of the relation between human and divine love, be applied as well to More's second marriage as to his first. These two stanzas come from his "Twelve Properties of a Lover," appended to his translation of the life of Pico della Mirandola.

> The first point is to love but one alone,
> And for that love all other to forsake:
> And whoso loveth many loveth none.
> The flood that is in many channels take
> In each of them shall feeble streamès make;
> The love that is divided among many
> Uneath sufficeth that any part have any.
>
> So thou that hast thy love set unto God
> In thy remembrance this imprint and grave:
> As He in sovereign dignity is odd,[1]
> So will He in love no parting fellow have.
> Love Him therefore, with all that He thee gave;
> For body, soul, wit, cunning, mind and thought,
> Part will He none, but either all or naught.

These verses lead me to a brief comment on the book in which they appear, published by More in 1510 under the title of *The Life of John Picus, Earle of Mirandula.* The writing of it follows More's decision to give up all idea of the cloister and to settle

[1] Unique.

down to the practice of law and to marriage. It was a rendering into English from the Latin of Pico's nephew.

A minor point of interest may be touched on first. The book is dedicated to Joyeuce Leigh, otherwise Joyce Lee, who was sister of More's friend Edward Lee, who was destined to succeed Wolsey as Archbishop of York. Joyce had become a Poor Clare (or a Minoress, as was the term then used in England), yet her membership in that very strictly enclosed order did not prevent More's sending her his book with its dedicatory letter as a New Year's gift, telling her it was "such a present as may bear witness of my tender love and zeal to the happy continuance and gracious increase of love in your soul."

I suspect that it is Joyce who appears (as do Wolsey and Dame Alice) under thin disguise in one of the stories in the *Dialogue of Comfort,* written thirty years later. There the nun is called to the grate of the convent parlor to talk to her brother, a doctor of divinity. She proceeds to give him "surely good counsel (saving somewhat too long)" until she paused to remark that she marvelled that so learned a man could not of his charity give so simple and unlearned a soul as herself some fruitful exhortation. "By my troth, good sister," said her brother, "I can not for you, for your tongue hath never ceased, and said enough for us both." We shall meet Edward Lee again; it is pleasant to recall that More's first book was dedicated to his sister.

Much more important than this, of course, is the revealing fact that, as Cresacre More tells us, his great-grandfather chose Pico della Mirandola as a model for his own life. Very modestly More set no saint before him for emulation, though Pico was a fair approximation to one, but a layman like himself. Pico was like him, too, in having come close to taking the monastic habit, and in being a scholar—an excellent exemplar of the best side of the Italian Renaissance. Regarding this, W. H. Hutton has a fine passage which catches much of the purpose of the Christian humanist. "In him," writes Dean Hutton, "no keen eye could detect the subtle flavour of a pagan life, nor was his Christianity cold, unsympathetic or unreal. His abilities were remarkable even among his contemporaries, and his energy and devotion were as extraordinary.... The favourite of Lorenzo de' Medici, he was also the friend and disciple of Savonarola. ... There is much similarity between Pico and More. Both were keen classical scholars, tinged with the mysticism of Renaissance imaginings, men of wide interests, bent on bringing the Divine Spirit into every sphere of human thought.... The Italian humanist was penetrated with the sense of the beauty and the mystery of life. ... To him it did not seem that Christianity was less true because Paganism was so beautiful, and the same thought was never absent from the mind of More."

That is a very good summary of what humanism meant to Thomas More and his friends, but as the term has been used in so many senses, and as it will be used frequently in this book, it might be advisable at this point to elaborate a little further, so that the sense in which I use the term may not be misunderstood. First of course there is that simple meaning retained in the term, the "humanities," the study of the classics of Greece and Rome. To many of the first humanists that was all that was involved: to them humanism was ancient literature, more particularly that in Greek. And though later when people spoke of the "New Learning," they were disposed to equate this with Protestantism, there was no necessary connection between the two things at all, nor commonly even so much as an accidental one. The tendency of one of the main branches of humanism was rather in the direction of paganism, but often of paganism at its most corrupt.

But again, this was not in the least necessary, even though it is understandable enough how this should be the effect of the art and literature of paganism upon many minds. The deeper sort of humanist perceived that paganism at its noblest pointed towards the Christian revelation—is not this almost the central theme of the *Utopia?*—and even divined the corruptions of paganism to be an unconscious dissatisfaction with the best that paganism could attain, and therefore a kind of confused and left-handed search for God.

Further, as the eccentricities of that sort of neo-paganism palled —and it was capable of little except eccentricities—humanism simmered down to what most people now probably think of as being, to quote the *Encyclopedia Britannica's* definition, "any system of thought or action which assigns a predominant interest in the affairs of men as compared with the supernatural or abstract." Such a concept, however, hardly belongs to the humanism of the Renaissance, of whatever variety. All one need say about it is that, had it been presented to a man like More, or any of his friends, they would have at once said that the real humanist was obliged to take God into account, and was unable to think of man as sufficient unto himself.

It ought to be obvious that the other concept narrows the horizon instead of broadening it. But the devout humanist could hold that, thanks to the stimulation of the newly discovered treasures of ancient Greece, philosophy could be more profound and have better scientific tools at its command. Plato, on the one hand, and a writer like Galen, on the other, opened new vistas. And as scholasticism was for the time-being petrified, there was a disposition, even among the most Catholic of humanists, unjustly to disparage it. Here was something not only fresher and more exciting than the syllogistic method, it was also something far more poetical. And the charm of Greek culture made men long for the poetical and despise as pedestrian stuffiness the compendiums that had only too often comprised the whole intellectual baggage of the philosopher and the theologian.

The humanist judgment on this point was altogether too sweeping. Yet it should be remembered that it did eventually aid in the revivification of scholasticism itself. The immediate necessity was the opening up of the Greek Fathers, for they were discovered along with the Greek poets and philosophers. And the discovery of the Fathers meant the possibility of a better understanding of the Scriptures.

None of this had any vital connection with Protestantism, as is proved by the career of Thomas More and his friends Erasmus and Colet. But it is true that Protestantism, at its higher intellectual levels, was quick to take advantage of the "New Learning" and even to try to appropriate it to its own use. There was something analogous here to the way the new politics and the new economics were soon given a Protestant slant. But in their case there was a natural affinity to Protestantism in its earlier phases; in the case of the New Learning itself there was no affinity at all but merely the same kind of seizure of opportunity by the religious reformer as was shown by the rich and powerful in another field. A strange but all but irresistable combination came about by which an absolutist monarch was supported, on the one side, by the scholar and, on the other, by the Machiavellian politician. Probably no humanist foresaw this outcome, or wished for it; and it is certainly hard to see how any human interest was well served.

Against such a deflection of humanism from its true purpose More fought a battle which ended only in his death on the scaffold. But there is another aspect of false humanism to which More was equally opposed. Humanism thought of itself, quite rightly, as an integration of the whole personality, and at its best did aim at a universality of knowledge directed to a single end. Some of the discoverers of the ancient pagan learning found it all too easy to develop their personality by abandoning restraint; nothing human was to be alien to them—least of all human vices. More was as far removed as it is possible to be from humanists of this stripe. There have been more versatile men than he; not many, but there have been some. But it would be hard to think of a man who more completely rounded himself out as a human being. And here we come back to God, and to man's place in relation to Him. More, with all his gayety and high spirits, never forgot the first fact about man—that he is a god in ruins. Not for a moment did he forget the fact of original sin. Hence his hair-shirt and his constant brooding over the Four Last Things. It was precisely because he saw that fallen man never can be altogether integrated until he is with God, that his personal integration was as near to perfection as it was. The complete man is the saint, and More set out to be a saint. In the course of doing so he was able to exercise his immensely versatile talents. At the end of it all he showed a constancy to principle that called for most absolute courage—and so became a hero. His humanism was crowned by martyrdom.

All this could not have been clear to him from the outset. But from the outset he was on the right road and he never left it. And for him this was not the road travelled by the monk but by the man in the world, yet not of the world; this man achieving the greatest position open to him, but taking it reluctantly and giving it up gladly. And in this process his taking of Pico della Mirandola as his model and his writing of Pico's life mark a very decisive stage.

What More translated is hardly a biography so much as a series of biographical notes about a typical but rather curious person—learned, as More was not, in Hebrew and attempting an impossible synthesis of Christianity and cabalistic lore. But under it all was a simple and familiar Catholic feeling, which perhaps shows itself nowhere so clearly as in its close. "Now" it runs, "since it is so that he is adjudged to that fire from which he shall undoubtedly depart into glory, and no man is sure how long it shall be first, and maybe the shorter time for our intercessions, let every Christian body show their charity upon him to help to speed him thither where, after the long habitation with the inhabitants of this dark world (to whom his godly conversation gave great light) and after the dark fire of Purgatory (in which venial sins be cleansed) he may shortly (if he be not already) enter the inaccessible and infinite light of heaven, where he may in the presence of the sovereign Godhead so pray for us that we may the rather by his intercession be partners of that unspeakable joy which we have prayed to bring him speedily to."

The book was written at the house named the Barge at Bucklersbury, near Walbrook, where Thomas More had taken his young wife—a part of London, where as Shakespeare reminds us, the herb-sellers had their fragrant booths. There the busy lawyer soon found himself, to use Cresacre More's expression, "clogged with wife and children"—a condition which one might suppose would have put an end to his scholarly and literary pursuits, but which did nothing of the kind.

Though his eminence as a lawyer had to wait until the next reign, the reputation he was already winning is proved by his appointment in 1503—when he was only twenty-five—as "reader" or lecturer in law at Furnival's Inn. Though this position was not as illustrious as that of a reader at an Inn of Court, such as he afterwards obtained, it assured success in his profession. And even before his marriage he was sent—probably by the city of London, where he was already immensely popular—as one of its Members to Parliament. He had a further qualification—proved by his lectures at St. Lawrence Jewry—that of an ability in public speaking rare in those days. Though one may doubt whether he was a great orator—for his was not an emotional nature and he lacked the "golden voice"—he had what, for practical purposes, served almost as well. "It would be difficult," Erasmus wrote to Ulrich von Hutten, "to find anyone more successful in speaking extempore, the happiest thoughts being attended by the happiest language, while a mind that catches and anticipates all that passes, and a ready memory, having everything as it were, in stock, promptly supplies whatever the time or occasion demand." To this I think we are safe in adding one of the best gifts of the public speaker—the ability to get in touch with the audience. Such at least one would infer from More's style of writing, with its fund of amusing stories and its intimacy. And the best gift of all was surely his, an evident sincerity, without which many a golden tongue betrays a shallow mind and a false heart. More had humor and homeliness and ready wit, not to mention knowing what he was talking about. These qualities soon made him, and kept him, almost the idol of his native city.

These very gifts, however, got him into serious trouble with King Henry VII. According to Roper, who is most circumstantial, More, almost alone, dared to oppose, as too large, a grant of money demanded by Henry when the Princess Margaret was married to the Scots King. About this, however, there may be some confusion, for Margaret's marriage was in 1503, and Parliament did not meet till the following year. Also there was a belated request for "reasonable aid"—that is, the customary grant—for the knighting of Prince Arthur, who had died in 1502. The *Rolls of Parliament* do show that there was opposition, which was no doubt all the stronger because of the general irritation against the fiscal methods of Empson and Dudley. So the grant was scaled down from £90,000 to less than £40,000, greatly to the anger of a King who was notorious for his avarice. As he could find no ground upon which he could punish the "beardless boy," Thomas More, for his part in the matter, Henry, according to Roper, "devised a causeless quarrel against his father, keeping him in the Tower until he had made him pay to him a hundred pounds fine."

Roper's story continues that when Thomas More encountered Richard Foxe, the Bishop of Winchester, shortly afterwards, the Bishop advised him to confess his offence and ask the King's pardon. Fortunately More happened to run into Richard Whitford, at that time Foxe's secretary and afterwards a Bridgittine monk and a devotional writer. As soon as Whitford heard of the Bishop's advice he exclaimed that Foxe's intention was to trap More; to admit any fault would give the handle he wanted. "My Lord," Whitford added with a shrewdness completely cynical, "to serve the King's turn, will not stick to agree to his own father's death." If this was really so, the King and the Bishop were a pretty pair of scoundrels.

A sequel to the tale is given by Stapleton. "Seven or eight years later Henry VII was dead, and Dudley, for the evil counsel he had given to that monarch, was condemned to death. As he was being led out to execution, More went up to him and said, 'Well, Mr. Dudley, in that matter of the exactions was I not right?' 'Oh, Mr. More,' he replied, 'it was by God's guidance that you did not acknowledge your fault to the King, for if you had done so you would most certainly have lost your head!'" This would seem to indicate that More's opposition in Parliament was to the general program of tax exactions, as conducted by Empson and Dudley, rather than to a special grant for Prince Arthur or the Princess Margaret, though this may have provided him with the immediate occasion for his protest. Roper adds, "Had the King soon after not died, [Sir Thomas More] was determined to have gone over [the] sea, thinking that being in the King's indignation, he could not live in England without great danger."

Roper is vague about this phase of the matter, and there are some discrepancies regarding dates. Yet he would seem to be substantially accurate, for More did more than "think" about going abroad for a time; we know from the letter he wrote to Martin Dorp (or Dorpius) in 1515 that he actually did so. In that letter he wrote: "You seem to set so much by [the universities of] Louvain and Paris, that, as regards dialectics at least, you think they are banished from the rest of the world. Now seven years ago I was in both those universities, and though not for a very long time, yet I took pains to ascertain what was taught there and what methods were followed. Though I respect both of them, yet neither from what I saw then, nor from what I have since heard, have I found any reason why, even in dialectics, I should wish any sons of mine (for whom I desire the very best education) to be taught there rather than at Oxford or Cambridge." This statement does not of course prove that More went abroad to escape from Henry VII, and in fact Stapleton says that he did so "to see the country as was customary with young Englishmen of rank." However, that could have been merely the professed motive, one that it would have been more prudent to give out than an admission that he was actually seeking refuge abroad.

One interesting incidental fact emerges from this visit of More's to the foreign universities. He mentions in his letter to Dorpius the high estimation he acquired at Paris for the teaching of Jacques Lefèvre d'Etaples, generally known as Faber Stapulensis. This scholar later leaned strongly towards heresy, but he was sufficiently orthodox in 1508, and during that "safe" period his casually dangerous speculative opinions would be likely to pass unnoticed. More's judgment on Faber, however, probably was intended to apply only to his dialectical method, but he praised him for the restoration of "true philosophy, founded upon that of Aristotle." It is at all events apparent that More's objection to the sterility of a philosophy whose futility was like that of a man milking a he-goat into a sieve held by another man was not meant as a comprehensive description of scholasticism as such but as a hit at its degeneration into logic-chopping. What Faber had been doing, much to More's approval, was to concentrate on the content of Aristotle rather than the logical devices of a scholasticism in temporary decline. The critical texts of the *Physics* and the *Ethics* and the *Metaphysics* and the *Politics* he was issuing rightly seemed a restoration.

This visit of More's to Paris and Louvain was, as he says, brief. For the rest of the time he lived, as quietly as possible, in London. But though he loved the city of his birth, he was often distressed by what he saw of the vices that were now springing from its growing wealth. His social analysis of these evils was to be given in the *Utopia,* but in a letter which we can date as just prior to 1504 the young humanist lawyer expresses something of the misgivings already in his mind when writing to John Colet. "I cannot blame you," More tells him, "if you are not tired of the country where you see simple people, ignorant of the wiles of the town, and wherever you turn your eyes, the beautiful face of the country refreshes you, the soft air exhilarates you, the sight of the sky delights you." His "dear Colet" was therefore urged to return, "Come for the sake of your native city, to which you owe the care due to a parent," and he adds, "Come for my sake." The service he specifically wished from Colet was that of a Father Confessor, a function being performed in Colet's absence by Grocyn. This humanist scholar was above everything else a devout Christian.

CHAPTER SIX

A Man Born for Friendship

WHEN Henry VIII succeeded to the throne in 1509 Lord Mountjoy—or more probably, Ammonius, in Mountjoy's name—wrote an enthusiastic letter to Erasmus. One often has to discount the somewhat flowery style in vogue among the humanists, but this letter undoubtedly did convey what everybody felt: "Heaven laughs and the earth rejoices; everything is full of milk and honey and nectar. Avarice has fled the country. Our King is not after gold, or gems, or precious metals, but virtue, glory, immortality. . . . Just lately he was saying that he wished he were more learned. 'That is not what we want from you,' I said, 'but that you should foster and encourage learned men.' 'Why, of course,' he said, 'for without them life would be hardly life.' " The letter was designed to induce Erasmus to return to a country which would now be so propitious to men of his stamp. More wrote in a similar persuasive strain.

If hardly any words can seem more savagely sarcastic, when read in the light of subsequent events, than those just quoted, it did really appear that, with the passing of the very unpopular and avaricious Henry VII, the night had also passed. Little was it realized that where the father had scourged with whips the son would scourge with scorpions, or that England was to experience under Henry VIII the worst tyranny in its history. How could that be imagined of the eighteen-year-old King with his almost feminine—some said, angelic—good looks? The young, golden-haired, six-foot-four athlete reminded More of the legend of Achilles in woman's disguise.

Nor was this flattery. We cannot but think of the burly and bearded and bloated satyr of Holbein's famous painting. But *that* Henry, though no doubt latent in the youth who ascended the throne, had yet to manifest himself. The fact that he already sweated profusely could be masked—as later it could not—by the use of heavy musk. What appeared to be hearty health was the first hint of gross lubricity.

Yet Henry's immense ability was not something credited to him by flatterers but an undeniable fact. And he was very much in the humanist tradition in combining learning with artistic gifts. His training in theology was due to the expectation that his brother Arthur would be King, and Henry had been thought of as Cardinal-Archbishop of Canterbury. Of his learning in divinity he was justly proud. But he was also a composer of music, some of whose charming pieces are still performed, though his Masses have been lost. And he was quite the best poet in England's royal line. Even those who smile, recalling his adventures with women, to read the lyric opening:

> Green groweth the holly, so doth the ivy.
> Though winter blasts blow never so high,
> Green groweth the holly.
>
> As the holly groweth green
> And never changeth hue,
> So I am, and ever hath been,
> Unto my lady true —

must admit that the lines come close to being first-rate.

These were the accomplishments that were admired by men like More and Mountjoy. To the populace at large Henry's athletic prowess perhaps made more appeal. It delighted the people that their king was the best tennis-player in England, and its most ardent hunter. He threw every wrestler until Francis I threw him at the Field of the Cloth of Gold. But Francis was the younger man, and by then Henry had a syphilitic sore on his leg.

At first even his martial ambitions met with popular approval, however dubiously his advisers (with the exception of Wolsey) regarded his hopes of emulating the exploits of the fifth Henry. These came to be unpopular only when the French wars brought crushing taxes and no gain. And it was observed that Henry VIII took good care never to expose his person in battle and that he showed, in the feverish way he moved from place to place to avoid any kind of epidemic, a fear of death that was excessive—at any rate in the conqueror he wished to be.

These things, however, were as yet far in the distance. So also were those matrimonial proceedings of his which have made it necessary for some people to think hard before remembering whether it was Henry VIII who had six wives or Henry VI who had eight! He married, shortly after the accession, his brother Arthur's widow, Katherine of Aragon. She had long resided in England, and was extremely popular there, giving a further popularity to Henry. More in 1501 was among the crowds that lined the streets and strained out of the windows to see the young Spanish Princess make her public entry into the city by the side of the fifteen-year-old Arthur. Here, everybody supposed, were the future King and Queen. More never forgot the radiant face he saw that day, and thought that Katherine lacked nothing that the most beautiful girl should have. But probably enough even then she possessed little more than the charm of youth and the evident goodness and nobility which should have been possessed by a daughter of Isabella the Catholic.

The cementing of the Spanish alliance was so eminently desirable that Henry VII, upon Arthur's death, actually proposed to marry his daughter-in-law—a sure proof that he considered her such only in name. The avaricious old king was so anxious to keep her rich dowry, that he would have married the girl had not Queen Isabella vigorously expressed her horror at such a mating. In the case of Henry VIII, on the other hand, though a papal dispensation had to be obtained because of Katherine's previous nominal marriage, there was general rejoicing. And the happiness of the royal couple during their first years made them all the more beloved of their subjects. Henry at this time seemed to be the very embodiment of the ideal of kingship.

But Henry had also a great deal of personal charm. Nor would it be just, in view of what we know of the capriciousness and tyranny of his later years, to think that what he had was really *fausse bonhomie*. Though the King's good humor could change in an instant to terrible rage, and though he did more or less deliberately use his charm to suit his own purposes, turning it on or off at will, he never lost a certain hearty affability. Nor did he ever employ that most detestable of combinations, affected geniality and affected piety. He was genuinely likeable, as he was genuinely devout. Except for this he would not have wrought such havoc. The center of his character was, rather than his sensuality (which did not exceed that of many kings whose reputation is better than his), an infinite and almost infantile egotism. His only development—except for cunning—was degeneration from the promise of his youth. The root of his malady was an absolute certainty that he was in conscience bound to do everything to which he took a fancy. He never grew up, but only grew more corpulent. He died emotionally immature.

All these things, of course, were as yet hardly hinted at. The new reign augured a happy prosperity from the start, and was soon crowned with the glory of military success. In the same year (1513) when the French were defeated at the bloodless "Battle of the Spurs," most of the Scots nobility fell round their King at Flodden. And for Thomas More Henry's accession opened a door which had been shut against him while the old King was alive. Now he began to forge upwards. As Hutton puts it, "he sprang, almost at one bound, into fame." Though he did not come immediately under Henry's personal notice, and so far owed nothing to direct royal favor, the popularity he enjoyed among Londoners insured his prosperity.

In spite of his youth—he was still in his early thirties—he became one of the busiest and most successful of English lawyers, so that Roper was able to say, "There was at that time none of the King's courts of the laws of the realm, any matter of importance in controversy, wherein he was not at that time with one party of counsel." His probity was proverbial. Stapleton assures us that from widows and orphans he would take no fees. Nor would he accept a case of whose justice he was not sure. Even so, it was his custom to dissuade clients from litigation if possible, and if in this he could not succeed, to tell them how most economically to present their cause. In spite of this—perhaps in part because of it—he made a substantial income, for Roper says that "he gained without grief not so little as four hundred pounds by the year." To translate Roper a little, this means that More made without undue strain more than an income of from six to ten thousand pounds a year in modern values. But he always showed himself without ambition and indifferent to money. Erasmus was to write: "No man was ever more free from avarice. He would set aside from his income for his children what he thought sufficient, and the remainder he used bountifully."

In addition to his private practice More held offices, early in life, which indicate the esteem in which he was regarded by his profession and by his fellow-citizens. On September 3, 1510, he was appointed Under-Sheriff of London, a position he valued so highly, because of the opportunities it gave him to serve his native city, that he clung to it long after Henry VIII came forward with flattering offers. Also it was an appointment that did not involve much work, as the Sheriffs' Court sat only on Thursdays. His duties were to act as legal adviser to the Court, where he was, in effect, if not in title, the actual judge.

In the autumn of the following year he was chosen as reader or professor of law at Lincoln's Inn, and was given the same profitable honor for the Lent Term of 1515. It clearly indicated his high reputation among his fellow-lawyers. He was in no need of having his fortunes pushed by the King, and would in fact have preferred to follow a quiet legal career on the strength of his own abilities. But of course all this—especially because it was so richly supplemented by other talents—marked him out for the royal favor and made another sort of career inevitable.

Erasmus's description of More and his manner of life belongs to this period, and was given most fully in the famous letter written in 1519 to Ulrich von Hutten. Yet what Erasmus said then applies almost as well to the later More. For there probably never was a man of more settled and orderly habits, or one whose character changed less—a point that should be remembered when we hear suggestions about the hardening of the intellectual arteries he is supposed to have suffered in middle age. The truth is that, so far from there being any essential difference between the Utopian and the Lord Chancellor, there was no essential difference between the law student and the Lord Chancellor, only a steady mellowing and maturing. Even his long imprisonment in the Tower, though it broke his health, seemed to make his heart younger and lighter than ever. So what Erasmus has to say of him in 1519 is also an excellent description of the Lord Chancellor of 1530. That the letter to Hutten was written after a twenty-years' friendship is a sufficient guarantee of its accuracy and fullness.

More is pictured by Erasmus as of medium height, well proportioned—"with such perfect symmetry as to leave nothing to be desired"—light complexioned, with a faint flush of pink under the whiteness of his skin, and with dark brown hair. Though we often hear of his laughing, Holbein showed his face as grave, the artist's eye seizing upon that as the essence of his being. We also know that many of his best jokes—especially those from which he wished to extract further entertainment by having them taken seriously—were tossed out in what is called "dead-pan" style. Only a mischievous flicker could be noted in his eyes. These were gray, flecked with golden spots, "a kind which betokens singular talent, and among the English is considered attractive." Erasmus thought that none are so free from vice as those with eyes the color of More's. We may be sure that candor and innocence shone there.

Erasmus said that an air of joy always surrounded him, and thought his aspect "better framed for gladness than for gravity and dignity, though without any approach to folly or buffoonery." The observant friend noted that one of More's shoulders was a little higher than the other, a result of his being so much hunched up over his desk. Partly because of this posture, but partly because of absent-mindedness, More's gown was generally pulled a little out of its strict folds. The same carelessness sometimes resulted in his going out, even when he was Lord Chancellor, with shoes that needed mending. Then, no doubt after protests from his wife and daughters, he appointed one of his servants to see that he was reasonably well spruced up. This servant—who was probably John Harris, his secretary—was nicknamed by him his "tutor." Though More never admitted it, one suspects that he welcomed having in same small matter one to whom he could render the virtue of obedience.

"I never saw anyone," continues Erasmus, "so indifferent about food." The same was true of drink. He preferred water, yet not to seem singular or morose, he used to hide his abstemiousness from his guests by drinking very small beer. And he drank it out of a pewter vessel so as to conceal how exceedingly little he took. When a toast of wine was offered, he only touched the vessel with his lips. "He likes to eat corned beef and coarse bread much leavened, rather than what people count delicacies. Otherwise he has no aversion to what gives harmless pleasure to the body. He prefers milk diet and fruits, and is especially fond of eggs." All of which surely means not that More actually relished these things better than daintier food, but that by professing a special fondness for them, he could avoid any appearance of asceticism.

Erasmus further describes More as always dressing simply, except on the occasions that demanded a velvet gown and a gold chain. And he ignored "all the ceremonious forms in which most men make politeness to consist." He hated constraint and loved equality in social relationships, seeking the soul of courtesy, which is kindness, rather than artificial etiquette. With which Erasmus comes to the center of his theme. "He seems born and framed for friendship, and is a most faithful and enduring friend. He is easy of access to all; but if he chances to get familiar with one whose vices admit no correction, he manages to loosen and let go the intimacy rather than to break it off suddenly. When he finds any sincere and according to his heart, he so delights in their society and conversation as to place in it the principal charm of life. . . . In a word, if you want a perfect model of friendship, you will find it in no one better than in More."

Another characteristic of this man was his detestation of all modes of "killing time." In his household no cards or dice were permitted, and his gentle nature made him abhor the hunting that was such a passion of his age. He even disliked tennis, as a waster of golden hours. Yet so far was he from being severe in temperament that merriment seemed to be a part of his nature. The word "merry" was constantly on his tongue. "In human affairs," Erasmus wrote of him, "there is nothing from which he does not extract enjoyment, even from things that are most serious. If he converses with the learned and judicious, he delights in their talent; if with the ignorant and foolish, he enjoys their stupidity. . . . With a wonderful dexterity he accommodates himself to every disposition. As a rule, in talking with women, or even with his own wife, he is full of jokes and banter." Though learned and witty men frequented his house, and meals began with the intoning of a passage of scripture, monastic style, the clowning of the fool was afterwards permitted as part of the conversation. He took pride in showing his guests his menagerie of curious animals and birds. In the Holbein family group we see that the marmoset was given the run of the house as though it were a kitten.

Mrs. More (Mrs. Middleton when More married her) is described by Erasmus as "a vigilant and active housewife with whom he lives as pleasantly and sweetly as though she had all the charms of youth. You will scarcely find a husband who by authority or severity has gained such ready compliance as More by playful flattery. What indeed would he not obtain when he has prevailed on a woman already getting old"—in 1519 she was almost fifty, seven years older than More—"by no means of a pliable disposition and intent on domestic affairs, to learn to play the harp, the monochord, and the flute, and by the appointment of the husband to devote to this task a fixed time every day." But in that household even the servants were pressed into the domestic orchestra or the part-singing. England was about to become the musical center of Europe. Erasmus concluded: "There seems to be a kind of fateful happiness in this house, so that no one has lived in it without rising to higher fortune; no member of it has ever incurred any stain on his reputation."

This account may be amplified by another letter written by Erasmus—to Budé, the famous French humanist. "It has been said," he remarks, "that learning is unfavourable to commonsense. There is no greater reader than More, and yet you will not find a man who is more complete master of all his faculties, on all occasions, and with all persons, more accessible, more ready to oblige, more quick-witted in conversation, or who combines such true prudence with such agreeable manners."

There were details of More's manner of life that escaped even the keen eye of Erasmus. To nobody but his daughter Margaret did he confide the secret of his hair-shirt, though Dame Alice discovered it, for we hear of her going to More's parish priest, Father John Bouge, asking him to order More to discontinue wearing it. The rather fussy and self-indulgent Erasmus would be among the very last people to be informed on such a point. Indeed, some wonder has often been expressed that, between men who were in many respects so dissimilar, a friendship so close and so completely undisturbed should have existed. One must suppose that though More could not have failed to observe his friend's faults, he decided that these could be overlooked. More had to make allowances for the stratagems a scholar had frequently to employ in those days for procuring the help of patrons without whom it would have been impossible to pursue his career. If it comes to that, More himself, when it was a question of helping Erasmus, was not, as he cheerfully admitted, above a white lie or a little harmless trickery, as when he contrived to smuggle money to Erasmus out of England in contravention of the law. The best possible certificate to the general good character and fundamentally sound purpose of Erasmus was that he retained More's friendship to his dying day. This needs to be said because Mr. Hollis shows himself vindictively intent to stress the worst that can be said of the great Dutch scholar. Here he seems to have taken over that late sixteenth-century tradition according to which Erasmus really was guilty of laying the egg hatched by Luther. If so, then the fact that a large part of that egg, *The Praise of Folly,* was produced in More's house and at his instigation, makes a canonized saint at least to some extent responsible. And the other main part of the Erasmian egg, his edition of the New Testament, was dedicated to the Pope. As a later Pope offered to make Erasmus a cardinal, this fact might be added to the others and used in rebuttal against the detractors of Erasmus.

It is, however, quite true that *The Praise of Folly* was later placed on the Index. But the prohibition was not so much because it was objectionable in itself as because changed circumstances made it possible for people to draw out of that satire things that Erasmus had never intended. In the same way the passage of time can change circumstances once again. Father Bridgett points out that the satire of Erasmus is "moderate compared with that of many previous writers whose faith and loyalty to the Church have never been called in question." I confess that the book seemed to me, when I reread it recently in Hoyt Hopewell Hudson's translation, sufficiently innocuous.

In 1510, in which year the *Moria* was written in More's house, Erasmus, though Luther and his egg had not yet been heard of, at least felt it advisable to make the explanation: "Some critics may complain that these trifles are too frivolous for a theologian[1] and too aggressive for a Christian—but when we allow every department of life to have its amusements, how unfair it would be to deny to study any relaxation at all, especially if the pastime may lead to something serious." As for More, in days when *The Praise of Folly* was being used as ammunition by the early reformers, he wrote a defence of it on the ground that it merely reproved faults and follies—doing so jestingly—and maintained

[1] Erasmus prided himself upon his theological attainments, though these have sometimes been disallowed. As against this is the fact that John Fisher, the Bishop of Rochester and a canonized saint, wished to take him as his theologian to the Council of the Vatican.

that it could still do good if rightly used. "But," he admits, "in these days, in which men by their own default misconstrue and take harm out of the very Scripture of God, until men better amend, if any man would now translate *Moria* into English, or some other works either that I have myself written ere this, albeit there be none harm therein, folk yet being given to take harm of that which is good, I would not only my darling's books, but mine own also, help to burn them both with mine own hands, rather than folk should (though through their own fault) take any harm of them, seeing that I see them likely in these days so to do."

At one time Luther and his unsavory young henchman, Ulrich von Hutten, had hopes of drawing Erasmus to their side. One may wish that Erasmus had been more prompt in his disavowal, but when he spoke out in 1520 it was to say most emphatically: "Christ I know, Luther I know not. The Roman Church I know, which in my opinion does not differ from the Catholic. From it death will not tear me away unless it be torn away from Christ." *His* egg, he declared, had been intended to hatch a chicken; what Luther had hatched from it was something very different. As for More, he was to write even more explicitly: "Had I found in Erasmus, my darling, the shrewd intent and purpose which I find in Tyndale, Erasmus, my darling, should be no more my darling. But I find in Erasmus, my darling, that he detesteth and abhorreth the errors and heresies that Tyndale plainly teacheth and abideth by, and therefore Erasmus, my darling, shall be my darling still."[2]

More had to defend Erasmus many times, sometimes when he was directly attacked, but sometimes also when the attack was oblique and delivered not so much against the man as against the cause for which he (and More himself) stood. A defence of this sort once or twice had to be made when the attacker was a friend

[2] Stapleton, who like many men of his time was puzzled by More's friendship with Erasmus, quotes only the first sentence that I have given, paraphrasing the second as "As he could not excuse the fact, at least, for friendship's sake, he excused the intention." Obviously More does much more than that. Nor is there any proof for Stapleton's assertion that More ever asked Erasmus to make any retractation.

of More's. It was so when Edward Lee, the future Archbishop of York but then Dean of Colchester, discovered, as he thought, heresy in Erasmus's *Annotations of the New Testament*. This was a situation that called for all of More's tact. He therefore begged Erasmus not to retaliate and promised Lee that, should *he* ever be attacked, he would find a defender in More. "You ask me, my dear Lee," he wrote, "not to lessen my affection for you in any way. Trust me, good Lee, I shall not. Although in this case my sympathies are with the party which you are attacking, yet I trust you will withdraw your troops with perfect safety. I shall ever love you and I am proud to find that my love is so highly valued by you." It might be a little invidious to remark that this defender of orthodoxy, according to the concepts of the "old school," did not stand firm against Henry in 1534, for (Fisher excepted) every one of the bishops yielded to the King. But at least it cannot be unfair to point out that the only two very prominent men who were prepared to be orthodox, as far as the scaffold, were the humanists More and Fisher. Grocyn and Colet died in 1519 and Linacre and Lily three years later, thereby escaping a test under which they might have failed. More and Fisher, the "advanced" men, did not fail.

More had a number of other controversies with scholars—real and bogus—of the old-fashioned sort: men who were inclined to equate a receptivity to ideas of reform and a larger intellectual horizon with theological unsoundness. Thus to an unidentified monk he wrote: "I wonder at the unbounded leisure which you find to devote to schismatical and heretical books. Or have you so few good books that you are obliged to consume your short leisure on bad ones? [The supposedly "bad" ones of course were those by his friend Erasmus]. If the books are good, why do you condemn them? If they are bad, why do you read them? As you gave up the care of the world, when you shut yourself up in the cloister, you are not one of those to whom leave is given to read bad books for the sake of refuting them. . . . Not only do you spend good hours on bad books, but you consume much time, as it appears, in talk and gossip worse than bad books; so that I notice there is no kind of rumour or calumny which does not find its way straight into your cell."

In the same vein, but at greater length and more powerfully, he addressed a letter the previous year (1518) to the Fathers and Proctors of the University of Oxford, this time doubtless speaking with the King's approval if not at the King's personal instance. Somebody had been preaching a course of Lenten sermons at the University, attacking not only Greek studies but, for good measure, the Latin classics as well. "What right," More demands, "has he to denounce Latin, of which he knows little; Science, of which he knows less; or Greek, of which he knows nothing? He had better have confined himself to the seven deadly sins, of which perhaps he has closer acquaintance. Of course we know that a man can be saved without securing learning. Children learn from their mothers the essential truths of Christianity. But students are sent to Oxford to receive general instruction. They do not go there merely to learn theology. Some go to learn law, some to learn human nature from poets and orators and historians—forms of knowledge useful even to preachers, if their congregations are not to think them fools. Others again go to universities to study natural sciences and philosophy and art: and this wonderful gentleman is to condemn the whole of it under one general sentence. He says there is nothing of importance except theology. How can he know theology if he is ignorant of Hebrew and Greek and Latin? He thinks, I presume, that it can all be found in the scholastic conundrums. These, I admit, can be learned with no particular effort. But Theology, that august Queen of Heaven, demands an ampler scope. The knowledge of God can be gathered only out of Scripture—Scripture and the early Catholic Fathers . . . and if he fancies that Scripture and the Fathers can be understood without a knowledge of the languages in which the Fathers wrote, he will not find many to agree with him."

Unfortunately there were plenty of people who did agree with this Oxford preacher. A man of the same type held forth in a similar strain in a sermon delivered before the King, who, still fancying himself as a patron of learning, summoned the preacher afterwards for reproof. Quailing before the royal eye, the anti-humanist orator, though he could not explain away his diatribe against literary studies in general, made an egregious exception in the case of Greek. He was not altogether opposed to that, he said, as it was derived from Hebrew!

That man of course was simply an ignoramus. But there were clever men who were almost as absurd. One of these was a foreign visitor, a sharp forger of syllogisms, who boasted at the table of Bonvisi, the Italian scholar merchant who was More's friend, that he could take either side of any question. He proceeded to prove that he could do so, and on all the subjects that were introduced. Upon this empty and conceited fellow, much to the enjoyment of all the other guests, Bonvisi proceeded to take a subtle revenge. Noting that the visiting monk was merely a disputant by profession, and had little knowledge of the Scriptures, he proceeded to invent, off hand, a number of biblical quotations, gravely citing chapter and verse. Now the logician was hard put to it to defend himself. As he could not refuse the authority of the texts the ingenious Bonvisi was citing, he had to say, "Yes, but I understand the passage in *this* sense," and when Bonvisi still maintained his ground, the theologian asserted that the interpretation he gave was that given by the famous commentator, Nicholas of Lyra. He was quite unaware that Bonvisi and his humanist guests were all laughing at him.

What More was affirming was the true humanist position which, as he wrote in his letter to Oxford University, makes the knowledge of natural things a road to heavenly contemplation. But he was also defending his friend Erasmus, who was the chief target aimed at by all those who rejected secular knowledge as useless. Even before he had any inkling of the storm that was about to blow out of Germany, he saw clearly that the new age needed a presentation of the truths of Christianity that would include and integrate all that was native to man. Some of the worst enemies of religion he recognized to be those who looked upon themselves as its staunchest defenders.

As early as 1507 Thomas More had an encounter with one of these people, when he was on a visit to his sister Elizabeth Rastell at Coventry. He had hardly dismounted from his horse when the question was propounded to him whether anyone could be damned who said the rosary daily. He laughed at this but was warned that he had better be careful, as there was a holy and learned priest in the neighborhood who was preaching such nonsense. More continues with: "I was immediately invited to dinner, and accepted the invitation and went. There enters an old friar with head bent, grave and grim; a boy follows him with books. I saw that I was in for a quarrel . . . At last they asked my opinion. As I was obliged to speak, I told them what I thought, but only in a few words and without emphasis. Then the friar pours out a long prepared speech which might have made two sermons." It was in vain that More pointed out that "though you may easily find a king ready to pardon something in an enemy at the prayers of his mother, yet there is nowhere one so great a fool as to promulgate a law by which to encourage the audacity of his subjects against himself, by a promise of impunity to traitors, on condition of their paying a certain homage to his mother." More saw quite clearly that, if men really believed this pious but foolish friar, they might come to feel themselves safe in the practice of their vices; in fact, he was told that just that was happening. Though he approved of the practice of those who invoked Our Lady by means of the rosary, he could not approve of using the rosary for magical purposes.

But not all the opponents of the new learning were so ridiculous as these men. One with whom he got into a little controversy in 1515 was Martin Dorp of the University of Louvain. And in this case he encountered one whose mind was not closed to reason and who ended by publicly admitting that More and Erasmus were right and that he had been wrong. This drew from More congratulations upon so rare a magnanimity. "It is well-nigh impossible," More told him, "to extort a retractation even from the most modest. Almost all men are so stupid with false shame that they would rather show themselves fools, than acknowledge that they were such once; while you, who have so much cleverness, learning and eloquence, that even if you were to defend something quite improbable or purely paradoxical, you would be able to convince your readers; you, I say, caring more for truth than appearances, prefer to tell all the world that you were deceived, rather than go on deceiving. Such an act will bring you eternal glory."

This particular controversy was conducted, even from Dorp's first protest—made directly to Erasmus concerning his *Praise of Folly*—with good temper on both sides; therefore a satisfactory thrashing out of the questions at issue was possible. What Dorp stood for was the old-style teaching of theology, in which the Scriptures and Fathers were usually left unread, except in so far as they were quoted in the compendiums. More's argument was simply in favor of going directly to the texts themselves instead of relying on text-books. It was in this letter to Dorp that he told his story of the logician so adroitly tripped up by Bonvisi.

Controversies of this sort, however, rarely make very exciting reading, even though they are not quite without modern application. But they were very much to the point at the time, and the Protestant revolt might have had a very different ending had the Church possessed more champions of the type of More and Erasmus, men who desired to integrate all knowledge with the Christian revelation and to reform what cried for reform in ecclesiastical practice. From this time on More was constantly being drawn into controversy, little as it was to his taste, partly to defend his "darling," when Erasmus was attacked by obscurantists, but also to help spread the enlightenment so badly needed. Not until he was clapped into the Tower in 1534 was he able to abandon the role circumstances fastened upon him; then he did so with a sigh of relief.

Though, in accordance with the controversial style of the time,

More was sometimes obliged to use a method of argumentation that was foreign to his gentle nature, at least this much must be said for him: only once was he involved in any purely personal issue. This was when he was really angry with Germain de Brie (or Brixius) who, after writing a poem that disparaged the English in the course of celebrating the exploits of a French ship in the war of 1512, produced in his *Antimorus* a personal attack on More, as he had patriotically come to the English defence. Erasmus, a friend to both men, intervened in the quarrel between two humanists who were showing themselves all too human. "I do not see," he wrote to More, "how [sound learning] can survive, unless the body of scholars, their ranks joined shield to shield, defends it against the stubborn attacks of our barbarians . . . . Not the least part of your reputation is due to the gentleness of your character and the sweetness of your manners, and I would wish nothing of it to be lost. I beg you to make allowances, and not to make ill-tempered and provocative accusations, but to fight with reason, not bitterness. Nevertheless I would much prefer you to keep silence, so that the whole affair may be forgotten." To this appeal More responded by saying, "The fact that De Brie is your friend will weigh more with me than that he is my enemy." But for once he had shown himself touchy. That he did so only once, in spite of frequent provocation, should be remembered.

Yet it is perhaps not perfectly accurate to say that More's onslaught on Brixius is the solitary instance of personal annoyance; there was another, though in his case More was prompted rather by a desire to make a clever jest than by a feeling that he had been injured. More, upon receiving from Peter One-Eye, Erasmus's secretary, the portraits of Erasmus and Peter Gilles in diptych painted by Quentin Matsys—portraits still in existence—had published a Latin epigram comparing his friends to Castor and Pollux. An unknown friar had objected that Castor and Pollux were not friends but brothers, something that one might think More could have safely allowed to pass without comment.

But an epigram came into his head and he retorted in the lines rendered by Father Bridgett:

All brothers are not friends you truly say,
For friars are brothers, yet what friends are they?

I confess to finding a kind of edification in these lapses—such as they are—from good humor. This is because they show that More's serenity of temper was not wholly a natural quality but a disposition acquired by effort. His son-in-law, Roper, who lived with him for sixteen years, was to say that never once had he seen More "in a fume." And another member of his household told Stapleton that he lost his temper only twice. It would appear from the Brixius incident that his amiability was, at least in part, the result of self-conquest, constantly renewed. This is all the more remarkable when we consider, first, that scholars, almost more than poets, are an irritable tribe, and secondly, that More soon obtained positions of authority in which he could have vented his ill-humor with impunity, He was indeed the most genial and gentle soul—a man born and framed for friendship.

One other fact should be born in mind, a fact not perceived by Henry during their long and close association. Amiability commonly goes with weakness; the man who wishes to please is not the one most likely to adhere at all costs to principle. Gentleness commonly goes with timidity, and the time was to come when the King was to count on More's quickly yielding under pressure. It was then that More showed that his lovable disposition had nothing soft about it. Having mastered himself, he was able, in an almost total isolation, to master the utmost in fear.

CHAPTER SEVEN

An Essay in History

THE title of what may be called the first—at all events the first notable—essay in English history, is headed in the 1557 folio of More's *English Works* edited by Judge Rastell: "THE HISTORY OF KING RICHARD THE THIRD (UNFINISHED) WRITTEN BY MASTER THOMAS MORE, THEN ONE OF THE UNDER-SHERIFFS OF LONDON, ABOUT THE YEAR OF OUR LORD, 1513. Which work hath been before this time printed in Hardyng's Chronicle, and in Halle's Chronicle, but very much corrupt in many places, sometimes having less, and sometimes more, and altered in words and whole sentences: much varying from the copy in his own hand, by which this is printed."

In spite of Rastell's declaration that he used More's own manuscript, More's authorship has frequently been questioned since 1598, when Queen Elizabeth's sprightly godson, Sir John Harrington, remarked that he had heard that the book was really by Cardinal Morton. As to this it is sufficient to say that whoever was the author, it was not Morton. For he died in 1500 and the book contains references to events that occured in 1509 and 1513. There is some reason to believe, however, that Morton did write a Latin life of Richard III, and that More may have used this. In the book as we have it, there are a number of incidents that Morton would have been in the best position to record. But More could have obtained these, and much else, from listening to the Archbishop's conversation during the two years when he was a page at Lambeth. Though the chronological references do not prove More's authorship, at least they rule Morton out, and there is no other claimant. The only doubt that can now arise would be a faint flicker of wonder that More in his other English works is sometimes inclined to be verbose and that *Richard III* is Tacitean in its terseness. But such a doubt has little, if any weight, in face of the evidence presented by Professor Chambers in a long introduction he contributes to the first volume of the Campbell edition of More's *English Works* and an extended note supplied by him to Dr. Hitchcock's edition of Harpsfield.

Two questions remain to be touched on briefly before coming to an examination of the book itself. One springs from the fact that the book exists in a Latin as well as an English version, and that neither can be described as a translation of the other in spite of their close relationship. The supposition must be that the Latin was designed for circulation on the continent, and the English for consumption at home. Mr. W.A.G. Doyle-Davidson, in an essay on this textual problem, concludes that neither version as a whole precedes the other, but that they are parallel, being written side by side at the same time. He admits, however, that if one version is prior to the other, priority must be given to the Latin. My own feeling is that the Latin did come first, and that this accounts of More's terseness. What can no longer be contested is that both versions were produced by the same writer.

The other question is as to why More left the book unfinished. One theory is that he was disappointed in it. This idea does not strike me as having much force. For though writers are not always the best judge of their own productions, and often have some favorite that the rest of the world regards with less than their own fondness, they are seldom mistaken about their very best work. And stylistically at least *Richard III* is just that. Stapleton is surely in error in telling us that More wrote it "only to practice his pen."

Another theory is that as More drew nearer to his own times he was approaching what might be dangerous ground, and so felt it safer to desist. This does not seem to me to hold water: had More thought this, he would not have begun at all. Moreover, how was he likely to offend Henry VIII by rounding out a story which ends with the dramatic death in battle of Richard III, defeated by Henry's father? The book could not have been other than flattering to the Tudors by exhibiting them as the liberators of England from a bloody tyranny. The simplest and most reasonable supposition would seem to be that More was obliged to lay the book aside under pressure of business, and then discovered, when free to take it up again—if he ever *was* free—that the effort of breathing life into a composition that had been allowed to become "cold" was repugnant to him.

Another suggestion I offer for what it is worth, is that if More really did have before him a Latin life of Richard III (now lost), written by Morton, and that if he were drawing upon this for his own work, he stopped where he did because that was where Morton himself stopped—perhaps because of being interrupted by failing health. Though More may well have remembered scraps of Morton's conversation, telling what he knew of the intrigues that led to Richard's overthrow, these may have been too fragmentary to weave into a coherent whole. There was no other source from which More could have obtained information so direct and personal and authentic.

But whatever the reason for the book's remaining unfinished, it can hardly be gainsaid that it is the most notable piece of English prose produced during the reign of Henry VIII. Other writers of his time were good at exposition and argumentation—as was More himself—but only More had mastery of narrative. In this, in fact, and in dialogue was his main power. Chambers claims not a bit too much when he says that with More's *Richard III* "begins modern historical writing of distinction."

Mr. Hollis finds the book "a consideration of the general nature of sovereignty." In my view, though I admit that such considerations are suggested by the story, it seems that More did not consciously have this as his thesis. His central theme is rather the instability of fortune, and even its treachery to those who are most confident in their ascendant star. Perhaps nowhere is this indicated more powerfully than in the passage upon Lord Hastings, which Shakespeare drew upon (along with much else from More's *Richard III*): "In riding towards the Tower, the same morning in which he was beheaded, his horse twice or thrice stumbled with him almost to falling, which thing, albeit each man wot daily happeneth to them to whom no such chance is toward, yet hath it been of old rite and custom observed as a token notably foregoing some great misfortune . . . . The same morning ere he went up, came a knight unto him, as it were by courtesy to accompany him to the Council, but of truth sent by the Protector to haste him hitherward, with whom he was of secret confederacy in that purpose. . . . This knight when it happed the Lord Chamberlain by the way to stay his horse and commune a while with a priest whom he met in the Tower Street, broke his tale and merrily said to him: 'What, my lord, I pray you come on. Whereto talk you so long with that priest? You have no need of a priest yet'—and therewith he laughed upon him, as though he would say, 'ye soon shall have.' " Hastings was aware that that very morning the kinsmen of the Queen were to be executed at Pomfret, for he had himself given his assent to this; but he had no inkling of his own fate, or that his own head was to fall before the Protector dined that day. "Oh, good God," More exclaims, "the blindness of our mortal nature: when he most feared, he was in good surety; when he reckoned himself surest, he lost his life, and within two hours after!"

It is one of the great scenes of literature when the unsuspecting Hastings was accused of treason by Richard and condemned out of hand, but I pass it over to quote instead More's description of Edward IV and his mistress Jane Shore. "He was a goodly personage and very princely to behold," wrote More of Edward, "of heart courageous, politic in counsel, in adversity nothing abashed, in prosperity rather joyful than proud, in peace just and merciful, in war sharp and fierce, in the field bold and hardy and nevertheless no further than wisdom would, adventurous . . . . He was of visage lovely, of body mighty, strong and clean made; howbeit in his latter days, with over liberal diet, somewhat corpulent and burly and nevertheless not uncomely. He was of youth greatly given to fleshly wantonness, from which health of body in great prosperity and fortune, without a special grace, hardly refraineth. This fault not greatly grieved the people." That is a vignette as excellent as the one of Hastings: "A good knight and a gentle, of great authority with his Prince, of living somewhat dissolute, plain and open to his enemy, and secret to his friend; easy to beguile, as he that of good heart and courage forestudied no perils; a loving man, and passing well beloved: very faithful, and trusty enough, trusting too much."

Even more moving are the pages on Jane Shore, our chief source of information regarding that lady. Morton had seen her in the prime of her beauty and so cannot be imagined as writing in the following terms: "Proper she was and fair, nothing in her body that you would have changed, but if you had wished her somewhat higher. Thus say they that knew her in her youth, albeit some that now see her (for she yet liveth[1]) deem her never to have been well visaged. Whose judgment seemeth to me somewhat like as though men should guess the beauty of one long departed by her scalp [skull] taken out of the charnel house: for now she is old, lean, withered and dried up, nothing left but rivelled skin and hard bone." More continues, drawing no doubt on Morton's recollections: "The King would say that he had three concubines which in three divers properties diversely excelled: one the merriest, another the wiliest, the third the holiest harlot in the realm, as one whom no man could get out of the church lightly to any place, but it were to his bed . . . The merriest was this Shore's wife, in whom the King took special pleasure, for many he had, but her he loved, whose favour, to say truth (for sin it were to belie the devil), she never abused to any man's hurt, but to many a man's comfort and relief. When the King took displeasure, she would mitigate and appease his mind; where men were out of favour, she would bring them in his grace; for many that had highly offended, she obtained pardon; of great forfeitures she got men remission; and finally, in many weighty suits she stood many men in great stead, either for none or very small

[1] She died in 1527.

rewards, and those rather gay than rich: either for that she was content with the deed self well done, or for that she delighted to be sued unto and to show what she was able to do with the King, or for that wanton women and wealthy be not always covetous. I doubt not that some will think this woman too slight a thing to be written of and set among the remembrances of great matters: which they shall specially think, that haply shall esteem her only by that they now see her. But meseemeth the chance so much the more worthy to be remembered, in how much she is now in the more beggarly condition, unfriended and worn out of acquaintance, after good substance, after as great favour with the Prince, after as great suit and seeking to with all those that had business to speed, as many other men were in their times, which be famous now only by the infamy of their ill deeds. Her doings were not much less, albeit they be much less remembered because they were not so evil. For men use, if they have an evil turn, to write it in marble; and whoso doth us a good turn, we write it in dust: which is not worst proved by her, for at this day she beggeth of many at this day living, that at that day had begged if she had not been."

There is surely no need for me to say that the style of that is magnificent, or to point out the shrewdness and humor and tenderness mingled in More's portrait of this woman. And that he wrote of her at all—"too slight a thing to be written of and set among the remembrances of great matters"—shows, what is all the more remarkable in those days of bare chronicling, that he had an eye for the significant details in human life. Had he lived in another age, More might have been a novelist.

There is another little exercise in contemporary history, one introduced in passing both in his *Dialogue Concerning Heresies* (1528) and his *Supplication of Souls* (1529). He reverts to it again in his *Apology* of 1533 to tell us that he knew Richard Hunne, the man whose case made such a stir at the close of 1514, and revealed so much about the anti-clerical feeling in London just prior to the outbreak of the Reformation in Germany.

The truth about this complicated case need not concern us, and it would in fact be impossible to decide now with any certainty whether Hunne, who was awaiting trial for heresy in the Lollards' Tower, was murdered (as the inflamed popular mind believed) or committed suicide. More definitely believed it was a case of suicide, and he had opportunities for hearing and weighing the evidence. Our only present concern is More's account of the kind of witnesses who came before the Commission to go into the matter at Baynard's Castle. And this no doubt gives us incidentally a good idea of his own judicial practice. His view of the affair was that taken by the authorities, for the King, at the appeal of the Bishop of London, quashed the indictment against those accused of having murdered Hunne—Dr. Horsey, the diocesan Chancellor, the sumner of the Bishop's court, and the bell-ringer of the prison. All that need be said here about this once-famous mystery story is that the most mysterious of all its features was why the ecclesiastical authorities should go to the trouble of murdering a man whom they were sure they could burn for heresy.

Yet, most of the witnesses were positive that Hunne had been hanged in prison and was not a suicide. One of these said that he had examined the body and could tell, because he had "another insight in such things than other men have." When the Commissioners said to him that they could not understand how this could be, as his employment (that of an officer to the King's Almoner) surely could not give him more specialized knowledge than a professional hangman, and *he* could not tell this from merely looking at a body, the witness replied that he had seen many such bodies. "How many?" one of the Commissioners asked, "a hundred?" He said, "Nay, not a hundred." "Have ye seen four score and ten?" At this question he pondered, as one who was in doubt, before admitting, "Not fully four score and ten." At this the Commissioners sharply dropped their figures, and asked whether he had seen twenty. This time without hesitation he answered, "Nay, not twenty," and yet he had been in doubt about the ninety. Fifteen and ten, also brought his "Nay." They brought him all the way down to three, to which he said that he had seen as many "and more too." In the end it came out that the only such body he had ever seen was that of "an Irish fellow called Crook Shank, whom he had seen hanging in an old barn." They let him go with the comment, possibly made by More himself, "that because he was not yet cunning enough in the craft of hanging, it was pity that he had no more experience thereof by one more!"

Another witness asserted that he had heard a priest say that if Hunne had not pleaded praemunire he would not have been sued for heresy. The cleric was sent for and questioned. He answered that what he had actually said was that if Hunne had not been accused of heresy he would not have tried to find shelter behind the law of praemunire—a very different matter. Yet the original witness was so thick-headed that, upon hearing this, he supposed his own testimony fully corroborated. "Lo, my Lords," he exclaim, "I am glad ye find me a true man! Will ye command me any more service?" One of them (again it may have been More) answered: "I have espied, good man, so the words be all one, it maketh no matter to you which way they stand: but all is one to you, a horse mill and a mill horse, drink ere ye go and go ere ye drink." In a daze he refused what he thought was an offered drink, and went off leaving them laughing.

Still another witness declared that he had been "by a right honourable man informed, that there was one had showed a friend of his that he could take him by the sleeve that killed Hunne." This man was sent for and said, "This gentleman did somewhat mistake me. But indeed I told him that I had a neighbour that told me he could do it." This man in his turn declared that he had not said quite that, "But I said indeed that I know one which I thought verily could tell who killed him." At this one of the Commissioners said, "Well, yet with much work we come to somewhat. But whereby think ye that he can tell?" The answer was, "Nay, forsooth, my Lord, it is a woman. I would she were with your Lordships now." To which the reply came, "Well, woman or man, all is one, she shall be had wheresoever she be." The witness assured them that she would tell them wonders, "for, by God, I have wist her to tell of many marvellous things ere now .... Forsooth, my Lords, if a thing had been stolen, she would have told who had it. And therefore I think she could as well tell who killed Hunne as who stole a horse." The Commissioner thought so too, but he inquired *how* she could tell. Upon this it came out that the witness "could never see her use any worse way than looking in one's hand." When they came at last to the mare's nest at the end of the long road, they found an "Egyptian" who had been living at Lambeth but who had gone "over sea now." Several hours had been spent in discovering a gipsy palmist—and she was not there to deliver her divinations!

Now note the sequel. It makes one wonder whether there is much value in the most logical of demonstrations. The use that Foxe made of the Hunne case need not be quarrelled with. He wished to make the flesh of Protestants creep, that being his trade; and belief persisted in London that Hunne had been murdered. But in the very same year in which More recorded what had happened at Baynard's Castle (1528), Simon Fish wrote his *Supplication of Beggars.* In it he used the proof More had given as though it showed the opposite. "Had not Richard Hunne," he wrote, "commenced action of praemunire against a priest, he had been alive, and none heretic, at all, but an honest man." Whether this was a stupidity akin to that shown by the witnesses of whom More gives such a racy account, or merely plain dishonesty, must be uncertain. But as the Commissioner said, "It is all one"; fools are sometimes just as much of a nuisance, and just as dangerous, as rascals. Misunderstandings (or misstatements) of this sort made More's subsequent task as controversialist—which had also to be that of contemporary historian—so very difficult and so very thankless. However, we get some amusing pages out of it all—and in *Richard III* a masterpiece.

CHAPTER EIGHT

The Utopian

In the summer of 1515 More went for the first time on an embassy abroad. As it was a commercial treaty that had to be negotiated, he was probably appointed at the instance of the Lord Mayor and the London Aldermen, for no man more enjoyed the confidence of the city. During his absence he was allowed to retain his office of Under-Sheriff and to have a deputy. Among those with him on the embassy were Cuthbert Tunstall, later to be Bishop of London, and Richard Sampson, who also became a bishop but who was at this time Vicar-General for Wolsey in the see of Tournai, one of several bishoprics held by the insatiable pluralist Cardinal.

Sampson wrote to Erasmus giving a very pleasant account of More on this mission. "No one," he wrote, "could surpass our young friend More either in learning or in gaiety of temper. I need say nothing of his good nature and merry friendliness in everyday life and the honourable uprightness of his conversation and conduct." More himself, however, upon his return to England, dictated a letter to Erasmus in which he humorously grumbled about the inconveniences of having been sent. The office of ambassador, he said, never pleased him, and seemed less suitable to laymen than to priests, as these had no wives and children to leave at home. "Besides," he went on, "when a priest is sent out, he can take his whole household with him, and maintain them at the King's expense; but when *I* am away, I must provide for a double household, one at home, the other abroad. A liberal allowance was granted me by the King for the servants I took with me, but no account was taken of those I was obliged to leave at home. You know what a kind husband I am, what an indulgent father and considerate master, yet I have never been able to induce my family to go without food during my absence, even for a short time!" He had expected to be away only for a couple of months, but these stretched into six, and at the end of the two months Tunstall had to write to Wolsey, "Master More, as being at a low ebb, desires by your Grace to be set on float again."

One of those who accompanied More was John Clement, who is mentioned in the *Utopia* as "my boy" and who functioned as secretary. Three years later he became a professor of Greek at Oxford and was later celebrated as a physician. He eventually married More's adopted daughter, Margaret Giggs. Tunstall is also given a complimentary mention in that famous book.

Two other friends figure more largely there, though one only in the letter to him appended by Peter Gilles to the book. This was Jerome Busleiden, a Councillor of Charles V and a rich cleric of Brussels who was the founder of the College of the Three Languages at Louvain. Gilles himself is, along with More, a partaker in the conversations with the Utopian traveler, Raphael Hythloday. In what is obviously the living image of him in the Matsys painting Peter is seen as a young man, by no means handsome but with so much intelligence and delicacy and kindness in his face that it is easy to understand the warm affection that came to exist between him and his newly-made English friend. "In all my travels," More wrote to Erasmus, "there was nothing I liked better than my intercourse with your host, Peter Gilles of Antwerp, a man so learned, witty, modest, and so true a friend, that I would willingly purchase his company at the cost of a great part of my fortune." It was under the stimulation of this friendship, and undoubtedly as a result of things tossed out in conversation, that the *Utopia* was produced. Nor is it impossible that More and Peter actually did meet and talk with a Portuguese sailor who had made a voyage near enough to Japan to have brought back an account, however vague, of that fabulous country. But of course we can also trace many of More's ideas to Plato's *Republic,* Plutarch's

Lives and St. Augustine's *City of God,* with the main literary source being Amerigo Vespucci's *Voyages.*[1]

Everybody knows (or should know) that the second part of the *Utopia* was written first. It is in this that Thomas More gives his account of the Utopian commonwealth. Had he allowed that to stand by itself, it would be not quite unreasonable to suppose—as many people still do—that he aimed only at producing a *jeu d'esprit* for the entertainment of Peter Gilles. Even there, however, he ends with a fierce denunciation of society, as it existed, as "a certain conspiracy of rich men," and of "the princess and mother of all mischief, Pride." And though he puts these words into the mouth of Hythloday, and indicates his belief that not all the customs of Utopia were based on sound reason, his general approval of the society Hythloday described should be sufficiently plain. But what seems to me to put his serious intention beyond all question was his adding to the second book, which contains his fable, the first book in which he applies that fable to the social conditions in England. Though he continues to use Peter and himself as foils to Raphael, so that they figure as the exponents of a cautious reserve, it should be always noted that More allows Raphael most of the conversation, and almost all of its force.

[1] The More family was definitely interested in promoting colonizing projects, such as are indicated in the *Utopia* itself. John Rastell, who was married to More's sister Elizabeth, seems to have been the first Englishman to have attempted a scheme of this sort, as distinct from mere exploration. Cabot, who was in command of a Bristol ship, had authority to take possession of whatever he discovered on the American mainland, but did nothing of this sort, though he did of course prepare the way by his search for the North-West Passage in 1509. On the other hand, six months after the publication of the *Utopia,* Rastell set off from Greenwich in the *Barbara,* largely financed by Thomas More and Sir John More. The project came to nothing because of the mutiny of the crew, who proposed turning pirates. When Rastell refused to join them, they put him ashore in Ireland and sold his ship at Bordeaux. But his son John, the brother of the editor of More's *English Works* in 1557, did sail later to Labrador. The Rastell-More idea appears in the *Utopia,* where it is said that the Utopians "count this the most just cause of war, when any people holdeth a piece of ground void and vacant to no good nor profitable use, keeping other from the use and possession of it, which notwithstanding by the law of nature ought thereof to be nourished and relieved." Henry VIII, however, let the golden opportunity of colonization slip in favor of his expensive and abortive French wars.

The first book (written, as I again remind my readers, second) does another thing very skilfully. In this part More authenticates his story, and so successfully, as he mentions with amusement in his dedicatory letter to Peter Gilles, that many people took it as a relation of actual fact. Dr. Rowland Phillips, the Vicar of Croydon, was so stirred that he wanted to get himself made a bishop in order to head a band of missionaries to a people who seemed so ready to accept the Christian faith.

To the first book I will come later. But as the second book is better known—being unfortunately the only one that most people read, thus missing a good deal of More's point—I remark that even Hythloday, while holding Utopia up as a model for all societies, indicates that he does not admire all the Utopian customs. For instance, he calls at least one of these customs "fond and foolish"—that of presenting prospective brides and grooms to one another naked, so that no complaints could be made later on the ground of unknown physical defects. And as a Christian he did not find it necessary to say that he did not approve of the Utopian right of suicide or of the Utopian divorce laws, strict though these were as compared with our own. Even less should it be necessary for me to say that these did not meet with More's approval. The account given is simply that of a highly organized pagan society, which Christians might study with profit, but which they were not called upon to imitate in every detail.

Yet even considered as pagans the Utopians have often been misunderstood. A fundamental matter here is the Epicurean philosophy commonly supposed to prevail among them. Yet one would think Hythloday was quite explicit when he said, "They think not felicity to rest in all pleasure, but only that pleasure that is good and honest. . . . For they define virtue to be life lived according to nature, and that we be hereunto ordained of God. And that he doth follow the course of nature, which in desiring and refusing things is ruled by reason. Furthermore that reason doth chiefly and principally kindle in men the love and veneration of the divine majesty." What we really have described for us is a social order devoid of everything luxurious and in which morals are so sternly enforced that a second offence of adultery is punished with death. In Utopia the pleasures most valued are those of the mind, and the mainspring of society is religion.

Another misunderstanding—this time of More himself—relates to the Utopians' religious tolerance. It has resulted in the supposition that More was advocating principles to which, when he became Lord Chancellor, he was sadly unfaithful. This is a matter which will have to be treated at greater length in a subsequent chapter. It is enough to say now that the Utopians were free to hold what religious opinions they pleased, so long as they did not force those opinions down their neighbors' throats. If they were contentious in religious argument they were either banished or sentenced to slavery. From this they could eventually emerge, like the other Utopian slaves—the malefactors—by good behavior. On the other hand, continued truculence resulted in death. Even so, there were, as there always must be, limits to religious toleration; it did not extend to those who denied Divine Providence and the immortality of the soul. From such all civic rights were withheld.

As against this, More did seize his chance of attributing to the Utopians his own private likes and dislikes. Thus he shows them as condemning all hunting and dice-playing (as he forbade them in his own household), and of getting all their entertainment—humanist style—from going to lectures or in improving conversation. But he also gives them a special fondness for fools, as he had this himself. Their exclusion of lawyers may have been introduced impishly in the hope of seeing old Sir John jump out of his skin when he read about it. We can also believe that he was artfully slipping in his own views when he said that the Utopians "have priests of exceeding holiness, and therefore very few." We know that he often advocated, as a prime means of religious reform in England, the ordaining of fewer and better men to the priesthood. It implies no antagonism to priests, as such. Nor can we suppose that, because the pagan Utopians had priestesses, More was suggesting the ordination of women to the Christian priesthood. So also it is impossible to credit a man who wore a hair-shirt with holding, with the majority of the Utopians, that while their sect of ascetics was holier, that of their non-ascetics was wiser. More perfectly understood that Christianity is essentially an ascetic religion, though few are called to its more rigorous practices. And all the Utopians were, in fact, more ascetic than most people would wish to be.

The *Utopia* has to be read in the light of More's rather voluminous writings, and of his own life and character, unless we wish to go astray. Yet a good statement of the many problems that arise —a statement only and not a final solution of those problems—is the one made by Sir James Mackintosh. "The true notion of the *Utopia,*" he writes, "is that it intimates a variety of doctrines and exhibits a multiplicity of projects, which the writer regards with every possible degree of approbation and shade of assent; from the frontiers of serious belief, through gradations of descending plausibility, where the lower are scarcely more than exercises of ingenuity, and to which some wild paradoxes are appended, either as a vehicle or as an easy means (if necessary) of disavowing the serious intention of the whole Platonic fiction."

As to the question: which of the Utopian customs did More admire and which did he condemn?—no answer can be given in a single chapter. The whole of this book must be taken as my commentary. But if one fact is remembered we shall avoid many errors: it is that the Utopians had only *natural* religion, but that their culture—derived, as More is careful to indicate, from Egyptian as well as Greek and Roman sources—disposed their minds to the acceptance of the Christian revelation, as soon as it was presented to them. This was of course good humanist doctrine. But it also is in perfect comformity with Christian psychology, which holds that grace builds upon nature—first the natural and then the supernatural—and that the pagan myths as well as the loftier speculations of the pagan philosophers prepared the road for Christ. *Teste David cum Sibylla,* as the tremendous Catholic dirge for the dead puts it.

It is rather surprising to note that the Utopians even had a strong inkling of the doctrine of the communion of saints, and this is something that should be borne in mind when we come to More's controversies with the early Protestants. He says of the Utopians that they suppose their dead, "to be present among them, when they talk of them, though to the dull and feeble eyesight of mortal men they be invisible . . . . And it were a point of great unkindness in them to have utterly cast away the desire of visiting and seeing their friends, to whom they were in their life time joined by mutual love and amity. Which in good men after their death they count to be rather increased than diminished . . . . Therefore they go the more courageously to their business as having a trust and affiance in such overseers."

Now perhaps I can approach what is the central question of the Utopian socialism, which might even be called communism were it not that that word has come to be identified with one brand of socialism.

Hythloday made it clear that nothing was a more effective argument in favor of Christianity in presenting it to the Utopians than that common ownership was once general among Christians and was still practised among the best Christian communities —that is, the monastic orders. And Hythloday is very definite in his opinion that, in this respect at least, so-called Christians may learn a good deal from the Utopians. For though he is not prepared to defend all their laws, "this thing," he says, "I verily believe, howsoever these decrees be, that there is in no place of the world a more excellent people, neither a more flourishing commonwealth."

In the discussions that occurred, More and Gilles took the line that, though a common ownership of everything might be desirable, it was not feasible. It must also be said that More at the end of his life made in his *Dialogue of Comfort* a defence of the existing economic order which could be taken, if it were allowed to stand alone, as the kind of crude advocacy of the advantages of capitalism which might be spluttered out by Colonel Blimp or the stupider of country squires. In that late book of his More raised, for the first time, so far as I am aware, the favorite objection used by the heckler of the socialist soap-box orator (and I am quoting More): "If all the money that is in this country were tomorrow next brought together out of every man's hand, and laid all upon one heap, and then divided out unto every man alike, it would be on the morrow after, worse than it was on the day before." But no socialist has ever suggested such a proceeding, or would be likely to deny that the effect of such a division would be the one that More indicates. It seems to me that we must not press that page from the *Dialogue of Comfort* too far. More was thinking only of conditions as they were. In saying that the rich man's substance is the well of the poor man's living, he was pointing out what should be, and what would be, if every rich man used his wealth as a trust—as *he* used *his* wealth when he had it. Though it may be rash to claim him as a socialist it would be a much worst error to think of him as a defender of the capitalist system. Certainly he showed, in the first part of the *Utopia,* which he added to the second in order to bring the application home to his own England, that he was keenly aware of a very pressing economic problem. His treatment of it is the most important part of the whole book. Incidentally he lays his finger not only on the economic ills of his own age but also upon the causes that were so soon to insure the success of the Protestant Reformation in England, and therefore to insure its success throughout so much of the world.

In the form of a conversation between Hythloday and Cardinal Morton—a conversation of a kind that More must have heard when he was a boy in Lambeth Palace—he sums up the woes of his country in a phrase as strange as it is unforgettable: "Sheep are eating men."

This is very typical of More's mind, so little concerned with the general but nearly always with the specific. Even when abstract propositions are before him, it is his habit—because it is in accordance with his nature—at least to illustrate with some concrete and often very homely incident or anecdote. So now, instead of confining himself to a generalized denunciation of avarice—he fastens upon one notorious example of it, and its effects. He deals with the enclosure of the common lands which had been going on for some time and which, as More clearly saw, was working havoc, by dispossessing the many small arable farmers for the benefit of the large landowners to whose profit it was to make pasturage of what had formerly been put under the plow. "Thus," Hythloday tells the Cardinal, "the unreasonable covetousness of a few hath turned that thing to the utter undoing of your island." He states the case even more strongly: "Your sheep that were wont to be so meek, and so small eaters, now, as I hear say, be become so great devourers and so wild, that they eat up, and swallow down the very men themselves. They consume, destroy, and devour whole fields, houses and cities. For look in what parts of the realm doth grow the finest, and therefore the dearest wool, there noblemen, and gentlemen, yea and certain abbots, holy men no doubt, not contenting themselves with the yearly revenues and profits, that were wont to grow to their forefathers and predecessors of their lands, not being content that they live in rest and pleasure nothing profiting, yea much noying the public weal, leave no ground for tillage, they enclose all into pasture; they throw down houses; they pluck down towns, and leave nothing standing, but only the church to be made a sheephouse. . . . Therefore that one covetous and unsatiable and very plague of his native country may compass about and enclose many thousand acres of ground together within one pale or hedge, the husbandmen be thrust out of their own, or else either by covin or fraud, or by violent oppression they be put besides it, or by wrongs and injuries they be so wearied, that they be compelled to sell all; by one means therefore or other, either by hook or by crook they must needs depart away, poor silly [simple] wretched souls, men, women, husbands, wives, fatherless children, widows, woeful mothers, with their young babes, and their whole household small in substance, and much in numbers, as husbandry requireth many hands. Away they trudge, I say, out of their known and accustomed houses, finding no place to rest in." What can such people do, he asks, but steal? Then according to the ferocious laws—which receive as ferocious a castigation—when caught they were hanged.

Here Hythloday is the speaker, yet one cannot but recognize the indignant and pitiful tones of More's own voice. It is no wonder that Hythloday went on to say: "I do fully persuade myself that no equal and just distribution of things can be made, nor that perfect wealth shall ever be among men, unless this propriety [private property] be exiled and banished. But so long as it shall continue, so long shall remain among the most and best part of men the heavy and inevitable burden of poverty and wretchedness." Though More, when he hears Hythloday recount this conversation, says that he is of a contrary opinion regarding private property, it is impossible to believe that, at the very least, he sympathized with Hythloday's socialistic solution. One suspects, indeed, that this device of mild dissent is used by More as a matter of prudence. One catches the note of irony in Peter Gilles's voice when he comments: "Surely it shall be hard for you to make me believe that there is better order in that new land than is here in these countries that we know!" One can perceive that not only here, but in the devastating things More says about government, as it was being exercised according to the principles of the new school of statecraft, under the cloak of dialogue he made his satire sharp. And this was a time when the radical dogs did *not* get the worst of the argument.

What we can, nevertheless, take as More's own opinion, is his moderate summary: "If evil opinions and naughty persuasions cannot be utterly and quite plucked out of their hearts, if you cannot even as you would remedy vices, which use and custom hath confirmed: yet for this cause you must not forsake the ship in a tempest, because you cannot rule and keep down the winds. No nor you must not labour to drive into their heads new and strange informations, which you know shall nothing be regarded with them of clean contrary minds. But you must with a crafty wile and a subtle train study and endeavour yourself, as much as in you lieth, to handle the matter wittily and handsomely for the purpose, and that which you cannot turn to good, so to order that it be not very bad."

In that and other passages, where More urges caution, what he said might almost be taken as the program of socialism of the Fabian type. And in this connection it is interesting to note that the Marxist, Karl Kautsky, in his book *Thomas More and the Utopia,* though completely puzzled by More's Catholicism, and therefore in several respects misunderstanding him, claims him confidently for the socialist side. Not only that: this canonized saint of the Catholic Church has even received another kind of canonization in Moscow as one of the chief forerunners of the proletarian revolution!

It is also very interesting to note, and instructive as well, that both More and Peter Gilles were so struck with Hythloday's ideas and range of information that they urged him to offer his services to some king. Hythloday brushes the suggestion aside. It would be quite useless to do this, he declares. He would soon either be driven away or made a laughing-stock. Kings, he assures More and Gilles, do not seek the advice of a man like himself, for their one idea is to enlarge their dominions, by fair means or foul, and never how to govern well what they already have. But More, in order to avoid giving offence to Henry VIII, makes Hythloday speak only of what service under the *French* king might mean, though clearly all that he says can be applied with even greater force to Henry. This though the social evils which Hythloday had just been discussing were those of England. But where such a discussion would pass with Henry, and even accorded with one part of Wolsey's domestic policy, More's whole object would have been defeated had he allowed Hythloday to aim a shaft at the English monarch. Yet there may have been a hope in More's heart that Henry would apply to himself the satire shot at the King of France, and perhaps desist from the course upon which he had already begun.

Therefore Hythloday asks what good his counsel would do, when all the French King's advisers were racking their brains to tell him "with what craft the King may still keep Milan, and draw to him again fugitive Naples, and then how to conquer the Venetians, and how to bring under his jurisdiction all Italy, and then how to win the dominion of Flanders, Brabant, and of all Burgundy." He would be advised "to conclude a league of peace with the Venetians, so long to endure, as shall be thought meet and expedient." Another councillor would propose that he hire German mercenaries, or the Swiss. Another again would suggest that the Emperor be appeased with gold, "as with a most pleasant and acceptable sacrifice." Whatever the suggestions were—to make peace with the King of Aragon by restoring him his own kingdom of Navarre, or the hooking in of the King of Castille "with some hope of affinity or alliance," or secretly pensioning some of his peers—they would all be sure to be insincere. But that England should not be left invidiously unmentioned, it is brought in as the poor inoffensive country, against whom "the Scots must be had in a readiness" so that should the English "stir never so little" they might at once attack them. Hythloday asks the direct question: supposing he did advise such a king to live peaceably, "Master More, how think you it would be heard and taken?" To which More can only answer, "So God help me, not very thankfully."

Hythloday had not yet finished. He then proceeded from foreign to domestic policy—driving the dagger to the hilt against Henry's own proceedings, though still speaking ostensibly of the French King. Supposing the King needed money. Well, he would be counselled to enhance its nominal value (that is to adopt inflation) when he had to pay any, "and again to call down the value of coin to less than its worth [deflation] when he must receive or gather any." Another counsellor would suggest a war, with which, as a pretext, the King could obtain special grants, and then "when it shall please him, make peace with great solemnity and holy ceremonies, to blind the eyes of the poor community, as taking pity and compassion forsooth upon man's blood, like a loving and merciful prince." Another counsellor would advise digging out "old and motheaten laws" which, because they had long been forgotten, every man had transgressed. The king could exact heavy fines for the breaking of these laws, "for there is no way so profitable, nor more honourable as that which hath a show and colour of justice." The time was not very far distant when Henry was to do precisely this with regard to praemunire, which though not quite obsolete, was used only when it was convenient to use it. Then, because of what Wolsey had done with Henry's express sanction, the whole English Church had to ransom itself. And More was to find to his personal cost how Henry contrived to proceed to the grossest injustice under "a show and colour of justice."

Through the mouth of Hythloday he has his say about the new statesmanship, and reprobates the notion that it was to the King's interest to keep his subjects poor, or to think that the "stout courage" of his subjects could be subdued by poverty, "taking from them bold and rebelling stomachs." The riches of his people, rather than his own treasury, was his surest safeguard. "The commonalty chooseth their king for their own sake, and not for his sake." He was therefore advised "to live of his own"—that is, to avoid all unnecessary taxation, and to run his government with the vast endowments provided for that purpose.

But all this was of course lost upon Henry, who perhaps was too infinitely egotistical even to imagine that it could possibly apply to himself. More, however, had spoken; and though it was completely in vain, so far as all his immediate purposes were concerned, he had produced one of the great books of the world.

It is perfectly evident, from the way that his contemporaries received the *Utopia,* that they took it to be a work offered for the correction of society and not merely a delicious trifle tossed over his shoulder for the entertainment of humanists. Yet the humanists were not so dense as to credit More with the approval of all the Utopian customs he described. Peter Gilles himself (and he should know) in the letter to Busleiden appended to the book, says that More had "well and wittily marked and bared all the original causes . . . whereof both issueth and springeth the mortal confusion and utter decay of a commonwealth, and also the advancement and wealthy state of the same." Budé wrote to Lupset: "We are greatly indebted to Thomas More for his *Utopia,* in which he holds up to the world a model of social felicity. Our age and our posterity will regard this exposition as a source of excellent doctrines and useful ordinances, from which states will construct their institutions." And Erasmus told Hutten: "He published his *Utopia* for the purpose of showing what are the things that occasion mischiefs in commonwealths, having the English Constitution especially in view." Busleiden wrote to More: "The world has never seen wiser, more perfect, or more desirable institutions." Stapleton, without any of the embarrassment that comes over many Catholic writers of our own time when they touch on the *Utopia,* collects a number of such comments from contemporary humanists, all in much the same vein. Of these perhaps the most interesting is one made by John Paludanus of Cassel to Peter Gilles: "You may see in Utopia, as in a mirror, all that pertains to a perfect commonwealth. England has certainly many excellent men. For what may we conjecture of the rest if More alone has performed so much, being first, a young man, and, then, so fully occupied with public and domestic business, and, lastly practicing a profession quite other than literature."

Alas, that opinion was much too sanguine. Three years before the *Utopia* appeared Machiavelli produced *The Prince,* and in Thomas Cromwell, recently returned from Italy and already in the service of Wolsey, he found a disciple whose advice was in the end to prevail with Henry VIII. More knew long before his death that it was the statecraft of *The Prince* and not that of the *Utopia* that was going to decide the destiny of England. But in 1516, and before, he also saw the plague of greed that was bringing about the enclosures of the common lands. He did not know that it was only beginning there, or that the new rich would conspire with the new statesmen to despoil the Church. And he died hoping that Henry's breach with the Church would not mean the permanent separation of England from the unity of Christendom. For there was no reason why this should have been permanent except that the holders of the monastic loot were desperately afraid that they would have to disgorge if ever England again became a Catholic country. Against this process the *Utopia* was a noble protest delivered in advance of the completed event.

Whether or not it be taken in a socialistic sense, the book is assuredly a tract against avarice. More at least shows, in his closing page, that he sympathized with the "community" of the Utopian way of life. While exercising some reserve, he dodges the necessity of expressing the disagreement he says he feels about some of its details, by remarking that Hythloday was tired from talking so much, and that dinner was waiting. But one can see that he admired the Utopians for being "without any occupying of money, by the which thing only all nobility, magnificence, worship, honour and majesty, the true ornaments and honours, as the common opinion is, of a commonwealth be utterly overthrown and destroyed." Not content with venting his scorn for conditions under which a "lumpish blockheaded churl" could have many wise and good men in subjection, only "because he hath a great heap of gold," he makes Hythloday give an edge to the parable by describing the derision the sight of bejewelled foreign grandees aroused in a people for whom the only use of gold was to make distinguishing emblems of infamy for criminals, trinkets for little children, and chamber pots.

One thing more: if the *Utopia* is a protest against the greed of a very vulgar age, it is also, in part, a protest against its "new" ideas—the "wave of the future." This hero of the communists, so far from being an "advanced" man was really reverting to the concepts that prevailed in an older England as against the new statesmanship and the new economics. It is not that More was hidebound to the past, and we should do this supple and broad-minded a man a serious injustice if we called him a reactionary. But it would be nearer the mark to think of him as that than as a revolutionary. Cant modern terms can have little meaning in his case. He was in the *Utopia,* as elsewhere, simply a Christian, affirming

Christian values. And his method was the highly original one of making those values appear all the fresher and more striking by picturing them as existing among a pagan people, guided only by reason, but whose attachment to such values put the so-called Christians of his time to shame.

CHAPTER NINE

The King's Friend

FOR ecclesiastics who went on embassies, as More wrote to Erasmus soon after his return, the King could always easily find rewards that cost him nothing by appointing them to rich benefices. It was not so easy to reward laymen, for in those days there was normally little taxation, and the King was expected to "live on his own." That is, he was supposed to provide out of his own treasury all the ordinary expenses of running the country, and to ask for subsidies only on extraordinary occasions, such as a war. Henry rarely did live according to this principle, and less and less as time went on; but the principle always enabled him to plead that he was short of funds when it was a question of paying people. Yet in More's case, he tried to recompense his services. The letter to Erasmus continues: "On my return an annual pension was indeed appointed for me by the King, and one by no means negligible [it was a hundred pounds]. Yet hitherto I have refused it, and I think I shall continue to do so because, if I accepted it, my present office in the city, which I prefer even to a better one, would either have to be resigned, or else retained not without some offence to the citizens, which I should be most loth to give." A conflict might arise between the privileges of London and the royal will, in which event a pensioner of the King would naturally be looked upon with suspicion.

More did in fact manage to hold the King off for some while longer and to remain Under-Sheriff. He wished to be, in so far as this was possible in those days, a free agent; and nobody was ever less keen on his own profit or advancement. Instead of wishing to take advantage of the opportunities now opening before him, he sought to avoid them. A man who had written as he had, in the person of Raphael Hythloday, understandably dreaded accepting favors from the Crown and getting obligated to services which he saw might be very far from his Utopian ideal.

But if he was reluctant to accept anything for himself, he had no hesitation when it came to asking for something for a friend. Thus Ammonius wrote to Erasmus to tell him: "[More] now haunts with us the smoky chambers of the Palace. No one is more punctual in carrying his morning saluation to my Lord of York." Wolsey had held out hopes that Erasmus would be given a canonry at Tournai, and it was for this or some other "fat benefice" that More was pressing. Probably, however, those who saw him in attendance at Whitehall, supposed that he, like the rest of the people there, was in quest of his personal profit.

Yet the King's service could not be permanently avoided, if the King insisted, as in this instance he did. To no monarch who ever lived were his wishes, or even his whims, more sacred than these were to Henry VIII. It was clear enough to More that he could, at best, only defer his fate. Of course neither he nor anybody else could have had the slightest idea as to what pinnacle of grandeur he would eventually come.

The eyes of the King and of Wolsey had probably been on him for some time; that was why he was chosen for the embassy to Flanders. And the efficiency of his work upon that embassy attracted further attention to him. But other things made his official employment more certain than ever. One was his masterly pleading in a case concerning one of the Pope's ships, which was claimed by the Crown as forfeit after having put into an English port. More obtained a decision in the Pope's favor and a greatly enhanced reputation for himself. Another thing, which was probably the main factor, was the part he played in the "Evil May Day" of 1517, something that lingered so vividly in the memory of Londoners as to figure largely in the play on More written by a group of Elizabethan dramatists, of whom Shakespeare was almost certainly one.

This famous riot, which so terrified law-abiding people, was at least in its origin, as More was to relate, hardly more than a prank on the part of a couple of mischievous apprentices. They, having started the trouble, got safely away when they saw that things were getting too hot, but not before they had instigated an attack upon the foreigners resident in the Blanchapleton section of the city. Feeling against the competition of these people had been growing for some time, and now suddenly it came to a head, with mobs surging along Cheapside and around St. Paul's, most of them young fellows shouting, "Clubs and prentices!" but few of them having any idea more definite than that it was good fun and exciting.

For many of them it proved to have an excitement little to their taste. An old statute was dusted off and used—again we have a confirmation of Hythloday on the current practice of kings; and on a charge that they had violated the King's safe-conduct to foreigners, about forty rioters were hanged out of hand on May 4th by the liberal Henry, thirteen on one gallows. Still more would have been executed had not the Lord Mayor and the Alderman, with the eloquent More as their spokesman—all of them in black—appealed to the King "to be good and gracious Lord unto them, and to accept them now being sorrowful and heavy." As a result of this plea, those under arrest were given the grace to come in a body to Westminster Hall in their shirts and with halters round their necks to beg the royal clemency. Pardon was indeed granted, but only after the Queen had pleaded for their lives, and the thoroughly frightened wretches—to the number of four hundred men and eleven women—were given a wigging on Henry's behalf by Wolsey. There were in addition to these a good many others who crowded into Westminster Hall, people not yet under arrest but who knew they would be arrested if the case were pressed. These too were all ready for the pardon, should it be pronounced, and the moment it came they stripped down to their shirts and put round the necks the halters with which they had come prepared. Yet no lives had been lost in the riot. It was merely that Henry VIII always got so scared at the slightest disturbance that he exacted a ferocious exemplary punishment.

More helped greatly in saving these people from the gallows. But on Evil May Day itself he had tried to restore order among the rioters, and nearly succeeded. Hall's *Chronicle* tells the story: "Thus they ran aplump through Saint Nicholas' Shambles, and at Saint Martin's gate there met with them Sir Thomas More[1] and others, desiring them to go to their lodgings. And as they were entreating and had almost brought them to a stay, the people of Saint Martin's threw out stones and bats and hurt divers honest persons that were persuading the riotous persons to cease, and they bade them hold their hands but they still strew out bricks and hot water. Then a Serjeant at Arms called Nicholas Downes which was there with Master More entreating them, being sore hurt, in a fury cried 'Down with them!' Then all the misruled persons ran to the doors and windows of Saint Martin and spoiled all that they found and cast it into the street and left few houses unspoiled."

The play that was written about More later in the century gives at some length the speeches he made to the mob, and though these are of course largely, if not wholly, fictitious, they show how firmly established was his reputation as a man at once compassionate and reasonable, and an upholder of authority. One of these speeches, made in reply to the call for the ejection of the foreigners, runs:

> Grant them removed, and grant that this your noise
> Hath chid down all the majesty of England.
> Imagine that you see the wretched strangers,
> Their babies at their backs, and their poor luggage,
> Plodding to the ports and coasts for transportation,
> And that you sit as kings in your desires,
> Authority quite silenced by your brawl,
> And you in ruff of your opinion clothed,
> What had you got? I'll tell you. You had taught
> How insolence and strong hand should prevail,
> How order should be quelled; and by this pattern
> Not one of you should live an aged man;
> For other ruffians, as their fancies wrought
> With self same hand, self reasons and self right
> Would shark on you; and men like ravenous fishes
> Would feed on one another.

1 This is by way of anticipation. More was not knighted until 1521.

But though that speech is imaginary, it was not in the least imaginary to represent More as in truth he was, a man whose whole thinking was based on order and the recognition of rightful authority. It also strongly suggests that the author of those lines had read the *Utopia,* and had in mind the passage about the pitiful plight of those dispossessed by the enclosures.

More did serve the King to the last limit of the loyalty to which he was entitled, and until it clashed with what was due to God. Though he could not have foreseen on how fundamental a matter the clash would occur, what he wrote in the *Utopia* makes it evident that he did at least fear that, as a servant of the Crown, he would be put in a position where he would appear to be supporting (or even advising) policies of which in fact he disapproved. He yielded in the end,—but not until 1518—and Erasmus wrote that the King had at last succeeded in "dragging" More to court. For emphasis he repeated, "*dragged* is the word."

When More did consent to accept the royal service, he wrote to Fisher, "Everybody knows that I did not want to come to Court, and the King often twits me about it; I sit as uneasily as a clumsy rider in the saddle." To Erasmus he had written of his innocent enjoyment of the fame the *Utopia* had brought him saying that he wished to be sovereign among Utopians, crowned with a diadem of wheat, clad in a Franciscan robe, and carrying as sceptre a few ears of corn. Instead, he had to wear fur and velvet and a gold chain. Erasmus regretted his friend's elevation, though he hoped that it would benefit himself, and he tried to console himself with the reflection, "Under such a king and with so many learned men for companions and colleagues, it may seem not a Court but a Temple of the Muses; still, we shall get no more news from Utopia to make us laugh, and I know that More would rather laugh than be carried in official state."

Even had More dared to reject the King's offers of place and profit, he could hardly have stood out forever against the ambition of the somewhat worldly Dame Alice. This he cleverly managed to indicate in his *Dialogue of Comfort,* in one of the many passages that are clearly about that rich character: "When her husband had no list to grow greatly upward in the world, nor neither would labour for office of authority, and over that forsook a right worshipful room when it was offered him, she fell in hand with him and . . . all to rated him, and asked him: 'What will you do, that you list not to put forth yourself as other folk do? Will you sit by the fire and make goslings in the ashes with a stick, as children do? Would God I were a man, and look what I would do.' 'Why, wife,' quoth her husband, 'what would you do?' 'What? By God, go forward with the best. For as my mother was wont to say, God have mercy on her soul, it is ever better to rule than be ruled, and therefore by God, I would not, I warrant you, be so foolish as to be ruled, when I might rule.' " To which speech, with its mouth-filling oaths, as characteristic of Dame Alice as of Lady Percy, her husband answered with mild amusement, "By my troth, wife, in this I dare say you say truth. For I never found you willing to be ruled yet."

She had her way in this matter. Though one can hardly describe so busy and successful a lawyer as a man who spent all his time drawing goslings in the ashes, it is understandable that Dame Alice wished to prod him on to take advantage of the opportunities that were opening for him. Yet as to that, More may well have intended for himself the words used by Hythloday when he was urged to take service under a king because of what he would be able to do in such a position for his friends and kinsfolk. To this Hythloday had replied: "As concerning my friends and kinsfolk, I pass not greatly for them. For I think I have sufficiently done my part towards them already." With the liberality shown he thinks they should be contented and not ask him to give himself "in bondage to kings." And when Raphael is asked to remember that "from the Prince, as from a perpetual well spring, cometh among the people the flood that is good and evil," and that no more valuable service can be rendered the commonweal than the wise advising of the Prince, Hythloday disclaims any qualification for such a task;

nothing, he said, would be accomplished, save that "in disquieting my own quietness I should nothing further the public weal."

More's short experience as an ambassador had disillusioned him. Hythloday is made to tell how the Utopians, as in their part of the world leagues between nations were so frequently broken, would make no leagues at all. How different, he exclaims sarcastically, from conditions in Europe, "especially in these parts where the faith and religion of Christ reigneth!" He indicates slyly that he is speaking of the Utopian hemisphere when he says that, the more solemn the ceremonies with which the pact is made, the sooner is it broken because of the discovery of some ambiguous clause that it contains, "which many times of purpose be so craftily put in and placed, that the bands can never be so sure nor so strong, but that they will find some hole to creep out at, and break both league and truth." Such fraud and deceit, he comments, if practised between private men in their contracts, would be regarded as detestable. Therefore it must be concluded that there are two kinds of justice —the inferior, suitable for ordinary people, and the superior, reserved for the rulers of kingdoms, among whom perfidy is "a princely virtue, which like as it is of much higher majesty than the other poor justice, so also it is of much more liberty, as to which nothing is unlawful that it lusteth after."

Yet these excoriating words, though put for the sake of prudence in the mouth of Raphael Hythloday, obviously express More's own views on the prevailing immorality of international politics. They were published in the year following his first embassy, and must have drawn further force from that fact. Nevertheless they did not prevent his being sent to Calais on another embassy in 1517 or his being advanced the following year to still higher office, and eventually to the highest place in England next to that of the monarch himself.

This could have meant that an attempt was being made to silence a dangerous critic. But though there is reason to suspect that More may have been made Lord Chancellor in 1529 as a means of "buying" him—in 1517 and 1518 it would seem that

Henry VIII had no other motive in mind except that of obtaining a distinguished man on his Council, one whose advice would be honestly given and perhaps be useful just because it was honest, but whose advice need never be followed. The author of a book that had made a sensation throughout Europe was regarded as an ornament, if nothing else. His reputation for incorruptible probity, even the opinions he had expressed in the *Utopia,* might be taken as a guarantee that the English government, of which he was now a member, was acting in good faith, and so leave that government all the more free to pursue its deceitful objects.

More was soon much more than a mere ornament to the Council. He became so close a personal friend of the King's that, had he wished to push his fortunes, he might easily have obtained a dominant voice in public affairs, though of course only on condition that he operated as other politicians do. It may almost be said that More was the only personal friend Henry ever had—for boon companions (of whom Henry had several) are rarely friends. Certainly More was Henry's truest friend, not only because of the excellent advice he gave but because he had a genuine affection for the King. This affection was returned, in so far as the royal egotist was capable of having any affection for anybody except himself. It was the intimacy that came to exist between the two men that made Henry so ragingly angry with More when More, in the end, found it impossible to accede to his wishes.

But no roles were further from More's thoughts, or his temperament, than that of the politician or the court favorite. Therefore he performed faithfully and well the duties which he was called upon to perform, but was so completely devoid of ambition that, so far from seeking further advancement, he would at any moment have been glad to relinquish all offices and to retire into private life.

Holding the views he did, More must have exercised considerable tact to avoid coming into conflict with the all-powerful Wolsey. The Cardinal held not only the Archbishopric of York, but also several other sees, the cathedral of not one of which had he so far seen, as well as a rich abbacy. As he was Papal Legate and Lord Chancellor he had effected such a concentration of authority as had never been known before, and this he exercised with immense energy and ability. Insatiably covetous, and of low morals[2], he was nevertheless just (even though he was willing to accept bribes), and was regarded as a friend of the poor. Hated, for good cause, by many people, he was of an affable, portly, full-blooded disposition, and had, like Henry, a good deal of charm at his disposal. His foreign policy was steadily directed towards the support of the papacy as a secular power, and he had ambitions of becoming Pope himself. But outside of that aim, he played—sometimes it would seem merely for the pleasure of exercising his own virtuosity, but later also for personal spite or personal advantage—a very devious game in Europe. In this at the last he overreached himself, and was preparing his downfall some time before his failure in the matter of the King's "divorce" became the immediate occasion of his ruin.

In 1518, however, his position seemed quite unassailable. Though there were occasional disagreements between himself and More, the two men upon the whole got on sufficiently well with one another, probably in part because More abstained from any attempt to use his friendship with the King for political ends. Yet Roper tells a story of how, when Wolsey was advocating in the Council the creation of a new office—that of Constable—for himself, which would have given him a still greater concentration of power, all those present subserviently accepted the proposal—with the exception of More. He was rewarded by being angrily told that he was a fool, to which he made the good-humored rejoinder, "God be thanked that the King has but *one* fool in his council," with which witticism the storm blew over. Also the proposal was dropped. That this is not recorded in any official document does not necessarily mean that what Roper relates is without founda-

[2] The son of his mistress, Miss Larke, was given rich ecclesiastical benefices, and her brother was appointed the Cardinal's confessor! The arrangement hardly suggests that Wolsey had much humor.

tion. But it may mean that Roper gave to what could have been a vague random suggestion a weight greater than it really deserved.

It would certainly seem that Roper—admirable fellow but somewhat too disposed to take his father-in-law's casual jests with unnecessary seriousness—was mistaken in what he says about Wolsey's wishing to send More on an embassy to Spain in the expectation that the Spanish climate would kill him, so that he would get rid of a man whom, according to Roper, the Cardinal more feared than loved. All this may be due to some facetious remark made by More when the man, sent in his place, actually did die, and another fell gravely ill—something like, "Oh, so that was what my Lord of York intended for me!" Roper's notion of an implacable animosity is contradicted by a state paper which shows that Wolsey at this time recommended that More be given a "bonus" of £100 because of his services. We also have More's letter thanking Wolsey for his good offices in this matter, and another letter which More, who was at the time acting as the King's secretary, wrote to tell Wolsey how pleased the King was with a letter the Cardinal had drafted for Henry. More tells him: "The letter which your Grace devised in the name of his Highness to the Queen [of the Scots], his sister, his Grace so well liked that I never saw him like anything better, and, so help me God, in my poor phantasy, not causeless, for it is for the quantity one of the best made letters for words, matter, sentences, and couching that I ever read in my life." More need not be suspected of flattery. Wolsey was in truth an extremely able man. But More knew that the Cardinal liked to be praised, and he was himself a kindly man willing to please when he could.

The main clash between Wolsey and More occurred when More, upon the opening of Parliament in 1523, was made its Speaker. In those days, when there was no cabinet whose members sat in Parliament, the Speaker was the connecting link between the King in Council and the House of Commons. Now, when the Cardinal demanded the huge subsidy of £800,000 for the prosecution of the war against France, a deputation called upon Wolsey saying that it could not possibly be raised. To this Wolsey "currishly answered that he would rather have his tongue plucked from his head with a pair of pincers than to move the King to any less sum." Then when reports of parliamentary opposition began to circulate outside, Wolsey angrily declared that "nothing was so soon done or spoken therein, but that it was immediately blown abroad in every alehouse." He determined to come to the Commons in person to overawe them. Roper continues: "Before whose coming, when after long debating there, whether it were better with a few of his lords (as the most opinion of the House was) or with his whole train royally to receive him there amongst them: 'Masters,' quoth Sir Thomas More, 'forasmuch as my Lord Cardinal lately, ye wot well, laid to our charges the lightness of our tongues for things uttered out of this House, it shall not be in my mind amiss with all his pomp to receive him, with his maces, his pillars, his poleaxes, his crosses, his hat, and Great Seal too; to the intent that, if he find the like fault with us hereafter, we may be the bolder from ourselves to lay the blame on those that his Grace bringeth hither with him'; whereunto the House wholly agreeing, he was received accordingly."

Roper describes the scene when the Cardinal arrived. From the House was demanded what Wolsey called "some reasonable answer," and when the members remained silent, he demanded from this or that man singled out by him the reply he wished. All continued to preserve what the Cardinal told them was "without doubt a marvellous obstinate silence"; so he swung round on More and called upon him to speak the mind of the Commons.

Upon this More went down on his knees and explained that the members were abashed at the "presence of so noble a personage," but also said that "it was neither expedient nor agreeable with the ancient liberty of the House" to be forced to give a reply. Neither could he answer on behalf of the assembled members, he told the Cardinal, "except every one of them could put into his one head all their several wits." So Wolsey left in a rage without having received any satisfaction.

A day or two later, when More was in the Cardinal's palace at Whitehall, Wolsey said to him rather bitterly, "Would to God you had been at Rome, Master More, when I made you Speaker!" To this petulant remark More answered mildly, "Your Grace not offended, so would I too, my Lord." Then to calm Wolsey with a compliment, he began to speak of the gallery at Whitehall, in which they were walking, saying that he preferred it even to the one at Hampton Court. A little judicious praise was always advisable with the vainglorious Wolsey.

The question of the subsidy was settled by compromise, and More managed at once to defend the liberties of Parliament and to do what was expected of a Speaker as the initiator of business for the Crown. It was for these services that Wolsey made the recommendation, to which there has already been reference, that he be given a grant of £100, in addition to his salary as Speaker.

More upon being appointed to this office, delivered what Chambers calls "the first recorded speech for freedom of speech in Parliament." In this the new Speaker went a good deal further than the customary request for pardon in advance for any too great boldness on the part of the members. Yet even More did not claim freedom of speech as a right but merely urged that, if the members were afraid of being punished for too rash an expression of their views (such as he had suffered for in his youth), the King would lack the benefit that might come from untrammelled discussion. His speech, as reported by Roper, after the usual formal disclaimer of being unworthy of the Speaker's office—what was called "disabling"—ran in part as follows: "Therefore, most gracious Sovereign, considering that in your High Court of Parliament is nothing intreated but matter of weight and importance concerning your realm and your own royal estate, it could not fail to let [hinder] and put to silence from the giving of their advice and counsel many of your discreet Commons, to the great hindrance of the common affairs, except that every of your Commons were utterly discharged of all doubt and fear how anything that it should happen to them to speak should happen of your Highness to be taken." He therefore requested "that it may like your noble Majesty, of your inestimable goodness to take all in good part, interpreting every man's words, how uncunningly soever they may be couched, to proceed yet of good zeal towards the profit of your realm and honour of your royal personage." Though what the Speaker asked for on that occasion was a good deal less than what came afterwards to be taken for granted, it was the most that could be looked for at that time, and therefore has some importance in the history of the English Parliament.

But I have somewhat anticipated matters by recording first what came fairly late in Thomas More's official career. Before becoming Speaker of the House of Commons in 1523 he was made Master of Requests in 1518, and Under-Treasurer in 1521 (in which year he was also knighted). This was a position that approximates to that of Chancellor of theExchequer. In 1525 he was appointed Chancellor of the Duchy of Lancaster.

There is no special need to say anything regarding these positions, except that he discharged his duties with such dispatch and justice that he prepared the way for further advancement. So also with his various embassies, for those to Flanders and Calais in 1515 and 1517 were duly followed by others—to Bruges in 1521, to France in 1527, and the final one (the most important of all), that which resulted in the signing of the Treaty of Cambrai in 1529. These indicate merely that he was a trusted public servant, not that he was a great man.

Also there were diplomatic functions in England attended by him, as when he was among those who welcomed the Emperor Charles V at Canterbury, delivering in London the Latin oration before Henry VIII and his imperial guest. On this visit the versatile John Rastell, More's brother-in-law, distinguished himself by designing a kind of panorama, "a place like heaven, curiously painted with clouds, orbs, stars, and the hierarchies of angels." The climax came when there suddenly issued out of a cloud, "a fair lady richly apparelled, and then all the minstrels which were in the pageant played and the angels sang, and suddenly again," according to Hall's *Chronicle,* "she was assumpted into the cloud which was very curiously done, and about this pageant stood the Apostles." But though More may have helped Rastell prepare this spectacle, he could only have been disgusted by the fact, clearly understood by him, that the Emperor's visits of 1520 and 1522, like the lavish display at the Field of the Cloth of Gold, when Henry and Francis entertained one another and protested undying friendship, were utterly insincere. The three monarchs—especially Henry—were all busy double-crossing their allies. It may well have seemed to More a judgment of God when at the Field of the Cloth of Gold, as Stowe relates, "the wind began to rise, and increasing in the evening, it then of a sudden blew off the canvas heavens with the planets, and blew out more than 1000 torches of wax." For More the occasion was pleasant only because of a friendship formed with Guillaume Budé, the famous scholar who may be claimed as the founder of the Collège de France and of the Bibliothèque Nationale. More made him a present of two fine English greyhounds.

As he did at the English court, Thomas More moved among the gorgeously decorated personages present, a simple smiling figure, as plainly dressed as possible by contrast to their robes of brocade and velvet. At the opulent banquets—Henry disdaining beef as coarse, gorged on swans and peacocks, yet admitting pork and venison—he pretended to eat a little of the rich foods they set before him on plates of gold, and at the toasts he touched the costly wines with his lips. But he charmed everybody with his friendly courtesy and his brilliant talk. And all the time he must have been thinking of the derision with which his Utopians would have gazed at such empty splendors. Many others probably did so too, for the *Utopia* had made him a European celebrity.

Always scornful of pretense, he especially despised it when it had, as on these occasions, deceit and even malice. Though he could say nothing about his opinions concerning these lavish and essentially vulgar displays, as he was himself an official, there were times when he took an impish delight in exposing the vanity of coxcombs. Thus at Brussels, when he was on his embassy to Bruges, he encountered one evening a man who proclaimed himself ready to dispute upon any point of law or literature, a challenge no doubt aimed at the famous More. Upon literature this man might have made a good enough showing, but More punctured his windy bladder by propounding, as Stapleton relates (and also "Ro.Ba."), an obscure proposition peculiar to English law: "Whether cattle taken in withernam be irrepreviable." The braggart of course did not have the faintest notion as to the meaning of the terms. On another occasion, Ro.Ba. says, More offered a little challenge of his own. He had been humorously claiming as one of the highest merits of the English language the difficulty of pronouncing it, and then added: "Now I will speak but three words, and I durst jeopard a wager that none here shall pronounce it after me: *Thwaites thwackt him with a thwittle*. And no man there could pronounce it."

Right in the midst of all this pageantry, in 1522, More composed his *Four Last Things,* a book never finished because it had to be laid aside on account of pressure of business. It seems to me to reveal a good deal more about him than the fact that he held a number of offices under the Crown, the most striking fact of all being that it was composed by a man who was steadily rising in the world and who yet turned aside from its vanities to a consideration of man's true end. Here Mr. Hollis wittily says: "It is common for us to be told to lay up our treasures where neither moth nor rust doth corrupt; it is not so common to be told it by the Chancellor of the Exchequer." Mr. Hollis continues: "For a very short time no doubt the pursuers of the glittering prizes were shaken by Sir Thomas More's contempt for them, but they very soon learned to say with their old confidence, 'No one ever despised the prizes of the world except those unable to win them.' And if the objector said, 'What about Sir Thomas More?' they answered, 'Oh, well, Sir Thomas More,' as if to repeat were to reply to an argument, as if everybody knew that Sir Thomas More, simply because he despised the world, was an oddity and therefore the generalization that no able man despised the world still held good."

That is not only witty but sensible, and yet I wonder whether anybody *can* shrug off the issue with an "Oh, well, Sir Thomas More. . . ." For More was not in the least eccentric, and that he wrote what Chambers calls "the grimmest of all his books" while Under-Treasurer, still gives one reason to pause. What can never be got around is the fact that the man who wrote it proved his absolute sincerity not only by renouncing the greatest prize obtainable by an Englishman, but also that he suffered death rather than be unfaithful to his principles. Perhaps Professor Chambers in using the word "grim"—which Miss Routh also uses in this connection—thinks of what More wrote as a manifestation of medieval piety in its sterner aspects. But one cannot dismiss things of this sort merely by calling them macabre or wringing one's hands that More completely believed in hell, or what he called "the deadly life of everlasting pain." In *The Four Last Things* More intended to give his readers salutary fear. I, for one, hope that he will continue to do so.

Of all sure facts the surest is that "we never ought to look to death as a thing far off, considering that although he make no haste towards us, yet we never cease to make haste towards him." With this in mind More presents here an idea that almost became an obsession with him, that we are all of us prisoners under sentence of death. Though he may have overworked this notion at times—as in the book written while he was jailed in the Tower, his *Dialogue of Comfort*—a good purpose is served if it forces us to reflect upon Death and Judgment, Hell and Heaven. "This medicine," More writes, however, "though men make a sour face at it, is not so bitter as thou makest for. For well thou wottest, he biddeth thee take neither death nor doom, nor pain, but only to remember them, and yet the joy of heaven to temper them withal." To such as do have in mind the prospect of paradisal joys, the "grimness" of which Professor Chambers and Miss Routh complain, serves to add an exquisite point. What *is* really terrifying is the worldliness of spirit that makes many a man, as More reminds us, arrange, even on his death-bed, for his fine funeral. "Instead of sorrow for our sins and care of heaven [the devil] putteth us in mind of provision for some honourable burying—so many torches, so many tapers, so many black gowns, so many merry mourners laughing under black hoods, and a gay hearse, with the delight of goodly and honourable funerals: in which the foolish sick man is sometimes occupied as though he thought he should stand in a window and see how worshipfully he shall be brought to death." As More remarks, the Dance of Death pictured in old St. Paul's cannot stir our imaginations as much as does what we feel (or should feel) deeply graven in our own hearts.

All this comes from an extremely busy lawyer who was rising, in spite of himself, rapidly upwards in the world. The grimness is that of the most cheerful man in all England. It is also that of the most popular man of his time. If *The Four Last Things* shows nothing else it shows his versatility. For along with the major offices More held, he was at one time or another during this period, a Commissioner of Sewers and a kind of health officer for Oxford during the plague of the "sweating sickness." Also (and no doubt more to his taste) he occupied the position of High Steward of Oxford University in 1524, adding to this, in the following year, that of High Steward of Cambridge as well. In this capacity he was obliged to try students guilty of serious offences.

But he was not only a disciplinarian; as one might expect of a man of More's character, he delighted in taking part in the university debates. In these, as Roper tells us, few men could stand up against him, but when More perceived that he had got them into difficulties, he would not press his advantage, lest he should discourage the disputants, but "ever showing himself more desirous to learn than to teach, would he by some witty device courteously break off into some other matter, and give over." Than which, zest of argument being what it is, nothing could have proved a more delicate kindness.

What took more time than anything else was his obligation of being in almost constant attendance upon the King. Most people would have envied him for this, but More sighed whenever he had to travel in the wake of Henry, who was forever moving from place to place in order to avoid the sweating sickness. Though in this Henry was a bit morbid, there is no doubt that the danger was real. Wolsey was several times attacked, and both Colet and Ammonius died from this strange sickness which struck suddenly and killed at the first onset and on the first day all those destined to succumb.[3] Even More thought it a little hard when he was sent to Calais just at the moment that the epidemic had crossed the Channel to that uninteresting little town.

When the King was at Greenwich or Westminster, More could slip away for a few days to Bucklersbury or, after 1524, to the house he built at Chelsea.[4] He came to discover that it was not merely official business that necessitated his being with the King but rather more the pleasure that Henry took in his society. At night the two friends would go on the leads of Greenwich Palace, and there More would discourse on astronomy, with the heavens sparkling overhead. More often the King would summon him into his private apartments, as soon as he had heard Mass—usually the pious monarch heard two, and sometimes five—in order to enjoy his witty conversation. He would be sent for again at dinner which was at that time eaten at noon, if not earlier—to entertain the King and Queen. He learned that it was advisable to be less amusing, if he was ever to get any time for his wife and children. Therefore he artfully contrived to lessen by degrees—it had to be done by degrees so as not to arouse Henry's suspicions—the effervescent ebullience of his natural disposition.

Even when he was at Chelsea he could not always escape the

[3] It was due entirely to unsanitary conditions. Osler says that it existed in the early nineteenth century. The main symptom was a heavy sweat.

[4] In 1523 he bought Crosby Hall, an odd fancy of his, perhaps springing from its association with Richard III, when he was Duke of Gloucester. But it is not certain that More lived there. In any event it could only have been for a short time.

King. Roper tells the famous story of how (probably in 1525) his Majesty dropped in to dinner unannounced. Afterwards the burly Henry walked in the pleasant garden for a full hour with his heavy arm round More's neck, much to the delight of Roper and no doubt even more to that of Dame Alice. Roper concluded: "As soon as his Grace was gone, I, greatly rejoicing thereat, told Sir Thomas More how happy he was, whom the King had so familiarly entertained, as I never saw him do to any other except Cardinal Wolsey, whom I saw his Grace once walk with, arm in arm. 'I thank our Lord, son,' quoth he, 'I find his Grace my very good lord indeed, and I believe he doth as singularly favour me as any subject within this realm. Howbeit, son Roper, I may tell thee that I have no cause to be proud thereof, for if my head could win him a castle in France (for then there was war between us) it should not fail to go."

More had never been under any illusions about his friend. Only two years later began that train of events which were to bring him to the block on Tower Hill.

CHAPTER TEN

The House of Happiness

St. Thomas More may almost be said to have merited canonization for the perfection of his family life, were he not canonized as a martyr. Indeed, some people, remembering how sharp was Dame Alice's tongue, and how short her temper, might even suggest a new sanctoral classification specially for him—that of husband and martyr. This, however, would be unfair not only to Lady More but to Sir Thomas as well. It is sufficiently evident that he relished to the full his wife's racy character, and it is likely enough that she felt all the more free because of this to indulge her idiosyncrasies. Though she is not just the woman one would picture as the wife of a saint, she may nevertheless have contributed to making him one. In any event there is no need to commiserate with him on her account. She made him a good wife, of the practical housewifely sort (which was what he had in view when he married her), and what she accomplished as a step-mother was as necessary to the family as the light and fragrance he shed upon it. She and her husband were undoubtedly much happier than the majority of people whose love story is far more romantic than theirs.

This needs to be said as her due, and we shall see more of her later in this chapter and at the end of this book. Yet one thinks—and rightly—primarily of More as the father of his children. It was in their society, and especially in that of his favorite daughter, Margaret Roper, that his tenderness most beautifully flowered. Admirable as was his public life, even more excellent was his private life as lived with his family.

English family life was far from being at its best at this time. We have seen how Thomas More in his youth had little of it, and how he was deposited on Archbishop Morton's doorstep when he was a boy of twelve. Though in his case this was of immense benefit, one suspects that John More may have been thinking of his own convenience rather than of his son's good. Certainly many children during the reigns of the Tudors were farmed out in this way because they were regarded as a nuisance at home. It may well be that, because of what Thomas More had lacked as a child, he determined to be the kindest of fathers to his own children. So far was he from following the domestic traditions then current that, not even in the case of his son John, did he permit so much as attendance at any school, though the best of London schools, St. Paul's—founded by his friend Colet and with Lily as its High Master—was within easy walking distance from his house at Bucklersbury. Instead he set up a school in his own home, engaging for John and the three girls, and his adopted daughter Margaret Giggs and his ward Anne Cresacre, who was to be the bride of his son, the very best of available tutors, several of whom became university professors.

But, indeed, everybody in that household, including the servants, made part of the *familia,* and More, though still a relatively young man at the time of his death, presided as the paterfamilias, even when old Sir John More was living there. Dorothy Colley, for instance, though she was Margaret Roper's maid, was clearly as much of a daughter as a servant. This was even more true of John Harris, More's secretary, whom Dorothy eventually married, as it was of the earlier secretary, John Clement, who took Margaret Giggs as his wife. The strong attachment of other servants to Sir Thomas comes out only incidentally, but we may suppose that it existed among them all.

Not only is this true, but the deep mark put by More upon the minds of the members of his household is very evident and very significant. All of those we hear of after More's death remained true to his principles, several of them preferring to live abroad, in the bitterness of exile after the accession of Elizabeth, in order to be able to practice their religion freely. One member of the family, Giles Heron, the husband of Cecily More, even suffered at Tyburn; and though he appears to have been brought to that fate largely through personal spite, the charge against him was that of much the same sort of "treason" for which his father-in-law had been condemned to death.

Several of these cases are quite remarkable. Thus the adhesion of Wiliam Rastell to the Catholic faith is all the more striking when we remember that he sacrificed a judgeship and that he was the son of John Rastell, More's brother-in-law, who lost no time in conforming to the Henrician religious system. So also is the case of John Heywood, wit and dramatist and the grandfather of John Donne, rather instructive. He publicly recanted in 1544 in the face of otherwise certain death, but he afterwards repented and joined others of More's circle on the continent, dying there a very old man with a jest on his lips. To the priest who sought to console his last moments with the reflection, "The flesh is weak," he retorted, "Verily, you seem to reproach God for not having made me a fish!" He married Joan Rastell, a daughter of More's sister Elizabeth. Two of their sons became Jesuits and men of some distinction, and both died in exile.

Chambers has described the household as a "small patriarchal, monastic Utopia." Perhaps the term monastic may be allowed to pass, though it hardly seems to apply to the marrying propensities of the Mores, but at least there was a religious discipline probably not to be found in any such house in England. More's later position demanded a number of personal retainers, among whom must be numbered the eight rowers of his barge. Yet none of these were allowed to be idle at such times as they were free from their ordinary duties. At such hours they were expected to practice singing, or playing musical instruments, including the organ; and for healthful recreation to each one was assigned a part of the large garden as his special care. To all, dice and cards were absolutely forbidden. And the young men and women lived in separate wings of the house so as to safeguard their morals.

They all also took part in the family prayers, being assembled morning and evening when More was at home in the oratory he had built near his Chelsea mansion. There, kneeling, they recited three psalms, including the *Miserere,* which were followed by the *Salve Regina* and the *De Profundis* for the repose of the dead. On Sundays they were obliged not only to attend Mass faithfully, but to be present in church by the time Father John Larke, More's appointee at Chelsea, and a martyr in 1544 (he is now beatified), appeared at the altar. The whole Divine Office was said by the entire household at Christmas and Easter.

Meals, as described by Stapleton, began with the reading of a passage of Scripture, "intoned in the ecclesiastical or monastic fashion," followed by a page or two from the commentaries of Nicholas of Lyra. This continued until More, like the superior of a religious community, gave the signal for conversation with the *Tu autem, Domine.* The reader at table was generally one of the daughters of the house, with John Harris officiating on the occasions when the devotions were longer.

If this sounds a little formidable, it must be remembered that the reading at table lasted only a few minutes and that the rest of the meal passed in highly diverting talk, Henry Patenson the clown bandying jests with Sir Thomas. As we can see from More's writings, even those of a devotional character, he had a vast fund of "merry tales" at his command. If some of these had a moral, they were not the less amusing on that account. The mischievous tricks of the pet monkey served sometimes to illustrate the devices of the devil. In that family, virtue was made to seem not only lovely but easy. And if More often told them not to count upon being carried to heaven on feather beds, he also used to say that God was lifting them to Him by their chins. One may surmise that More himself had a playful way of lifting them up like this.

More's wit, however, was commonly exercised not with a moral object but simply for the simple pleasure he derived from it. When a member of the Manners family once said to him, a little rudely, with a spiteful reference to his rapid rise from obscurity, *"Honores mutant Mores,"* More instantly capped the witticism in English with, "True, indeed, my lord, but *Mores* in English is not *More* but *Manners,"* a repartee with more edges than one. Similarly when More requested a debtor to repay what he owed, and was reminded by the man that he was destined to die, "God knoweth how soon, and then he would have little use for money," adding *"Memento morieris,"* he got the retort, "Of course you mean, *Memento Mori æris*—remember More's money." The tradition of such things was treasured by the family, and jests that Roper and Harpsfield and Stapleton overlooked were saved for us in the pages of Cresacre More.

But Thomas More's jocular habit, though always to be borne in mind as part of his character, is of course of less importance than other facts about him. His intellectual distinction, his moral integrity and his piety are the basic elements in his make-up, even though they must be said to draw a special quality from his friendly and humorous way of being a great man and of being a saint. We know from Stapleton that he personally used to visit the families of poor neighbors, "helping them not with small gifts but with two, three, or four pieces of gold, as their need requireth." When the dignity of the Chancellorship forbade him from doing this himself, he used to send members of his household out on charitable missions, the task being commonly laid on Margaret Giggs. "Moreover," says Stapleton, "in his parish Chelsea, he hired a house in which he placed many who were infirm, poor, or old, providing for them at his own expense. In her father's absence, Margaret Roper took charge of these." Into his home he took a widow named Paula who had spent all her money in litigation, but indeed he seems almost to have kept open house for his poor neighbours, and, says Stapleton, "the rich were rarely invited, the nobility hardly ever." A letter of his to Dame Alice, dated September 3, 1529, from Woodstock, where he was in attendance upon the King, is specially revealing of his generosity. He had heard from his son-in-law Heron of the burning of his barns at Chelsea, and as some of his neighbors' barns had also gone up in fire, along with all that they contained of the year's harvest, he tells Alice to be of good cheer, "and take all the household with you to church, and there thank God both for what He hath given and for what He hath taken way from us, and for that He hath left us, which, if it please Him, He can increase when He will." Yet so far from offering only a pious reflection—that alone would have been admirable under the circumstances—he tells her, "I pray you to make some good ensearch what my poor neighbours have lost, and bid them take no thought therefore; for, and I should not leave myself a spoon, there shall be no neighbour of mine bear no loss by any chance in my house." Rastell in printing this letter in the *English Works* adds that the fire was not the fault of any of More's servants but of a neighbor's carter.

Such benefaction must have cost a great deal of money. Yet it is hard to believe that "Ro.Ba." could have been correct in writing: "His ordinary alms, as yet to be seen in his book of accounts amounted yearly to one thousand pounds; his extraordinary were as much, and sometimes more; sometimes two, three and four thousand pounds a year." Such expenditures would, in modern values have amounted to several hundred thousands of dollars a year, and More's official salary was never very large, though of course it was supplemented by considerable court fees.[1] What we do positively know is that More spent his entire income upon maintaining his household and his charities, and that upon his fall from office his income from lands—the only investments he had ever made—was small and that the value of his plate was negligible. It would have been easy for a man in his position to have enormously enriched himself; he did nothing of the kind.

More's personal piety was of the most devoted kind, but was concealed as far as possible. Stapleton, who shows in his preface that he considered himself to be writing the life of a saint, says that "as regards the service of God, he lived almost the life of a monk." Every day he recited, in addition to the morning and evening prayers said with his household, the seven penitential psalms and the litanies. Fridays he set apart as days of recollec-

[1] "Ro.Ba." as printed in Wordsorth's *Ecclesiastical Biography,* Vol. II, p. 149. The author does not actually say that he himself saw this book of accounts, though that is the implication. However, those accounts are not in existence, so there is no means of checking the matter.

tion; these he spent in his oratory. Every day he heard Mass, and whenever any important business was pending, or at any crisis in his life, he was confessed and received Holy Communion. Had he lived in our times he would unquestionably have been a daily communicant, but that practice was almost unheard of in those days, even in monasteries.

In his parish church of All Saints he sang in the choir—not well, but possibly no worse than other members of the choir, and he often served Mass or carried the cross in processions. Once the Duke of Norfolk, calling upon him unexpectedly, found him in church and was disgusted to see the Lord Chancellor acting as verger. "God's body, Master More," he expostulated with him afterwards, "God's body, a parish clerk!" More was utterly unmoved by the reproof. On Rogation Days, when the procession went tiring distances round the fields, he refused to ride but followed on foot.

Then there was his practice, begun in youth and continued to the last day of his life, of wearing a hair-shirt. And what may sound even more shocking to modern ears, he regularly scourged himself with a "discipline." This article has disappeared, but the hair-shirt may still be seen in the convent of Newton Abbot in Devonshire. Stapleton described it as knotty, "like a net, much rougher, I should think, than are commonly the hair-shirts of religious." Once young Anne Cresacre, his future daughter-in-law, caught sight of it on a hot summer day when Sir Thomas was sitting in his doublet and hose. She giggled at the sight, and when More noticed the source of her amusement, he was filled with confusion. The only person who was supposed to know about this shirt was his daughter Margaret; she was told because she was entrusted with laundering it once in a while. But Dame Alice must also have known, because we hear of her, early in her marriage to More, going to Father John Bouge and asking him to get More to lay it aside.

Yet into that pious Catholic family came William Roper, who as Harpsfield writes, "at what time he married with Mistress

Margaret Roper was a marvellous zealous Protestant." We must suppose that More was in ignorance of this, for we cannot imagine that he would have allowed his dear Margaret to take a heretic as husband. At all events Roper soon became belligerent in his heresy: "Neither was he content to whisper it hugger mugger, but thirsted very sore to publish his new doctrine . . . and thought himself very able to do so, and it were even at Paul's Cross." He had read a couple of Luther's books and was taken with the characteristic Lutheran concept of justification by faith alone, though it is not easy to square this with what Harpsfield says about his "immoderate fasting." But perhaps young Roper was making up his own private heresy as he went along. At all events he had been hob-nobbing with the German merchants of the Steelyard (a badly infected spot) and had been talking so unguardedly that Wolsey heard of the matter and summoned the young man before him. In the end the Cardinal, out of deference to More, let Roper off with a friendly warning, while those with whom he had been associating were obliged to "carry their faggot" at Paul's Cross as a public recantation.

More of course was horrified, and did his best to argue with his son-in-law, but all to no purpose. He said to Margaret one day as they were walking in the garden, "Meg, I have borne a long time with thy husband; I have reasoned and argued with him in those points of religion, and still given him my poor fatherly counsel: but I perceive none of this able to call him home; and therefore, Meg, I will no longer argue nor dispute with him, but will clean give him over, and get me another while to God and pray for him." What argument was powerless to effect, prayer accomplished. Roper returned to Catholic practice, to which he was faithful until his death in 1578.

More's prayers were also efficacious in Margaret's case when, probably about the same time, she came down with the dreaded sweating sickness. What were recognized as the sure signs of death—"God's marks" they were called—were seen by the doctors, and the worst sign of all was a sleep from which she could not be roused. At this point More went to his oratory to pray for her recovery in spite of everything. He did not only pray, though; he drew upon his reading of medicine, in which, like many humanists, he was well versed. He suggested that the doctors try a remedy they had not thought of. Margaret got well, and her cure was attributed to her father's prayers. Afterwards he said that had she died he would have retired from public life. The relationship between them is the classic story of love between father and daughter.

Dame Alice, who had brought up all of More's children, has been badly treated by several of More's biographers, and some of More's friends made what were, to say the least, rather ungallant references to her. Ammonius was the worst in this respect, when he wrote of "the hooked beak of the harpy." He would seem also to have been unfair, for the Holbein family portrait shows her as plain, indeed, but having nothing remarkable about her nose—unless it was a bit long. Erasmus also felt, after one of his long visits to the Mores that, so far as Mistress More was concerned, he had outstayed his welcome. Yet it is only just to remember that Erasmus must have been a difficult guest, demanding all kinds of special attentions, needing carefully selected wines and salads composed in a particular way, hating English beer and being nauseated by the smell of fish. Probably, too, the delights of his conversation, though enjoyed by the children, were beyond Dame Alice's comprehension, though she may have picked up a little colloquial Latin from having heard it spoken so constantly round her. Under the circumstances, she should, I think, be credited with having shown a good deal of forbearance.

To call her, as somebody has done, the worst possible wife for a saint is a little harsh. Certainly she was no saint herself, but she was a thoroughly good woman. That More could write to her as he did after the burning of the barns, so sure of her kindness of heart, speaks volumes. She often appears in his works under a disguise easily to be penetrated and of course without disguise in the pages of Roper. It is More who, in one of his controversial works against Tyndale, brings her in as an example of one who i impervious to logic, though he does not fail to let us see that h enjoyed the way she countered scientific reasoning with an im- perturbable common sense. He had been trying to explain to he (according to the science then in vogue) that as the earth wa the center of all things, its precise center, if it could be reached was the point at which further progression down would mean a ascent. More explained this with a concrete illustration. Imagin a hole bored through the earth, and a millstone thrown down tha hole; when it got to the center it would stop, otherwise it woul be falling upwards. Dame Alice was impatient of such an argu ment and kept interrupting so often that he could hardly finish Then she had her say: "I will make you a like sample [example] My maid hath yonder a spinning wheel . . . . Come hither, thou girl; take out thy spindle, and bring me hither the whorl. Lo, sir ye make imaginations, I cannot tell you what. But here is a whorl and it is as round as the world is. And we shall not need to imagine a hole bored through, for it hath a hole bored through in deed. But yet, because ye go by imaginations, I will imagine wit you. Imagine me now that this whorl were ten miles thick on ever side, and this hole through it still, and so great that a millston were thrown in above at the other end, would it go no furthe than the midst, trow you? By God, if one threw in a stone n bigger than an egg, I ween if ye stood at the nether end of th hole five mile beneath the midst, it would give you a pat on th pate that it would make you claw your head, and yet should y feel none itch at all."

It will be seen from this, and many other passages in whic she appears, that her conversation was racy; and it is evident tha More relished it. As Roper did so too, it would seem tha "Mother" was regarded as a "character" by the whole househol for he catches the tone of her voice almost as well as More did No doubt she was a little difficult at times, and even something o a shrew. But More knew how to handle her. That he persuade a woman of her sturdy independence, not to say crabbedness, t learn music and perhaps study books, was a wonderful instance of his way of tactfully insinuating rather than commanding. Harpsfield describes her as "aged, blunt and rude," meaning middle-aged, and rough in manner rather than what we should understand by the word "rude." But he praised More's wisdom in choosing her for his second wife, saying that she was "spareful and given to profit," that is, an economical housekeeper. He also praised More's skill in managing her, writing, "He so framed and fashioned her by his dexterity that he lived a sweet and pleasant life with her"—and that, after all, is a great deal to have.

As a sample of her humor, Harpsfield relates how, once, after he had been to confession, she told her husband, "I have this lay left all my shrewdness [shrewishness], and will begin afresh." On this Harpsfield comments, "Which merry conceited talk, hough now and then it proved true in very deed, Sir Thomas More could well digest and like in her and in his children and thers." In that household there was a lot of banter. But in this Dame Alice could hold her own with anybody. She often "stole he show" even when the brilliant Sir Thomas was on the stage. When More wrote to Erasmus saying, "My wife desires a million f compliments, especially for your careful wish that she may live nany years. She says that she is the more anxious to do this as she vill live the longer to plague me," the joke was the clearest proof hat he was happy, and that so was she. But we must add that robably only a man of his gentle temper could have avoided eadlong clashes with the lady. He governed by love, and his rule as unquestioned, even by Dame Alice.

More's children were all fond of her, though they laughed at er eccentricities. That she took excellent care of them is shown the fact that none of them died—something very rare in that ge of high mortality among the young. And as Sir Thomas was ten away from home, it was she who had to see to it that the chilen kept at their studies, however little learning she may have had rself. At the end of his life, looking back upon his matrimonial fairs, he wrote in the long epitaph he composed for the tomb in

Chelsea church which he expected to occupy, and to which he had translated the bones of Jane, that he could not say which of his two wives he loved the most. He then quaintly added: "Oh, how well could we three have lived together in matrimony, if fortune and religion had suffered it. But I beseech our Lord that this tomb and Heaven may join us together." Though he wrote to Francis Cranefeld, one of Charles V's councillors, "I do not think it possible to live, even with the best of wives, without some discomfort," he knew very well that he had good reason to be gratefully attached to the somewhat tart-tongued Dame Alice.

Yet, that she may have been at bottom a very good-natured person is suggested by the drawing Holbein made in 1527 of the assembled family, the first stage of a painting which was completed but is now lost.[2] There Lady More is shown kneeling at a prie-dieu while the pet monkey is climbing up her dress. But Holbein may have decided that this was too improbable a situation in which to depict anyone, for he made the annotation, "this one sits." This, however, may have been merely to obtain a better balance for his composition. We are at any rate free to believe that Holbein had seen her at her prayers quite undisturbed by the queer dear little animal. When other animals, almost as queer, came into that household she seems to have raised no objection. Nor would her husband have felt free to gather his menagerie except with her approval.

More's relations with his children will be dealt with in the next chapter, and that apple of his eye, Margaret, appears in her

[2] Holbein had come to England in 1526 with a letter of introduction to More from Erasmus, and the tradition persists that More took him into his house at Chelsea, which is just what he would be likely to do. He wrote to Erasmus to tell him that the painter was a wonderful man, but added, "I fear that he won't find England as fruitful as he had hoped. Yet I will do my best to see that he does not find it absolutely barren." More was, as usual, much better than his word, and found him many commissions. It is hardly too much to say that More established his fortunes, though his greatest prosperity came on subsequent visits, some of them after More's death. He made drawings or paintings of many of the people mentioned in this book, including all of the Mores. Unfortunately one cannot be certain that his drawing which is supposed to be of Margaret Roper is really of her.

greatest beauty in the last year of his life. Here, a word or two should be said about old Sir John More. At the time Holbein depicted him (both in the family group and a separate drawing) he was over seventy and had been since 1518 a judge. He looks dryly humorous, but one might infer, even if one did not know of how he treated his son while Thomas was at Oxford, that he was a bit of a skinflint. In 1527 he was apparently without a wife and a home of his own, as he is shown sitting at his famous son's right hand. Yet he seems rather indifferent to the animated discussion of literature that is going on, and pays no attention to the passage Margaret Giggs is pointing out. All this is in perfect keeping with what we know to have been his views about mere literary affairs.

A couple of years after this picture was made, his son became Lord Chancellor. Then Sir Thomas did his father most signal honor, for he would, before going to his own court, go into that of the King's Bench, where Sir John was sitting, and there, kneeling down, ask his blessing. Perhaps this explains why a man who gave such filial devotion should have received it.

Beloved by his family, everybody seems to have been a friend of his, or is mentioned as such by Roper—even the man who conducted him to the Tower, and the Lieutenant there, and the official who brought him word that he was to be executed. Thomas Cromwell himself, though the contriver of More's doom, professed to wish him well, and probably did. He was of course only acting as the King's agent. As for the Duke of Norfolk, who sat with other friends of More on the panel of judges that condemned him to death, we often hear of him as being on most cordial terms with the man before them on July 1, 1535. What they did was done because of what they regarded as regrettable political necessity; none of them had any of the violent anger shown by the one who had been More's closest friend of all, King Henry VIII.

The popularity that More enjoyed was, in fact, something hardly without parallel. It is really astonishing when a man is held up by his contemporaries as the perfect illustration of all that is good—extending even to grammar. But that is what happened. Thus Robert Whittinton, writing a book on Latin prose composition in 1524, goes very much out of his way to say there: "More is a man of an angel's wit and singular learning. I know not his fellow. For where is a man of that gentleness, lowliness, and affability? And, as time requireth, a man of marvellous mirth and pastimes, and sometime of as sad gravity. A man for all seasons." Not content with this, Whittinton proceeds to use the passage to illustrate, first the straightforward statement of fact, then oratorically, again historically, and finally poetically with *Morus est vir prestans ingenii et eruditionis.* When writers of textbooks treat one of their contemporaries in this fashion it is a sign, not only that he is universally admired, but universally loved.

CHAPTER ELEVEN

Beaten with a Peacock's Feather

WHEREVER Sir Thomas More was, whether on one of his distasteful embassies, or in attendance upon the King in England, or engaged in official business, his thoughts were always with his children. Riding through the rain on horseback, over the rough and deeply mired roads of the time, he composed for them in 1520 a Latin epistle in verse. And of his letters that survive, the largest number, and the longest and most revealing, are those he wrote to them, either singly or to the whole group. Stapleton, who was able to use some of these letters in the writing of his book, says that they were falling in pieces from having been read so often.

But though More was immensely proud of the letters his children wrote to him, they have disappeared, and we can learn their contents only by what he says about them. Thus he writes to Margaret that he showed one of her letters to the Bishop of Exeter (John Vesey), and that he was so impressed that "he took out at once a gold coin which you will find in this letter. I tried in every possible way to decline it, but was unable to refuse to take it and send it to you as a pledge and token of his goodwill. This hindered me from showing him the letters of your sisters, lest it should seem that I showed them to obtain for the others too, a gift that it annoyed me to take for you." Similarly Erasmus tells Budé in 1521 how More made his children send him, as a family friend, specimens of their progress in study. "He bade them," he writes, "all write to me, each one without any help, neither the subject being suggested nor the language corrected, for when they offered their papers to their father for correction, he affected to be displeased with the bad writing, and made them copy out their letters more neatly and accurately. When they had done so, he closed the letters and sent them to me without changing a syllable.

Believe me, my dear Budé, I was never more surprised; there was nothing whatever either silly or girlish in what was said, and the style was such that you could feel they were making daily progress." Such a testimonial to the Latinity of More's daughters, coming from the celebrated Latinist, Erasmus, and made, not to More himself but another friend, carries very great weight. If there was nothing sent from More's son, John, this must have been because in 1521 he was still too young to have his work exhibited and not, as has sometimes been supposed, because John was a dullard.

As to this we have a number of proofs. Yet it is no doubt true that John was not so brilliant as the girls, especially Margaret, though she in turn seems to have been outshone as a scholar by More's adopted daughter, Margaret Giggs. It should be noted that John comes in for a special word of praise in an undated letter quoted by Stapleton. In it, writing to "his dearest children, and to Margaret Giggs, whom he numbers among his own," More says in one paragraph: "There was not one of your letters that did not please me extremely; but to confess frankly what I feel, the letter of my son John pleased me most, both because it was longer than the others, and because he seems to have given it more labour and study. For he not only puts out his matter prettily, and composes in fairly polished language, but he plays with me both pleasantly and cleverly, and turns my own jokes on myself wittily enough." As the girls had been, on that occasion, a little remiss—possibly because they had been engaged in some feminine activities in which John was not concerned—their father admonishes them to make no excuses, such as that they had to cut their letters short as the carrier was waiting, or that they had nothing to write about. "How can a subject be wanting when you write to me?" he asks, "since I am glad to hear of your studies or of your games, and you will please me most when there is nothing to write about, you write about that nothing at great length! This must be easy to you, especially for the girls, who, to be sure, are born chatter-boxes, and who have a world to say about nothing." This reproof, such as it is, may be taken as a good sample of what More admits he has sometimes done—beaten them with a peacock's feather. This was so pleasant to them that Margaret Giggs told Stapleton that when she was a child she deliberately used to commit some small offence now and then, merely for the sake of being playfully scolded.

More's kindness manifested itself not only in words but in the little presents he brought them every time he had been away from home. And his indulgence comes out in a letter to Margaret, in reply to one in which she had asked for money, "with too much shyness," he assures her, "from a father who is eager to give." He says he would gladly reward her with two gold coins for every syllable, but adds, "as it is, I send what you asked for; I would have sent more, but that, as I enjoy giving, so do I like to be asked and coaxed by my daughters, especially by you, whom virtue and learning have made dear to my heart. So the sooner you ask me for more, the more you will be sure of pleasing your father." He had praised his own father for having given him no money to spend at Oxford, or rather, said that his having been kept so short had been good for him. But his own practice was the reverse of old Sir John's.

He would not of course have approved of the foolish spending of money, though if there was any shop at Chelsea village where little cakes and comfits could be bought, the ascetic would no doubt have thought such spending pardonable. But what he mingled with his praises were frequent warnings against pride, and he told his children that "all we have, of God we have received; riches, royalty, lordship, beauty, strength, learning, wit, body, soul and all. And almost all these things He hath but lent us. For all these must we depart from, every whit again, except our souls alone. And yet that must we give God again also."

In one letter he tells Margaret: "I assure you that, rather than allow my children to be idle, I would make a sacrifice of wealth and bid adieu to other cares and business, to attend to my family, amongst whom none is more dear to me than yourself, my beloved daughter." It is very evident that, next to his religion, his love for his children was the governing passion of More's life.

Circumstances made him the head of a family of girls, for to his own three daughters must be added the one Dame Alice had borne to her first husband, and Anne Cresacre and Margaret Giggs. But boys were in the household from time to time—among them More's young brother-in-law, Thomas Colt, bequeathed to him by his father, with a sum of money for his support, as "my best Colt," and John Smith, a youth trained by More who served Erasmus for a while as servant and secretary. So John More was not left to languish entirely in a feminine society. But Sir Thomas More was primarily a father of women, and though the attention he gave to his children's education would have been notable under any circumstances, it derives special interest from the fact that he was chiefly concerned with the education of girls —something that few people bothered with in those days.

Here he was a good deal of an educational pioneer, and it should be pointed out that he never wished for his daughters a different sort of education than he himself had had or was giving to John. They studied not only the Greek and Latin classics but astronomy and mathematics and medicine and philosophy. Because of this his friend the Spanish scholar, Jean Luis Vives, who had come to England to draw up a plan of studies for Katherine of Aragon's daughter, the future Queen Mary, held up the More family as a model. "Their father," he wrote in his *Instruction of a Christian Woman,* "not content only to have them good and chaste, would also that they should be well learned, supposing that by that means they should be more truly and surely chaste." Regarding this More himself says: "Renown for learning, when it is not united with a good life, is nothing less than splendid and notorious infamy." It is a principle which completely separates him from those humanists who sought no more than the revival of pagan learning, and whose lives were often exemplifications of paganism at its most corrupt.

More set forth his views at considerable length when writing to

William Gunnell (or Gonnell), a young priest who was one of a line of carefully selected and able tutors, all of whom no doubt had the same guiding ideas impressed upon them—that the minds of the girls under his charge were to be developed in exactly the same way as the minds of those of the other sex, and that, in the cultivation of virtue, which was superior to book learning, pride was above all else to be shunned. More begs his "dearest Gunnell": "to warn my children to avoid the precipices of pride and to walk in the pleasant meadows of modesty; not to be dazzled by the sight of gold, nor to sigh for those things which they mistakenly admire in others; not to think more of themselves for the possession of gaudy trappings, nor less for the want of them; not to spoil by neglect the beauty that nature has given them, nor to heighten it by artifice. Let them put virtue in the first place, learning in the second, and esteem most in their studies whatever teaches them piety towards God, charity to all, and Christian humility in themselves. . . . I fancy that I hear you object that these precepts, though true, are beyond the capacity of my young children, since you will scarcely find a man, however old or advanced, who is not stirred sometimes with the desire of glory. But, dear Gunnell, the more I see the difficulty of getting rid of this pest of pride, the more do I see the necessity of getting to work at it from childhood. For I see no other reason why this evil clings to our hearts so closely, than almost as soon as we are born, it is sown in the tender minds of children by their nurses, it is cultivated by their teachers and brought to its full growth by their parents, no one teaching what is good, without at the same time awakening the expectation of praise as the proper reward of virtue.

"That this plague of vain glory be banished from my children, I do desire that you, dear Gunnell, and their mother and all their friends, would sing this song to them, and knock and repeat it in their heads, that vain glory is a despicable thing, and that there is nothing more sublime than the humble modesty so often praised by Christ." That letter, which was no doubt studied by the children as much as by their tutor—for Stapleton obtained it from the

More family for use in his *Life*—derived its force from the fact that it was evident, from More's own example, that these were no mere words but something lived by him each day. An even greater force was afterwards given by the martyr's death.

It is perfectly evident, however, that More was much too good a pedagogue to deny altogether the value of praise as encouragement; and he was much too kind a man to withold it. What he wished was that everything should be referred to God. And in laying down principles for the guidance of his children, he applied them to himself. Professor Chambers penetratingly remarks, "I fancy that More's children (especially Margaret Roper, and the foster-child Margaret Gigs) did more for the Saint's education than anyone else ever did, even Erasmus or Colet."

But it must be emphasized that More did not content himself merely with laying down general principles. He went into practical details about their secular studies. For instance, there is this typical passage about the means for acquiring a good Latin style. "Whether you write serious matters or the merest trifles," he admonished his children, "it is my wish that you write everything diligently and thoughtfully. It will be no harm if you first write the whole in English, for you will not have much trouble in turning it into Latin; not having to look for the matter, your mind will be intent only on the language. That, however, I leave to your choice, whereas I strictly enjoin you, that whatever you have composed, you carefully examine before writing it out clean, and in this examination first scrutinize the whole sentence, and then each part of it. Thus, if any solecisms have escaped you, you will easily detect them. Correct these, write out the whole letter again, and even then examine it once more, for sometimes in re-writing, faults slip in again that one has expunged. By this diligence your little trifles become serious matters, for while there is nothing so neat and witty that it may not be made insipid by silly and inconsiderate chatter, so there is nothing in itself so insipid, that you cannot season it with grace and wit if you will give a little thought to it."

The Greek and Latin classics (and among these More, as a humanist of the broadest type, included some knowledge of the Fathers) formed only one of the subjects of study. To round out his children's education he saw to it that it ranged through all knowledge from music to medicine. And on one occasion, the fame of the dialectical accomplishments of these brilliant youngsters having reached the court—one may suspect because the proud father had talked about them—they were invited to stage one of the debates in philosophy, common at the time, "afore the King's Grace." We hear of this only from a letter written by John Palsgrave, who was tutor to the King's bastard son, the Duke of Richmond, and he adds, "I wish it were my fortune to be present." Yet this event, though unique so far as the court was concerned, was frequent enough in the More household. Let us hope the girls were not too abashed by the presence of the overpowering Henry to do themselves justice. In any event More must have found what is the greatest satisfaction to a good man, that his children were moral and intellectual miniatures of himself.

We hear of other tutors besides Gunnell. Among these were John Clement and John Harris, both of them also serving in turn as secretary to More, and Richard Hyrde, who wrote an introduction to Margaret Roper's translation of a work by Erasmus on the Lord's Prayer and who himself translated Vives' book on the education of women. Hyrde died in 1528 when serving on the commission, headed by Foxe and Gardiner, sent by Henry VIII to Rome that year. He was with them in the capacity of physician, for, like Clement, he combined Greek with medicine and was doubtless engaged by Sir Thomas More to teach his children for that very reason. Clement himself, after lecturing at Oxford in 1519, to a larger audience, as More told Erasmus, than had ever frequented any other lecturer there, afterwards turned to the practice of medicine, becoming eventually President, like Linacre before him, of the Royal College of Physicians. To be attached to More's household seems to have been a passport to distinction.

Another tutor, however, we hear of simply as "Master Drew";

still another, though referred to by Stapleton simply as "One Nicholas" was the well-known Bavarian mathematician and astronomer, Nicholas Kratzer. He had been a Fellow of Corpus Christi College at Oxford before going to Chelsea, and his portrait by Holbein may still be seen in the Louvre. He seems to have had a ready wit, for when Henry VIII asked him how it was that he spoke English so badly after having lived in England for thirty years, he countered with, "Pardon, your Grace, but how *can* a man learn English in thirty years?"

He appears to have been with the Mores only for a short time, taking the place, during his absence, of Master Drew. For upon Drew's return More wrote to his "whole school"—he often said that that was the most endearing title he could give them—"I think you can have no longer any need of Master Nicholas [in another he is just plain "Nicholas," which might suggest that he was accorded a little less than the respect the tutors usually received] since you have learned all that you can know about astronomy. I hear that you are so advanced in that science that you cannot only point the polar-star, or the dog-star, or any of the constellations, but also—and this requires a skilful and profound astronomer—among all those heavenly bodies, you can distinguish the sun from the moon!" Then having got off his little jest, More goes on to point the moral: "Go forward then in that new and admirable science by which you ascend to the stars."

But if Master Nicholas left after the return of Master Drew, he seems to have come back, for in a letter, undated like the other,[1] More writes to Margaret: "You tell me that Nicholas, who is so fond of you and so learned in astronomy, has begun again with you in the system of the heavenly bodies. I am grateful to him, and I congratulate you on your good fortune." He goes on to advise her to devote the rest of her life to medical studies and sacred literature, though without neglecting "humane letters and liberal science.

[1] This is due not to More's carelessness about dates, but to the fact that the good Stapleton, who made the only copies of these letters, apparently thought dates of letters unimportant.

The conclusion of this letter contains what is perhaps its most interesting passage: "It would be a delight, my dear Margaret, to me to converse long with you on these matters: but I have just been interrupted and called away by the servants, who have brought in supper. I must have regard to others, else to sup is not so sweet as to talk with you. Farewell, my dearest child, and salute for me my most gentle son, your husband. I am extremely glad that he is following the same course of study as yourself. I am ever wont to persuade you to yield in everything to your husband: now, on the contrary, I give you full leave to strive to get before him in the knowledge of the celestial system." From this it is clear that Margaret did not cease studying after her marriage, and that William Roper joined her in this. It was all the more commendable as he was a man of considerable means and one who came to be a Member of Parliament and a Protonotary of the Court of the King's Bench. Therefore his studies show his entirely disinterested desire of learning for its own sweet sake. And though we do not hear of the other sons-in-law, Giles Heron and William Daunce (or Dauncey), regularly following the courses of instruction, it would be fairly safe to infer that, in such a household, where virtue and scholarship went hand in hand, both united with wit and at their loveliest, they did not altogether neglect their opportunities.

It might be a little exaggerated to describe the house at Chelsea as a kind of domestic university—though most of the tutors were men who had been or were to be university dons—but it is mere fact that the courses of study attracted outsiders, even if only friends of the family were admitted. Among these was the young wife of Sir Thomas Elyot, the author of *The Book Called the Governor,* at this time Clerk of the Privy Council and in 1531 Henry VIII's ambassador to Charles V. And the variety of the subjects studied, and the distance they were pursued certainly far exceeded anything that could be called merely a school.

It is worth noting that More made excellent marriages for his children, and also for Dame Alice's daughter, though we can be sure that he did not allow material considerations more than the attention any prudent man should give them. Daunce was the son and heir of Sir John Daunce, an adviser in financial affairs to the Crown, and Heron was the son (also the heir) of Sir John Heron who had been Treasurer of the King's Chamber. John More was married to Anne Cresacre, a young heiress who was brought up in the family as More's ward. And Dame Alice's daughter was married first (in 1515) to a Thomas Elrington, who may have been a son of the Thomas Elrington who was employed by the Treasury, and secondly to Sir Giles Alington. Though none of these was what can be described as very rich, they were all fairly well-to-do. More was an unworldly man, but not so unworldly as to be unpractical. He evidently thought a sufficiency of means to be desirable. Moreover, he did not observe the Utopian rule under which no woman was permitted to marry before she was eighteen, or any man before he was twenty-two. When a good chance occurred for his children he took it. But we can at least be sure that he never consented to any marriage until he was sure of the character of those with whom his children were to ally themselves.

What is also worth noting is that all of More's children continued to reside with him after marriage, and that their children were born in his house, until there were no less than eleven grandchildren in that "small patriarchal monastic Utopia." It is evident, from what came out later, that they were not allowed to make any contribution to the expenses of the household. It is also clear that they stayed with Sir Thomas, not because economy was their motive, but because they could not bear to leave him.

Where in all the world could they find a pleasanter place to be than the comfortable house at Chelsea, with interesting people always coming and going, and where a sunny sweetness filled every day? Whenever the weather was fine the studies were in the garden, just as the discussions recorded in the *Utopia* took place on a moss-covered seat. With the silver Thames running softly at the end of the lawn, they read their books and had their discussions under the trees. The air was full of the sweet scent of the rosemary More had planted, "not only because his bees loved it, but because 'tis the herb sacred to Remembrance and therefore to Friendship." If, as has been surmised, the rosemary that still flowers in many a Chelsea garden springs from the rosemary More had brought to the garden of the house pulled down by Sir Hans Sloane in the eighteenth century, other still more beautiful blooms are fragrant with his memory. His children grew to be his friends and his disciples. In early life he had chosen older men to be his friends; now that he was growing into middle age, it was the young who clustered round him, finding in the mellowing More one perennially young of heart.

CHAPTER TWELVE

The Sword of Controversy

THOMAS MORE in the dedicatory letter of the *Utopia* explains to Peter Gilles the difficulties a busy man like himself encountered when he tried to write. "Whiles I do daily bestow my time," he says, "about law matters: some to plead, some to hear, some as an arbitrator with mine award to determine, some as an umpire or a judge, with my sentence finally to discuss. Whiles I go one way to see and visit my friend: another way about mine own private affairs. Whiles I spend almost all the day amongst others, and the residue at home among mine own: I leave to myself, I mean to my book no time. For when I am come home, I commune with my wife, chat with my children, and talk with my servants. All the which things I reckon and account among business, foreasmuch as they must of necessity be done . . . unless a man will be a stranger in his own house. . . . Among these things now rehearsed, stealeth away the day, the month, the year." The only time, he tells Peter, that he gets for literary work is the time he snatches from sleep and meat.

If this is true of the period when he was composing the *Utopia,* it was still truer when he came to occupy various public offices, each more exacting than the last. Yet the great volume of his writing was produced at that very time—another proof that the best man to turn to for a new task is the man who already has more than he can do. More managed it by rising at two in the morning, and giving the next five hours to study and writing and prayer. It is hardly surprising that the work of these years shows the effect of pressure and haste.

At the outset certain dates must be borne in mind. His unfinished *Four Last Things*—the last of his work to show anything like the compression of *Richard III*—was written in 1522. As he published during the following year his defence in Latin of Henry VIII against Luther, it may be inferred that he laid his own work aside in order to help the King. But, as from then until 1528 he produced nothing at all, it can only be because he found it impossible to do so. Similarly that he produced between 1528 and the time of his arrest in 1534 so vast a body of controversial writing, would indicate that this was because the need for it enabled him to perform the impossible. The difficulties to be overcome were, however, so great that his style suffered.

Nevertheless this controversial work of More has many great merits. One may find in it, perhaps better than anywhere else, a presentation of the issues involved, as they appeared to the men of his time. As such it has very considerable historical interest. But also scattered through these books there are exceedingly brilliant and entertaining pages, as well as autobiographical passages of the utmost interest. On the other hand, the arguments, though fresh when first presented, sometimes strike the modern reader as being a thrashing of the commonplace. And worse still, much of the writing is, as Tyndale and the other Protestant controversialists often complained, extremely prolix.

More, in his *Apology* of 1533, tried to answer this last objection by saying that it took much longer to refute heresy than to propound it. But this, though perfectly true, does not justify a disproportion so enormous that Dr. Arthur Irving Taft, the editor of that book for the Early English Text Society, estimates it as commonly in a ratio of twenty to one and sometimes of forty to one. Christopher Hollis comments on More's defence of his prolixity that "such a plea provokes the inevitable answer that it shows indeed why brevity is difficult but it does not show why it is not desirable."

Nevertheless, Mr. Hollis may be a little unfair in saying that More did not so much as understand that he could have been more effective had he seen that brevity is the soul of wit, for More is frequently very witty. His wordiness, though it may in part have been due to writing hastily at odd moments, was in the main due to a motive of charity much to his credit. Deliberately he sacrificed art to his purpose of saving souls.

Both art and charity might, no doubt, have been combined, but we can see what causes More's prolixity. It is because he is controverting books which were in many instances not before his readers, or even readily obtainable, that he felt obliged to quote from his opponents at great length, and then to answer them piecemeal; and he is so afraid that something might be overlooked that the smallest point is never allowed to pass. Unlike his King Utopus, who felt he could afford to be tolerant of all religious opinions, because truth would shine out by its own native force, he thought of "Tom Truth" coming into court unprepared, because he was so sure of the justice of his cause, and of then losing his case. As Dr. Taft says, "Though he were to argue against an heretical centipede, Sir Thomas would be determined to leave him not a leg to stand on."

This can be very tedious, yet it certifies More's zeal, and also his fairness. The editor of Tyndale's Works, Henry Walker, has confessed that he was often able to correct a corrupt text from More's citation of it. And More was rightly able to claim that frequently his comments give his opponent's arguments a clarity and force they had lacked before. It is no man of straw that he ever tries to knock down.

But before coming to these later works, his first essay in controversy must be glanced at. In 1517 Martin Luther had nailed on the church door at Wittenberg his famous list of theses. Of this far too much has been made, for these were only propositions for debate, such as were offered commonly enough, and asserted no positive heresy, whatever they might imply. But Luther was carried along much further than he had intended to go, and in the summer of 1521 was declared a heretic by the Pope. In the interval he had produced his *Babylonish Captivity of the Church.*

This was answered at once by no less a person than Henry VIII with his *Assertio Septem Sacramentorum adversum Martinum Lutherum,* a work which made Luther very angry but which deservedly won for Henry the title of Defender of the Faith, conferred by Leo X. Henry, though he has been accused of having written it to obtain a special title from the Pope, may be credited with sincerity. He is reported to have said "Would to God my ability were equal to my good-will, but I cannot but think myself obliged to defend my mother, the spouse of Christ." It has sometimes been questioned just how far this book was Henry's unaided performance. To which it is perhaps sufficient to say that Henry had received a theological training unusual in a monarch, as until the death of his elder brother, Arthur, he had been thought of as taking orders and becoming Archbishop of Canterbury. Though it is probable enough that he consulted Fisher, the Bishop of Rochester, an obviously sensible thing for a amateur theologian to do, as he certainly consulted More, the book is the King's and is an able performance.

More's part in it was later to be brought up against him by Henry. It was then that More explained: "after it was finished, I was only a sorter out and placer of the principal matters contained therein"—which I take to mean that he had tried to impart order to what may have been a rather confused manuscript. And Roper quotes him further as replying to the charge that he had craftily egged on the King to a defence of the papacy which Henry later came to regret, by saying: "When I found the Pope's authority highly advanced and with such strong arguments mightily defended, I said unto his Grace: 'I must put your Highness in remembrance of one thing, and that is this. The Pope, as your Grace knoweth, is a prince as you are, and in league with other Christian princes. It may hereafter so fall out that your Grace and he may vary upon some points of the league, whereupon may grow breach of amity and war between you both. I think it best, therefore, that the place be amended and his authority more slenderly touched.' 'Nay,' quoth his Grace, 'that shall it not be, we are so much bounden to the see of Rome that we cannot do too much honour to it.' " Which means that More had warned the King that it would be advisable not to assert too much spiritual authority for the Pope, lest at some later date he come into conflict with him as a secular sovereign. More himself was to admit that at this time his own concept of the papacy was that its spiritual jurisdiction, though historically necessary, was not derived directly from God. In this matter the orthodox King went beyond him. To use an anachronistic term for the sake of its convenience, in 1522 Henry VIII was a thorough-going papist, a Catholic of the most ultramontane type. He rejected More's advice and published his book as it stood.

When Luther replied to Henry with a book full of of scurillous and scabrous abuse, as it was beneath the dignity of the King to reply to such an attack, More kindly undertook to do so. But because he was rather ashamed of the bitter tone of his own rejoinder, he published it under the name of William Ross.

Nobody suspected that the gentle Thomas More was the same person as the violent "Guilielmus Rossius," especially as it turned out that there *was* a William Ross, who was just then on a visit to Italy and who providentially died there, just before the book was published. As he was unable to deny his authorship, More's secret was kept for a long while, and he took some pains to throw people off the scent by every now and then referring in his later English works to what Ross had written. Yet even under that pseudonym, he apologized in his *Vindicatio* for some of the expressions he had been obliged to use, writing: "I doubt not, gentle reader, that your fairness will pardon me if in this book you often read what causes you shame. Nothing could have been more painful to me than to be forced to speak foul words to pure ears. But there was no help for it, unless I left Luther's book utterly untouched, which is a thing I most earnestly desired." He added that for those who have disdained to read Luther, "there is no need for them, nor do I wish them, to waste their time over my book." Yet even with this disclaimer, one must sympathize with Dr. J. S. Brewer's sad dictum: "I should be glad to believe that More was not the author of this work. That a nature so pure and gentle, so adverse to coarse abuse, and hitherto not unfavourable to the cause of religious reform, should soil its better self with vulgar and offensive raillery, shocks and pains, like the misconduct of a dear friend."[1] That criticism, though upon the whole just, should be balanced with Algernon Cecil's reflection on More's book, "If the author was too careless of taste, the critic should not on that account be oblivious of circumstance."

Whatever may be thought of "William Ross," it must be said that in his controversial works directed against the English reformers, More, though seemingly a bit hard upon them, is actually very moderate when we consider the polemical style of the time. The shoe is really on the other foot, for Tyndale accused him as being a man "who knew the truth and for covetousness forsook it again," a base accusation that More was easily able to refute. To Tyndale's personal charge that he had accepted a huge subsidy from the clergy for being their champion, he replied with quiet explicitness and unruffled temper. But what *is* true is that he was horrified by heresy—especially the attack on the Mass—and was shocked that so many of the leading heretics had not only broken their vows of celibacy but had specialized in marrying nuns.

A horror of heresy may be something completely beyond many modern minds, but surely even a modern mind should have enough imagination to understand More's horror. Nor would there seem to be any logical escape from the proposition that, if the Church is what it claims to be, the repository of truth, doctrines opposed to her teaching are detestable. To More heresy appeared worse than treason, which does not usually seek to wreck the order of society, whereas heresy was, in More's view, essentially seditious in seeking to destroy the framework of Christendom. Again one must allow for what was in More's mind. To him the heretics were more subversive than even the communists are today, and they were advocating their destructive ideas with

[1] *The Reign of Henry VIII,* Vol. I, p. 609. I cannot refrain from remarking that More never ceased to be favorable to religious reform, though of course he never had any sympathy with "reform" of the Lutheran sort.

virulence. If one grants his premise, one must pardon him for speaking of their "devilish books."

Even so, the personalities in which he indulged rarely went beyond his reference to the Protestants as the "new brethren," which is surely mild enough, or his derisive use of the word "Friar" when speaking of those among the reformers who had been such. When they objected to this in the case of the former Augustinian Robert Barnes, More retorted: "I shall be content like as instead of doctor men call him heretic, so instead of friar to call him tother name, that every man calleth those that be run out of religion [out of a religious order]. Lo there I have fallen on a fair figure unaware, that I trow is called periphrasis, to avoid the foul name of apostate." Here of course he uses the word in the purely technical sense, applicable to a man who has deserted a religious order in which he has made profession.

He answers the charge that he handles the heretics "ungoodly and with uncomely words" by remarking that "it were very hard for me to handle it in such wise, as when I plainly prove them abominable heretics and against God and His sacraments and saints very blasphemous fools, they should ween that I speak them fair." For his own part he asks them, if they must be heretics, "let them yet at the leastwise be reasonable heretics, and honest, and write reason, and leave railing, and then let the brethren find the fault with me, if I use them not after that in words as fair and as mild as the matter may suffer and bear." All the same, More has little hope of this and adds, "In railing standeth all their revel."

A characteristic passage is the following: "Father Alphonse[2] the Spanish friar told me that the devils be no such deformed evil favoured creatures as men imagine them, but they be in mind proud, envious, and cruel. And he bode me that if I would see a right image of a fiend, I should no more but even look upon a very fair woman that hath a very shrewd, fell, cursed mind. And when I showed him that I never saw any such, and

[2] This probably was the confessor of Katherine of Aragon.

wist not where I might any such find, he said he could find four or five, but I cannot believe him. Nor verily no more can I believe that the fiends be like shrewd women, if there were any such. Nor as the world is, it were not good that young men should ween so. For they be so full of courage, that were the fiends never so cursed, if they thought them like fair women, they would not fear to adventure upon them . . . Nor to say the truth no more can I believe it neither, that the damned spirits have all their natural gifts as whole and as perfect as they had them before the fall." Then More makes his thrust at his antagonists. "But surely if they have, then (as I said before) God hath on Tyndale, Barnes, and Frith, and those other heretics, more showed his vengeance in some part, than he did upon the devil." Nevertheless, on the preceding page, when replying to their accusations that he had handled them roughly, he indicates that he had never said that "as for wit and learning they have none," but only denied these qualities to them as heretics. As such he cannot but regard them as other than pestiferous fools.

An objection he mentions as having been brought against his works is that he introduces into the most serious matters "fantasies and sports and merry tales." This he does not deny but merely remarks that, in the case of one writing as a layman, "it may haply better become him merrily to tell his tale, than seriously and solemnly to preach." But few people will now object to this; in fact many will regard More's homely humor as a redeeming feature in a too long-drawn-out argumentation. It was as much for this quality, as for his eloquence and learning, that Bishop Tunstall had asked him to take up the sword of controversy.

A favorite gibe of the brethren was that More was a "poet," from which it would seem that even in those days to give a dog that bad name was to hang him. But when Tyndale wrote in his *Answer,* "His eleventh chapter is as true as his story of Utopia, and all his other poetry," More made the rejoinder in his *Confutation*: "If poetry be as Tyndale calleth it, nothing but feigning and lying, then he is cunning enough, and can, I assure you, make as much poetry upon any part of scripture as any poet in England upon any part of Virgil."

Despite these amenities, the long duel between More and Tyndale must be considered what the *Dictionary of National Biography* calls it, the classic controversy of the Reformation, at all events between Englishmen. Some people have deplored with Miss Routh the throwing away of a great opportunity when Tyndale was refused Tunstall's backing for a translation into English of the Scriptures. Yet this was not due to any obscurantism. Tunstall firmly believed, as did most of the English bishops, that a vernacular Bible was in itself very desirable. The only doubt in their minds was as to Tyndale's fitness for so important a task.

In this, of course, they may have been mistaken, and though by the event of Tyndale's eventual openly professed heresy they seem to be fully justified, it is possible that had Tunstall given the help that was asked, Tyndale would have not fallen under Lutheran influences nor, under those influences, produced a New Testament that was decidely Lutheran in tone. But such speculations are idle; and it may well be thought that if a man's Catholicism is so shaky that he has to be held in the Church by showing him personal favors, he is hardly a man to be trusted. More, upon the publication of Tyndale's version in 1526, denounced it, accusing Tyndale of deliberately mistranslating a number of passages. To turn, as Tyndale consistently did, the word "Church" into "congregation" was, More asserted, a malicious attempt to deny that there was such a thing as a visible Church. "Congregation," as he pointed out, could as well apply to a gathering of Mohammedans or Jews as to Christians. So also with regard to "priests," always rendered as "seniors," and the reduction of "charity," with its supernatural meaning, to the natural "love,"[3] and "grace" to "favor" and "penance" to "re-

[3] This was to make *charity* less in order to make *faith* more, in the Protestant sense, and by this means assert the reformed doctrine regarding justification.

pentance." Tyndale attempted to deny any malice in this, but the heretical implications were too clear to be missed. There can be no doubt that Tyndale was using his translation to insinuate Protestantism.

It must be said that the King James version, when it came in the next century, did not as a rule use these renderings of Tyndale's however much may have been drawn from him in other ways. Though More may have been a little harsh in describing Tyndale's version as poisoned bread, so infected that it was impossible to scrape it clean again—for the frequent translations More makes of passages from the Scriptures do not greatly differ from Tyndale's, and a little editing might have rendered Tyndale innocuous—it was undoubtedly necessary to warn people emphatically, in the absence of any other satisfactory English New Testament, against what was really a party tract.

As such it was condemned by the bishops and publicly burned at Paul's Cross. At the same time Tunstall, according to Foxe the Martyrologist, tried to buy up all the copies being printed at Antwerp, using for this purpose (so Foxe gleefully records) a man named Augustine Packington, who was secretly in league with Tyndale. Foxe continues that when George Constantine was arrested for heresy he told More, "It is the Bishop of London that hath holpen us," for the high price paid for all copies of the first edition was used to print a second, meanwhile keeping Tunstall in funds. The story goes on that More, upon hearing this, answered, "Now by the truth, I think even the same; for so much I told the Bishop, before he went about it."

The English hierarchy probably was, as we can now see, ill advised in some of their methods of dealing with heresy. But at least they must be commended for good judgement in asking More to deal with the heretical books being smuggled into the country. For More's official position, his European reputation as a scholar, his universally recognized integrity, and his immense popularity among Londoners—the group most exposed to the heretical inroads—made him by far the best man for the purpose.

If some of his arguments have little application today, this is because the issue under debate no longer exists. For example, if he dealt at considerable length with the characteristic Lutheran assertion of justification by faith alone, he was only doing what a good controversalist should do, face the central problem. Tyndale had described good works as "popeholiness," for at that time, as Brewer points out, "Luther's most earnest remonstrances were directed not against bad but against good works, and the stress laid on them by the advocates of the old religion." Brewer adds: "If that religion had been in its practice so generally corrupt as it is represented to have been by modern writers, such denunciations were idle." But today, while the Catholic stress is precisely where it always has been—on faith *and* good works—one of the things one now hears most commonly in Protestant churches is that what men believe is of little importance, so long as they live good lives.

The first of More's controversial works in English appeared in 1528 and is his *Dialogue Concerning Heresies*. More did not pretend to be a theologian, and though Stapleton (who was one) testifies to his learning in this department, Hutton says that the *Dialogue* "owes all to its skill, nothing to its learning." What More had was enough, and more than enough, theological learning for his purpose, even if his frequent citation of the Fathers, or his being able once, in conversation with John Harris, to point out the exact reference to a passage in St. Thomas Aquinas, may not prove much more than that he was widely read and had a wonderful memory. Notable too is his knowledge of the Bible, which he draws upon freely and familiarly and most effectively. Nor can it be forgotten that while still a very young man he tackled that very difficult book, St. Augustine's *City of God,* in public lectures. Tunstall was well advised to entrust the defence of the Catholic Faith to More.

If there is a good deal in these controversial works of More's that is a bit tedious, and a good deal that has little bearing upon the problems of our own age, there is also in them much that is lively and amusing. Even at his driest, More is an examplar—

perhaps the first in English on the same scale—of a racy and colloquial style. His humor in fact seems on occasion to run away with him, and is sometimes broader than would be countenanced by modern taste, at all events in religious books. Thus when the "Messenger," who presents the Protestant side of the case in the *Dialogue,* interrupts More's remarks that the brethren teach that there is no need for a priest to hear confessions, but that anyone—man or woman—would serve as well, and says that, with a woman for a confessor, he would be willing to go to confession every week, More answers that the Messenger would doubtless tell a different tale to *her* than he would to a "foul friar"; also that tales are told to friars that few men would be willing to confess to a fair woman.

In the same way, More aims his shaft at the Lutheran stress on predestination by telling the story of a German robber who, when haled before a judge, pleaded that he had been predestined to steal, only to be answered by the judge that he also had been predestined—predestined to hang the criminal before him.

When the question of miracles was raised, the Messenger of course challenging the authenticity of those related of the saints, More gravely told him of a miracle he personally knew about. It occurred, he said, to authenticate it fully, in the parish of St. Stephen's, Walbrook. It seems that a young man and a young woman of that parish—both of them still alive and so able to corroborate this—married. That night the bride was escorted to her bed by the attendant women, after which the bridegroom was admitted. But that same night, or perhaps a little later, "except it happened a little afore . . . the seed of them twain turned in the woman's body into blood and after into shape of man child." Within the year she was delivered of a boy, "and forsooth it was not then passing the length of a foot." Yet now that child was an inch taller than himself! When the Messenger inquired how long ago this extraordinary thing had happened, More replied, "By my faith, about twenty-one years[4]."

[4] That comes from Chapter X of Book One of the *Dialogue Concerning Heresies.* Much too broad to quote is the tenth chapter of the next book.

Yet More does not content himself with his joke. He relates—now seriously—another incident for which he can vouch, as to how the twelve-year-old daughter of Sir Roger Wentworth was cured of what appeared to be demoniac possession after a pilgrimage to the shrine of Our Lady of Ipswich. She was then living as a nun in a convent of Poor Clares, and her case had been witnessed by many people of a kind in whom there could be "no pretext of begging, no suspicion of feigning, no possibility of counterfeiting, no simpleness in the seers."

In the year following the publication of the *Dialogue,* More published in reply to Simon Fish's *Supplication of Beggars* his own *Supplication of Souls.* Fish's trenchantly written little book, which was circulated with the secret connivance of the King, purported to be a petition from the paupers of England for the confiscation by the Crown of the endowments of the monasteries and hospitals, in order that the accruing wealth might be used for the public good. In order to justify the argument, Fish denied, on the one hand, the existence of purgatory, and, on the other, asserted that the wealth of the Church (in manorial holdings) was half of that of the entire country. As Henry was already meditating a confiscation of this sort, the book served his purposes very well. He did in fact, very soon after this, suppress the four great hospitals of London, though by later partially restoring the endowments of St. Bartholomew's, he officially became its founder!

More had little difficulty in showing that Fish's estimates as to the wealth of ecclesiastical holdings was enormously exaggerated, for though it was very large, it was only about half of what Fish said. He met the *Supplication of Beggars* with what purported to be a petition from the dead. This was based on the fact that the monasteries had been largely endowed to pray for the faithful departed, who, with the cessation of the monastic requiem Masses, would languish all the longer in purgatory. The souls are made to say in one place: "Much have many of us bestowed upon rich men in gold rings and black gowns, much in many tapers and torches, much in worldly pomp and high solemn ceremonies about our funerals, whereof the brittle glory standeth us here, God wot, in very little stead, but on the other side done us great displeasure." Therefore they mourn, not that they had given so much to the Church, but so little. They now see the bags of gold they had left behind like a bag of cherry stones laid up by a child and found by him as an old man—a treasure quite valueless!

As usual, More introduces humor into his argument. The departed souls hear their widows, now married again, saying to their second husbands, "God have mercy on my first husband's soul, for he was a wise and honest man, far unlike you." Upon which they comment, "Then marvel we much when we hear them say so well by us, for they were ever wont to tell us far otherwise." But he was greatly shocked by a proposal which would have deprived the souls in purgatory of the Masses for which they had supposed themselves to be providing by endowments left to monasteries. In the *Utopia,* even when writing about a pagan people and their regard for the dead, he had shown that he deeply felt, as Professor Chambers puts it, that "the noble living and the noble dead are branches of one society." At the same time, he who had so nearly became a monk in his youth, saw how beneficent an institution monasticism was, not only because of its "social" usefulness, but because the monks and the nuns and friars served the living by their lives of prayer and holiness, being the salt that preserves the earth. More also knew in his bones that, should there be any expropriation it would not be the poor that would benefit, nor even the Crown as the guardian of the common good, but those greedy new rich who were already casting their eyes in the direction of the wealth of the Church.

But though it was perhaps impossible for More to concede anything to Fish's argument, it must be admitted to be true that many monasteries had grown too rich, and that, even had the ecclesiastical endowments been somewhat pared down, the spiritual obligations of prayers for the living and the dead could have been retained. But More knew very well what was in the air and that Fish's thesis, however plausible it might seem, was thoroughly disingenuous. And it is no more than historical fact that the wholesale loot that so soon afterwards occurred came to be deplored as a social disaster even by many who least approved of "monkery."

More's arguments, here and elsewhere, laid him open to the charge that he was "partial" to the clergy, to which it was perhaps hardly a sufficient answer for him to point out that, as a twice-married man, he was forever made incapable of holy orders. But what he did reasonably maintain was that Fish's accusations, like those made by Tyndale and other Protestant controversialists, were too sweeping to be believed. It was, he said, as unjust to charge the whole clerical body with corruption because of the shortcomings of a few of its members, as it would be to assert the whole laity was rotten because some laymen were bad men. It is worth noting, however, that these early controversialists did not accuse the clergy so much of immorality as of sloth and covetousness and arrogance. Yet More did not deny that some immorality existed, especially in out-of-the-way districts in Wales, and in his *Dialogue* of 1528 had written: "Verily, were all the bishops of my mind, as I know some that be, ye should not of priests have the plenty that ye have." He went on to say: "The time was when few men durst presume to take upon them the high office of priest. . . . Now runneth every rascal and offereth himself for able." The remedy he offered was the Utopian one—fewer and better priests. This champion of the Church did not maintain that all was well with the clergy. He distinguished between reform and revolt, and with all his soul he hated heresy.

Late in his life he replied to a small anonymous book entitled *The Division Between the Spirituality and the Temporality,* now known to have been written by a lawyer named St. German, but whose identity More never discovered. Sometimes he even supposed that the man might be some disgruntled monk, for this time the attack was on the secular clergy rather than the religious orders; and throughout his book St. German claimed to be an orthodox Catholic.

This, however, only made the attack worse, and as the charges were insinuated rather than openly made, and avoided all naming of names and specific instances, using instead the *on dit* of "they say" or "some say," More dubbed the anonymous writer "Sir John Some Say." "Beside all the faults," More wrote, "that he bringeth in under 'some say' and 'they say,' [were] some that himself saith without any 'some say' be such as some say that he can neither prove and some, they say, be plain and open false." Despite the professed irenic intentions of the author, More accused him of seeking "to bring the spirituality in the more hatred, and to make the spirituality the more odious among the people," which was certainly the effect of what Sir John Some Say wrote. Of course, More freely admitted once more, the clergy had many faults, but he added, "I think every man's duty towards God so great, that very few folk serve Him as they should." If More rebutted this kind of anti-clericalism it was not because he was "partial" towards the priesthood, but because he saw that almost any attack made at that time on the clergy, glanced off individuals to fall upon the Church itself. No man was ever less priest-ridden than himself, no man was ever firmer in his Catholic faith.

These controversial works by More continued up to the time of his arrest, and culminated in the *Apology* of 1533, which is their summation, and perhaps the most interesting of them all because of the personal material it contains. That book will be touched upon later. It is sufficient to say at this place that during the years 1528 to 1533, the period when tension was increasing between the English King and the papacy, More was most careful to avoid raising the question of the Pope's authority. This was because More was well aware that he could serve the Catholic cause with his pen only so long as what he wrote was directed against those heresies of which Henry disapproved. He would have defeated his purpose by discussing the basis of spiritual authority, though he must have handicapped himself by ruling that issue out.

His services were so greatly valued by the English hierarchy that, at the instance of his friends, Tunstall and Vesey and John Clerk, the Bishop of Bath, the huge sum of four or five thousand pounds was collected and pressed upon him. At the time this was done, he had fallen out of the King's favor and was in straitened circumstances; yet he refused to accept anything, nor would he even allow the bishops to settle upon his wife and children the money they had collected. Roper mentions the amount that was offered, which More does not. But More in his *Apology* was to write: "I take God and them also to record, that all they could never fee me with one penny thereof, but (as I plainly told them) I would rather have cast their money into the Thames than take it. . . . I look for my thank of God . . . for whose sake I take the labour and not for theirs." Then he scornfully tosses over his shoulder, "I am both over proud and over slothful also, to be hired for money to take half the labour and busyness in writing, that I have taken in this gear since I began." Yet it was this man that Tyndale accused of having known the truth and forsaking it for covetousness!

He had long foreseen the troubles that lay ahead. Even before the "King's Great Matter" had reached its climax, when Roper was saying with sanguine satisfaction one day that the country "had so Catholic a prince that no heretic durst show his face," More agreed but added gloomily: "Yet, son Roper, I pray God that some of us, as high as we sit upon the mountains treading heretics under our feet like ants, live not [till] the day that we would gladly wish to be at league and composition with them and to let them have their churches quietly to themselves, so that they would be contented to let us have ours quietly to ourselves." At this Roper was shocked and said, "By my troth, Sir, it is very desperately spoken." To which More "merrily" replied in an effort to cheer him up, "Well, well, son Roper, it shall not be so, it shall not be so."

Events shortly after this began to bear out More's worst fears. And Roper records another conversation with his father-in-law. More said then: "Now would to God, son Roper, upon condition that three things were well established in Christendom, I were put in a sack and presently cast into the Thames." Roper asked him what those three things were and got the answer: "In faith, son, they be these. The first is that, whereas the most part of Christian princes be at mortal wars, they were all at universal peace. The second that, whereas the Church of Christ is at this present sore afflicted with many errors and heresies, it were settled in perfect conformity with religion. The third that, whereas the matter of the King's marriage is now come in question, it were to the glory of God and quietness of all parties brought to a good conclusion." It was the answer not only of a good Catholic but a good European, one who saw the necessity of preserving the unity of Christian society. Roper added, "As I could gather, he judged that otherwise it would be a disturbance to a great part of Christendom." If the words were said, as one would infer, in 1527, Francis I and the Emperor were at war again. It was also the year of the Sack of Rome, which left the Pope with a restricted freedom of action. And it was the year of the formal introduction of Henry's demand for the annulment of his marriage to Katherine of Aragon.

CHAPTER THIRTEEN

King Henry's Great Matter

IT SHOULD not be necessary to explain that what Henry VIII meant by the word "divorce" was merely a declaration of nullity, such as is still made frequently by Catholic diocesan matrimonial courts and, upon appeal, passed upon by the Rota in Rome. Yet when the learned Miss Routh speaks in a footnote on page 165 of her book of a "dissolution" it would seem that the real issue had better be stated again. A dissolution of marriage is something that the Pope is incapable of giving, and it would never have occurred to Henry to ask for it. What he did ask from Clement VII, and confidently expected to obtain, was a declaration that his marriage to Katherine of Aragon had never existed. What he actually obtained in the end (from Archbishop Cranmer) was, from the Catholic point of view, a divorce and, as such, inadmissible. But this Henry and Cranmer (not to mention the lady) considered an annulment. Its historical importance is that it resulted in a breach with the papacy and eventually the establishment in England of the Protestant religion, this last something Henry never foresaw and never wished.

Not even Froude can defend Henry in his matrimonial affairs, though Froude (and others), while deploring these, rejoice in the victory of Protestantism, whatever its sordid source. And some historians—for instance, even one of such a high standing as Professor A. F. Pollard—have made attempts to soften the shock by suggesting that the idea of the annulment had been floating in Henry's head since 1514, and so of course had nothing to do with Anne Boleyn. Pollard even gives references to six documents in the second volume of the *Venetian Calendar*—Nos. 479, 482, 483, 487, 492 and 500—in support of this, though usually only the first of these is ever mentioned. It is a letter from a Venetian banker named Vetor Lippomano, living in Rome, and runs: "It is also said that the King of England intends to repudiate his present wife, the daughter of the King of Spain and his brother's widow, because he is unable to have children by her, and intends to marry a daughter of the French Duke of Bourbon. He means to annul his own marriage, and will obtain what he wants from the Pope, as France did with Pope Julius." The other documents have nothing to do with the case. But even the letter just quoted is no more than an *on dit*, a mere piece of gossip, and is valueless as evidence. Nobody in England at this time or for a long while afterwards appears to have heard that in 1514 Henry was dissatisfied with Katherine, nor is there any record of a project then or at any time for a marriage between Henry and a daughter of the Duke of Bourbon. As for Katherine's inability to have children, several sons *were* born to the royal couple, though they were either still-born or died soon after birth. And when Mary was born in 1516 proof was provided (if any were needed) that a child could live. Henry was so pleased that he said, "We are both young; if it was a daughter this time, by the grace of God sons will follow."

What is true enough is that Henry was deeply disappointed in not having a viable male heir. For though three of the most glorious reigns in English history were under queens, they were all veiled by the future; the previous reign under a queen could not encourage Henry (whose claim to the throne was none too secure) in his hopes of founding a firm line. With this in mind the King in 1525 created his bastard by Elizabeth Blount, Lord Mountjoy's sister, Duke of Richmond and then Duke of Somerset. He was even mentioned in one document as King of Ireland. If the last of these honorifics need not detain us, the others are very significant. Henry VII had once held the titles of Richmond and Somerset, and Prince Arthur that of Somerset, from which it is evident that young Henry Fitzroy (who was also made Lord High Admiral and Lord Warden of the Marches, the last of which his father had been before him) was being groomed as Henry's successor. It was More's duty—one he could hardly have relished—to read the patent that conferred these titles upon the six-year-old boy. He was a likely lad, according to all accounts, and More was asked to advise the King about his education. But of course More would not have objected to accepting him as heir to the throne, providing he was the choice of the realm, any more than he subsequently challenged the right of King and Parliament to put Elizabeth, whose legitimacy he could not admit, in the line of succession before her half-sister Mary.

The situation changed only after Anne Boleyn's appearance upon the scene. Then Henry believed he could satisfy his own inclinations by marrying her and at the same time obtain a legitimate son. He could not feel any too easy about the acceptance of his bastard by the country after his death. The bastard, however, continued to be held in reserve until his death in 1536.

Henry contrived to keep his designs regarding Anne a dark secret for a while. When in May, 1527, Wolsey made his first move for the obtaining of an annulment, he supposed that the King would make a diplomatic alliance in accord with English foreign policy at the time and marry Renée, Louis XII's daughter and afterwards the famous Duchess of Ferrara. It was while Wolsey was in France with Sir Thomas More from July to September of that year that Henry took advantage of the Cardinal's absence to bring the business before the Roman Curia. Both Wolsey and More were greatly surprised to hear upon their return of what was afoot.

It was in September that the King, while walking with More in the gallery at Hampton Court, suddenly announced that he had discovered that his marriage with his brother's widow was so contrary to the divine law that "it could in no wise by the Church be dispensable." Henry produced a Bible and pointed to Leviticus XVIII, 16, and XX, 21. Both of these passages seemed to prohibit a marriage with a brother's widow, and the second pronounced the doom, "they shall be childless." (As Henry and his brother's widow had an eleven-year-old daughter, the King interpreted the childlessness as applying only to male children.) Against Leviticus there was a passage in Deuteronomy (XXV, 5-9) which made it a duty for a brother to beget children on his childless widowed sister-in-law. And to this passage Our Lord referred in an incident recorded of Him in three of the Gospels (Matthew XXII, 23-33, Mark XII, 18-27 and Luke XX, 27-38). There He swept aside the "poser" of the Sadducees, as to whose wife a woman would be in heaven who had been married in succession to seven brothers, by saying that there *was* no marriage in heaven. Regarding the duty inculcated by Deuteronomy, or of the apparent prohibition in Leviticus, He said nothing whatever.

Of these biblical texts King Henry took, as might be expected of him, the one that suited him best. In any event there was a question as to whether a law of the Old Testament was binding upon Christians of the New. Henry's contention was that it did bind them—that is, that Leviticus did, and Deuteronomy did not—and that therefore the papal dispensation issued at the time of his marriage to Katherine was *ultra vires*.

Henry had what was at least an arguable case. Moreover he had before him plenty of precedents of annulments, though not on this particular ground. There was the one referred to in the letter quoted from the *Venetian Calendar*, when Louis XII obtained from Alexander VI (not Julius II, as the Roman banker mistakenly says) the annulment of his marriage with Jeanne de Valois. Nearer home there were other annulments. His sister Mary had been married since 1515 to Charles Brandon, Duke of Suffolk, who obtained an annulment to make this possible. And in 1527 Henry's other sister, Margaret, who had been married first to the King of Scots, obtained an annulment of her second marriage. On one pretext or another—usually technicalities—such things had been obtainable by the powerfully placed. So, though Henry persuaded himself that his marriage with Katherine was contrary to the moral law, he felt that the quickest and safest course was to plead the insufficiency of the dispensation on the plea that it was issued in the supposition that the marriage between his brother Arthur and Katherine had been consummated.

This was something Katherine steadily refused to admit, thereby complicating what the King had expected would be a problem easy of solution. And when a further dispensation was found in Spain, covering this very contingency, Henry pronounced it a forgery, backed in this by his ambassadors to Spain, who had examined it. The original has been found since then in Vienna, and most modern historians believe it to be genuine. In any event the case does not depend upon its authenticity.

It is not necessary to argue the complicated matter here. But what might be pointed out is that Wolsey, in first seeking an annulment for the King, was actuated not only by his foreign policy but by personal spite towards Charles V, who had undoubtedly twice double-crossed him in his candidacy for the papacy. The first time was in January, 1522, when the Emperor's old tutor was elected as Adrian VI. The second time was in October, 1523. Then so as not to enrage Wolsey further, Charles did write letters to his agent in Rome backing the English Cardinal, and he sent copies of these letters to Wolsey to prove that he was receiving the imperial support. What he did *not* tell Wolsey was that the bearer of these letters was detained at Barcelona by secret instructions, and so arrived at Rome only after the election was over. With it went Wolsey's last chance of the triple tiara. After this he was prepared to go to almost any lengths in opposition to Charles. He now had a wonderful chance to even old scores. The Elizabethan Catholics, though they accused Wolsey of too much, were right in thinking that for his part in this matter, as for much else, he was largely responsible for the disasters that overtook the English Church.

Unluckily for Henry VIII (and also for Wolsey) the sack of Rome occurred in 1527, following which the Pope, Clement VII, was virtually a prisoner in the Emperor's hands. This is not to suggest that the Pope would have given a different decision in different circumstances, but circumstances forced him to a policy of procrastination which does him little credit. He played for time, hoping that Henry or Katherine or Anne would die before the case was settled, if only it were dragged out long enough, or that the King's infatuation for the Boleyn woman would cool. Yet he did issue secret instructions to Campeggio—who was commissioned to try the case in England with Wolsey—that, if the marriage between Arthur and Katherine had been consummated, the dispensation that had been given to Henry and Katherine could be declared invalid. He also undertook to abide by the decision of his Legates and not to permit a further appeal to Rome.

This document was to be destroyed after being read to the King, and as that was done we are unable to ascertain its precise wording, which may have been ambiguous by design. And it was issued before the discovery of the further papal dispensation permitting Henry to marry Katherine even if Katherine's previous marriage was more than nominal. But it was enough to make the King feel that he was being played with, and that his dignity was infringed when in the end the case was referred back to Rome. Not unnaturally he was extremely angry.

Moreover Henry had a conviction that, even if there were any doubt, the Pope should be willing to stretch a point in favor of a man who had always shown himself so strong a friend of the papacy. For not only had he been the most orthodox of monarchs, he had also been a faithful ally to the Pope (as a secular sovereign) in the manoeuverings of European secular politics. So firmly had he counted upon Clement's doing as he wished that, when in July, 1527, he sent his secretary, Dr. William Knight, to the Pope asking for an annulment, he asked, for good measure, that he might be given a dispensation for bigamy on account of the signal services he had rendered the Church.[1] Also he asked for a further dispensation—one that would have been needed had he obtained an annulment of his marriage to Katherine—on the ground of the first-degree affinity he had contracted with Anne by having had her sister Mary as his mistress. As Chambers puts it, "At the very

[1] Fortunately Wolsey managed to persuade the King that this particular demand would only make him look foolish, so it was dropped. One rather wishes, for the amusement of Clio, that it had been presented at Rome.

time that he was denying the power of the Pope to remove the one disability, he was seeking a papal dispensation to remove another" —and, one may add, a disability of an almost identical sort. But in truth the conscience of Henry VIII was an extraordinary article. In all this it is certain that he believed himself in the right. As Campeggio said, when reporting to Rome, an angel out of heaven would be unable to convince the King that his marriage to Katherine was valid.

The King was fertile in his expedients. Thus when unexpected difficulties arose over the "divorce," he took the suggestion of Cranmer—until then an obscure university don—and canvassed the universities for their opinions. Their canonists and theologians were to be regarded as a "scattered council," as a General Council of the Church could not be summoned to deal with the King's Great Matter. Oxford and Cambridge could hardly do otherwise than say what Henry wanted them to say. But abroad the universities of Bologna, Paris, Orleans, Angers, Toulouse, Ferrara, Pavia and Padua all decided for Henry in 1530, though it must be remembered that those commissioned to approach these learned bodies were instructed to spare no expense.[2] Nor were erudite but impecunious rabbis overlooked. As specialists in the Hebrew language, their opinions were well worth buying—especially as they were glad to take a fee of only twenty-four crowns.

It would probably be unjust to Henry to say that he thought More's opinion was also well worth buying, though doubtless the King supposed that, from a man in his service and who was his personal friend, he would receive full support. More, however, was very disinclined to express any opinion at all. But when Henry challenged him that day in the gallery of Hampton Court, he read

[2] The Italian Ghinucci, who was Bishop of Worcester, was very useful in these little transactions. Cf. Friedmann's *Anne Boleyn,* Vol. I, p. 115, and the *Venetian Calendar,* Vol. IV, No. 1251. At Padua Richard Croke offered £500 to the Canonists, and when they refused, raised his price, but in vain. He did, however, succeed in obtaining, at what price we do not know, an opinion from some of the Doctors of Divinity in Henry's favor. Others of the theologians refused to assent; nevertheless what Croke did get was sent to England as the opinion of the whole university.

the passages that were pointed out in the Bible and then, as Roper writes, "As one that had never professed any study of divinity, excused himself to be unmeet in many ways to meddle with such matters."

Henry was not satisfied with this answer and pressed More further, but his only reply was "foreasmuch as the case was of such importance as needed great advisement and deliberation, he besought his Grace of sufficient respite to consider it." The King had to agree to so reasonable a request and told him to consult Tunstall and Clerk, the Bishop of Bath. When More had done this, he made his report to Henry: "To be plain with your Grace, neither my Lord of Durham nor my Lord of Bath, though I know them both to be wise, virtuous, learned and honourable prelates, nor myself, with the rest of your Council, being all your Grace's servants, for your manifold benefits daily bestowed on us so much bounden to you, be, in my judgment, meet counsellors for your Grace herein."

But Henry was not to be put off. He wanted, perhaps above everything else, More's favorable opinion. In order to give him every chance of reversing himself gracefully, Henry from time to time reverted to the subject, asking More to consult the Archbishops of Canterbury and York (this of course was after Wolsey's fall, when More was Lord Chancellor and his friend, Edward Lee, Archbishop in Wolsey's place), and Dr. Nicholas Burgo, an Italian friar who had a high reputation as a theologian. Edward Foxe, later the King's Almoner, was also consulted. Yet More had to come back every time to his first opinion, which was that what he could gather from "St. Jerome, St. Augustine, and divers other holy doctors, both Greeks and Latins," did not support the King's view. This, Henry, as Roper relates, "as disagreeable with his desire, did not very well like of, yet were they by Sir Thomas More, who in all his communications with the King in that matter had always most discreetly behaved himself, so wisely tempered that he presently [for the moment] took them in good part, and oftimes had thereof conference with him again." Stapleton adds that More acted with so great a loyalty to Henry that, though ne read all the books that came to be published on the King's side of the case, "he would never so much as look at any published against the divorce." He even destroyed a book written by his friend, the learned Bishop of Bath, because it was among these. But willing as he was to be persuaded, he never could change his mind.

He had indeed every possible inducement to change it. Knowing Henry as he did, he probably foresaw what the outcome of the affair would be. For though at the beginning the King took More's reserve with a sufficiently good grace, More, like everybody else, grew increasingly aware that the woman behind the King was one of an extraordinarily determined character, and that her will was set upon nothing less than becoming Queen. The source of her hold over Henry was quite incomprehensible, but it was also quite unmistakable. She was vivacious and she was young, but she was without wit or beauty, except for dark eyes and a swan-like neck and long black hair. Wolsey, in reference to her swarthiness, used to call her "the crow of the night". Her charms were further offset by what some people described as a sixth finger on one of her hands, and by a high shrill laugh that grated on all nerves. Yet Henry was completely captivated by La Boleyn, who held him off for five years, refusing to become his mistress, as her sister had been, not because of any moral scruples, but because she wanted first to make perfectly sure of her prize. Only then, a few months before her marriage, did she yield to Henry's importunity. Meanwhile those who were known to be upholding the validity of Katherine's marriage—even not to deny its validity was enough —were well aware that they were incurring the animosity of a woman who would take her revenge when this was in her power. So whatever assurances the King gave as to his wishing only disinterested advice, those who understood his nature, with its violence, its caprice, its willingness to yield to a dominating influence (until he flared into rebellion), had every reason to fear.

Nor did Anne Boleyn stand alone. She was now the spearhead

of a party. It would not be accurate to describe them as that of the Protestants, but it was certainly that of the group who divined that the impending religious changes would be for their benefit. And the chaplain of the Boleyns was the resourceful Thomas Cranmer, who was already secretly a Protestant and who had married (this also was secretly) the niece of the Lutheran Ossiander while he was in Germany.

The Boleyns, because of their enmity against More, deserve a few words here. Thomas Boleyn (then Viscount Rochford and after his daughter's rise, Earl of Wiltshire) was not himself of particularly good family. His father was a wealthy merchant who served a term as Lord Mayor of London. There was, however, on his mother's side, a relationship with the great Norman-Irish family of the Ormondes, and the spruce little man had married a sister of the Duke of Norfolk. And the Howards were near enough to being royal to incur at the end of Henry's reign his jealousy. A cousin of Anne's was the poet, Henry Howard, the Earl of Surrey, who was beheaded; if his father was saved from the block, this was only because the King died the day before that set for his execution.

Anne's brother, who became Viscount Rochford when his father was created Earl of Wiltshire, was to be executed after her fall on what was probably a false charge of incest with her. His wicked wife, who brought this charge against him, was herself to die on the scaffold in connection with the behavior of Henry's fifth wife —another niece of the Duke of Norfolk's—Katherine Howard. Upon both commissions their uncle sat, and he gave his consent to their condemnation, as he did also to More's execution, though he was More's close friend. These things were a matter of political routine.

Anne fascinated other men besides Henry. Hardly had she returned from the French court when the poet, Thomas Wyatt, fell in love with her, as he records in a sonnet in which, however, he is careful to indicate a prudent withdrawal, because the lady had so clearly written in diamonds round her neck, "Caesar's I am." Young Sir Henry Algernon Percy, later the sixth Earl of Northumberland, was not so discreet as the poet. He was almost as infatuated as the King, so Henry had to instruct Wolsey, to whose household the young man was attached at the time, to send him packing. His father was also brought in to deal with the affair, and he, very much alarmed, threatened to disinherit his son. In the end Percy saw reason and, in order to remove all suspicion in the future, married the daughter of the Earl of Shrewsbury. The incident proved useful to Henry in 1536, when he argued that his marriage to Anne was invalid because of her precontract to this former flame. A second argument in 1536 was the first degree affinity created by Henry's liaison with Anne's sister. The King always liked to have such questions tidily disposed of before he disposed of his victims.

As to how far Anne Boleyn returned Percy's (or Wyatt's) passion is questionable, but it seems that she was perfectly willing to marry the man who would succeed to the earldom that made Englishmen sometimes call the Percies the Princes of the North. In any event, however, she soon saw that her ambition might reach towards a still greater position, and from then on everything she did was directed towards ousting Katherine as queen and taking her place.

Had she been allowed to follow what was in all likelihood the preference of her heart and marry Percy, she might have been a fairly good woman. As it is, though she may not have been guilty of all the adulteries of which she was accused—perhaps of none of them—she stands before us as a woman commonplace in everything except a ruthless will and the devastation she wrought in the history of England and of the world.

That she was not popular was perhaps only in part due to the view that everybody took of her as an upstart who was not very gracious to anybody. But still more it sprang from the people's love of Katherine of Aragon, and their perception that a monstrous wrong was being done her. Yet theirs was merely an instinctive feeling and had little or nothing to do with the religious questions involved. More was one of the few who, from the start, understood the real issue and who, though with the nicest prudence and circumspection, opposed the royal divorce and so prepared his own glorious doom.

CHAPTER FOURTEEN

Lord Chancellor More

IT WAS nevertheless the royal divorce that brought Sir Thomas More to the Chancellorship, an office that he had never sought and that he would have refused had he been free to do so. Even had he been ambitious, he was fully aware that he would be at a grave disadvantage in following in this office a man who had a wealth greater even than the King's and also the powers of the Papal Legate. Moreover he had to deal with a Parliament in whose House of Commons, as Fisher said in the Lords, the cry was all, "Down with the Church!" The breach that the new Lord Chancellor saw to be widening between the Crown and the Holy See would, at the very least, create great difficulties for him.

Yet More could not refuse. He did, however, remind Henry of what had been said when he first took office in 1518, "that his Highness spake unto him . . . the most virtuous lesson that ever Prince taught his servant, willing first to look unto God, and after God to him." To this, Roper continues, the King made the kindly answer "that if he could not therein with his conscience serve him, he was content to accept his service otherwise; and using the advice of his learned Council, whose consciences would well enough agree therewith, would nevertheless continue his gracious favour towards him, and never with that matter molest his conscience more." It was therefore with the distinct understanding that he was not to be asked to promote the annulment proceedings, that More consented to take the fallen Wolsey's place.

Wolsey represented in the popular mind all that was most arrogant, most luxurious, and most repressive in the ecclesiastical system. When he failed to effect what he had assured Henry was well within his powers of diplomatic management—the securing of the annulment—his doom was certain. Yet he had done everything within any man's capacity, and had even tried to get himself made Vicar-General for the Pope, when Clement was virtually a prisoner of the Emperor's, so that he might pronounce the decree Henry looked for. With Wolsey's failure, his enemies came at his heels like a pack of wolves.

Yet in spite of all his self-seeking, the English Cardinal had tried to serve the Church, as he had also tried to serve his King. A man of immense energy and ability, as well as of great geniality when he chose to exercise it, there were grave defects in his character as there was a grave limitation to his intelligence. Mr. Belloc describes this as a lack of vision. Wolsey saw keenly, none more so, the immediate consequences of any course of action, but he did not take long views. He several times told Cardinal Campeggio, that if the royal annulment were not obtained, the authority of the Apostolic See would be ended in England—a sound judgment. What he did not see until too late was that it was his policy of getting that authority concentrated, as never before, in his hands as Legate, that had made the Church so vulnerable.

Now, though everything had been done with the King's consent, Henry was able to invoke against him the statute of praemunire, and, indeed, to implicate in the penalties of the law, the entire kingdom. Only the King escaped, because, under the constitutional fiction, the King can do no wrong. Henry had therefore what he always liked to have, an opportunity for acting unjustly under perfectly legal forms. And as praemunire could be specially directed against the whole clerical body, he was in the position of being able to reduce it to a terrified compliance with his will. It was in these circumstances that More reluctantly took office.

The Chancellorship had previously, with only two or three exceptions in medieval times, always been held by an ecclesiastic. And it would seem that it may in 1529 have been offered to Warham, the Archbishop of Canterbury, who had been Chancellor from 1504 to 1515. But if this offer was ever made, it was only as a matter of form, and in the certainty that Warham would be sure to plead age and ill health. On October 25, 1529, the Great Seal was given, with universal approval, including that of Wolsey himself, to Sir Thomas More.

It has been suggested that this was an effort on Henry's part to win More over. Stapleton asserts this plainly, and Cardinal Pole, Henry's cousin, adds that "The course of events shows clearly that the King made More Chancellor with the intention of bribing him, that he might allow himself to be a party to the King's designs." It would, however, probably be nearer the truth to say that the King meant to keep his promise to More not to make him responsible for the divorce proceedings, but was too weak to keep his word. We do find him repeatedly returning to the very subject he had undertaken to leave alone, trying to extract from More an adhesion that More was never able to give. Even without that adhesion, More was useful because of his reputation of probity; the dirty work could be done by compliant tools (of whom there were an abundance) while the Chancellor stood in his glory, some part of which would cover the King and his ministers. As Algernon Cecil puts it: "If Cromwell was invaluable to his master as an *âme damnée,* More was in a position to serve the King with a soul already in the public eye no little blessed."

In accepting the chancellorship More may have hoped that he might be able to act as a brake upon the course of events. It was conceivable that a fortunate occasion would arise when he might even be able to persuade Henry to abandon his plans. Queen Katherine needed a friend, and though More had to proceed very cautiously, it was better for her that he should be in the chancellorship rather than a man more subservient to the King. In the *Utopia* he had spoken along these lines, in his own person telling Raphael Hythloday that the ship must not be abandoned in a tempest, "but you must with a crafty wile and a subtle train study and endeavour yourself, as much as in you lieth, to handle the matter wittily and handsomely for the purpose, and that which you cannot turn to good, so to order that it be not very bad."

Roper has described the scene that took place on October 26th when, between the Dukes of Norfolk and Suffolk, More was escorted through Westminster Hall to his seat in the chancery. Then the Duke of Norfolk made a speech in which he said that all England was beholden to Sir Thomas More for his services, and that he was worthy of the highest place in the realm, and how dearly beloved and trusted he was of the King. More rose to reply, "trembling with nervousness," says Stapleton, and protested himself as unfit for so exalted an office, "wherein, considering how wise and honourable a prelate had lately taken so great a fall, he had, he said, thereof no cause to rejoice."

Another speech of More's is reported by Hall as given at the meeting of Parliament on November 3rd. Then More, after remarking that the reason it had been summoned was "to reform such things as had been used or permitted by inadvertence, or by changes of time had become inexpedient," lashed out at Wolsey. The words recorded are these: "As you see that amongst a great flock of sheep some be rotten and faulty, which the good shepherd sendeth from the good sheep, so the great wether that is of late fallen (as you know), so craftily, so scabbedly, yea and so untruly juggled with the King, that all men must needs guess and think that he thought in himself that he had no wit to perceive his crafty doing, or else he presumed that the King would not see nor know his fraudulent juggling and attempts. But he was deceived, for his Grace's sight was so quick and penetrable that he saw him, yea and saw through him, so that all thing to him was open, and according to his desert he hath had a gentle correction, which small punishment the King will not to be an example to other offenders."

The authenticity of such speeches is of course open to challenge, and this one has so pained several of More's biographers that they cannot believe he would have used these ungenerous words of his predecessor. But though the actual phrasing used is in all likelihood not just the same as that given, we know from a letter from Charles V's ambassador to the Emperor that More did speak very severely of Wolsey. Two things should be noted, however; one is that Wolsey was assured of no more than a "gentle correction," which would be less than was prepared for other misdoers, and that in all these official speeches More was obliged to act as the mouthpiece of the King. Chapuys tells of another speech of More's in the House of Lords, when he reported the opinions of the universities on the divorce matter and declared that the King was motivated only by scruples of conscience and not "out of love for some lady." On this occasion the Bishops of Lincoln and London (Stokesley, now that Tunstall had not been transferred to Durham), "took it on their conscience that the marriage of the King and Queen was more than illegal", but Chapuys says that the Lord Chancellor, when asked to give his own opinion, "said that he had many times declared it to the King, and said no more." The reply was enough to make it clear that he himself did not approve.

The question had, however, "put him on the spot." And at other times too he needed all his tact and discretion to be at once faithful to the King and faithful to his own conscience. When the Emperor wrote him a personal letter, which no doubt asked his help for Katherine, More refused to receive it from Chapuys, as he would be bound to show it to the King. And it was not difficult for him to guess that this would not do the Queen any good.

Stapleton describes the public state of the Chancellor, "on his right a golden sceptre surmounted by the Royal Crown, as a sign of his power under the King, and on his left a book, as a sign of his knowledge of the law; the royal seal carried before him." More now took precedence even over the Dukes of Norfolk and Suffolk and the Archbishops. Yet he showed how little he valued such honors. In a characteristic passage written late in life, he said that when twenty men stood before him bareheaded it never kept his head as warm as his own cap. Though he had to submit to such things, whenever possible he continued to dispense with all formalities. We hear of him often holding court in his house at Chelsea, where he was always accesible to anybody who had a suit to bring before him. It reminds one of St. Louis administering justice under the oak at Vincennes.

No two men could have offered a greater contrast than Sir

Thomas More and the man who had immediately preceded him in the chancellorship. The essence of the difference was the pride of the one and the modesty of the other. In his chapter on flattery in the *Dialogue of Comfort* More gives a most amusing glimpse of Wolsey, of course disguised but not so disguised that he is not easily recognisable: "Glorious was he very far above all measure, and that was great pity, for it did harm, and made him abuse many great gifts that God had given him. Never was he satiate of hearing his own praise." Then More proceeds, in the character of Vincent, a young Hungarian noble, to tell how, on a visit to Germany, he was at table with a "great man of the Church," who had made an oration. The orator sat upon thorns until he obtained the desired flattery. When it was slow in coming, he bluntly demanded an expression of opinion from his guests. Upon this nobody present could eat a mouthful, as each of them was "in so deep a study for the finding of some exquisite praise. For he that should have brought out but a vulgar and common commendation would have thought himself shamed for ever." So all those present spoke in turn, beginning with the lowest at the board, as though "it had been a great matter of the commonweal, in a right solemn counsel." When Vincent was called on to speak his piece he thought he acquitted himself reasonably well. But the one who sat highest and who had to speak last was a doctor of divinity, and he knew that he would be expected to surpass the previous speakers. He was laboring so hard to think of the richest encomium of all that he positively sweated, "so that he was fain in the while now and then to wipe his face." He saw it was impossible to dish out any more luscious phrases of flattery than those already concocted, and yet the wily fox did after all beat everybody at that game. For when he was called on to speak, he did not say a single word, but drew a "long sigh with an oh from the bottom of his breast, and lift up his head, and cast his eyes into the welkin and wept."

More (as Vincent) was vastly amused, yet he admits of the speech Wolsey had made, "to say the truth it was not to dispraise.

Howbeit surely somewhat less praise might have served it, by more a great deal than the half. But this I am sure, had it been the worst that ever was made, the praise had not been less by one hair. For they that used to praise him to his face, never considered how much the things deserved, but how great a laud and praise themself could give his good Grace."

He continued with his stories of Wolsey by relating how one day he called a man who might be supposed to know something about the matter in question, as he had been several times an ambassador—which suggests that the man may have been More himself—and showed him a treaty he had drawn up, and asked him for his sincere opinion of it, saying, "I pray you heartily tell me the very truth." At this More, thinking candid criticism really was wanted, ventured to find fault with one of the details of the treaty, only to be rebuffed in great anger with, "By the mass, thou art a very fool!" More adds that the ambassador of course after that would never tell Wolsey the unvarnished truth again.

There was, however, one point of similarity between the two Lord Chancellors, apart from the broad fact that both men were of quite exceptional ability. This was that they both did what they could to arrest that process for the enclosure of the common lands denounced by More-Hythloday in the *Utopia*. Now More as Chancellor had the opportunity to adjudicate several such cases. One of these, cited by Miss Routh, shows that he compromised, but mainly in favor of village folk who had been using the common, when giving judgement in the Star Chamber. But in another he reversed a decision given by Wolsey in 1510 and ruled that the lord of the manor should retain the enclosure.[1] In both instances he acted, not according to abstract theory or his private prepossessions, but in conformity with what seemed to him just in the particular cases before him.

In respect to dealing with judicial matters, More far surpassed Wolsey in speed and efficiency. The Cardinal was a prodigious worker but he was not a professional lawyer, and he had to spend

[1] *Sir Thomas More and his Friends,* pp. 159 and 178.

most of his time on foreign affairs or ecclesiastical administration. The result was that when More took charge of the Chancellor's Court, he found it cluttered up with unfinished business, some of which had dragged on for twenty years. He disposed of it with such dispatch that there came to be a popular rhyme:

> When More some time had Chancellor been
> No more suits did remain.
> The like will never more be seen
> Till More be there again.

It has, however, been pointed out by the lawyers who have written on him that no great legal decision is connected with his name. Lord Justice Russell of Killowen even says[2] that he can find no contemporary report in official documents of any legal decision made by him, and though subsequent investigations by Professor Chambers and Miss Routh have produced several, these do no more than confirm some of the incidents related by Roper and others. What can be said is that More enhanced the already strong reputation he possessed for honesty and ability. Lord Russell does go on to remark that, "While it is not possible to describe More as a great chancellor from the lawyer's point of view . . . nevertheless, this may be truly said: that if to discharge judicial duties conscientiously, speedily and without favour, to make the machinery of justice work smoothly and efficiently, and to soften the rigours of the law so as to meet the rights of particular cases, are the marks of a great chancellor, then Sir Thomas More must be so described."

We hear from Roper how he dealt with the other judges. These were complaining of the way the Lord Chancellor was issuing injunctions, though More was sparing of these as compared with Wolsey. To smooth out the difficulties with his colleagues, More invited them to dinner, and afterwards went over with them all the injunctions he had issued. They were obliged to confess that, in his position, they would have acted as he had done. "Then

[2] *The Fame of Blessed Thomas More,* pp. 67, 72.

offered he this unto them: that if the justices of every court . . . would, upon reasonable considerations, by their own discretions (as they were, as he thought, in conscience bound) mitigate and reform the rigour of the law themselves, there should from thenceforth by him no more injunctions be granted." Roper also tells us—and he was a lawyer—that his father-in-law made a practice of reading every legal document himself that was laid before him, taking nothing for granted, and this extended even to the issuing of subpoenas. All of which indicates a scrupulous fairness and a desire to show all possible leniency consistent with justice.

We have a number of amusing stories about More as judge, and though some of these indicate only that he had a pleasant wit, others indicate a good deal more. Thus his son-in-law, Daunce, made the more or less humorous complaint that when the Cardinal was Chancellor the very door-keepers of his court "gat great gain," whereas More's son-in-law got nothing at all, because the Chancellor "was so ready himself to hear every man, rich and poor, and kept no doors shut from them." More laughed at this but said that he might find other ways to help poor Daunce, adding, "Howbeit, this one thing, son, I assure thee on my faith, that if the parties will at my hands call for justice, then, all were it that my father stood on one side, and the Devil on the other, his cause being good, the Devil should have right."

He was as good as his word, as another son-in-law, Heron, found when, "having a matter before him in Chancery, and presuming too much on [the Lord Chancellor's] favour," a flat decree was given against him.[3] Even Lady More found that her husband administered impartial justice with a wisdom worthy of Solomon. For once when a beggar woman came to Chelsea, claiming that a dog Dame Alice had recently bought really belonged to her, what the Chancellor did was to make the women stand at

[3] Professor Chambers points out that the details of this case are preserved at the Record Office, Early Chancery Proceedings, Bundle 643, No. 32: Giles Heron *versus* Nicholas Millisante.

opposite ends of the room and call the animal. When it ran to the beggar woman, Sir Thomas gave her a gold coin that would have bought three such dogs, so that everybody was pleased.

Though some of the other stories wear a rather apocryphal look, they nevertheless serve, as legends commonly do, to indicate More's contemporary reputation. We hear of a man named Silver being brought before him on a suspicion of heresy, and of More's remarking with a sly jest, "Silver must be tried by fire." He was so delighted with the rejoinder, "Ay, but quicksilver cannot abide it" that he let the man off. That tale is extremely doubtful, but a similar incident seems at least plausible. A lawyer named Tubbe had brought him a bill to which he had signed his name. The Chancellor gravely wrote what turned this into "A Tale of a Tubbe," with which the man departed, not looking at what More had done and supposing that his brief had been approved.

From "Ro. Ba." come the following, not used again, I think, by any biographer. A man who had lost a purse containing ten pounds, set up a notice about it in St. Paul's. Sir Thomas, seeing it by chance, wrote on it his name, as though he had been the finder. When the man came to him, More gravely wrote down his name and age and address and where and how he had lost his purse. Then he said, "My friend, I am sorry for your loss, but I have not your purse, nor I know not where it is." The man then asked him why, in that case, he had put his name on the notice, to which More replied, "Marry, to this end, that I may know thee again another time; for if you cannot keep your own purse, you shall not keep mine." But having had his little joke, he gave the man forty shillings towards his loss and told him to be more careful another time.

The other Ro. Ba. story is that More was presented with a very foolish book by its author. At their next meeting More asked the man whether he could turn it into metre. "Yea," said the author, and this he very quickly did. When he brought it again, expecting a reward, More asked him, "Is it the same book?" and was told, "Word for word; but that it is now in verse, before in prose."

Upon this Sir Thomas shot, "Then is it now a fair piece; before it had neither rime nor reason; now it hath at the least some rime, no reason." Doubtless there are authors who deserve such handling; all the same one wonders whether the kind-hearted More would have treated anybody like that.

An incident, as related by Stapleton and Cresacre More, would seem to be inherently improbable and may be an embroidering of something of which Sir Thomas tells in his *Four Last Things.* There he wrote: "I remember me of a thief once cast in Newgate, that cut a purse when at the bar, when he should have been hanged on the morrow. And when he was asked why he did so, knowing that he should die so shortly, the desperate wretch said, that it did his heart good, to be lord of that purse one night yet." It reappears as a story of how one of the magistrates on the bench with More—this if it happened at all, must have been while he was Under-Sheriff of London—when some pickpockets were brought before them, inveighed against the carelessness of people who made it possible for rogues like these to ply their trade. When the court adjourned, More sent for the thief and promised him immunity if, when the court reconvened, he would announce that he had some information he would whisper only in private. Then he was to go to the magistrate who had made the reproving speech and cut *his* purse while talking with him. As soon as this had been done, More said he would like to ask the magistrates to contribute to a collection he was taking up for "some poor fellow in danger of death." When reaching for his purse, the magistrate found it gone, "all who were present enjoyed the joke and appreciated the wisdom that was intertwined with More's humour." As used by the Elizabethan dramatists who wrote the play *Sir Thomas More,* the incident is told with psychological subtlety, and the cutpurse, greatly frightened when approached by More, says:

> Good Mr. Sheriff, seek not my overthrow.
> You know, Sir, I have many heavy friends
> And more indictments like to come upon me;

> You are too deep for me to deal withal.
> You are known to be one of the wisest men
> That is in England. I pray you, Mr. Sheriff,
> Go not about to undermine my life.

On the face of it, it seems most unlikely that Mr. Sheriff would have undertaken to get a man off from what was then a capital crime on condition that he commit another, even sportively. But More had such celebrity as a jester that, just as many witticisms are attributed to Talleyrand and many broad tales to Lincoln for which neither are responsible, all kinds of stories were fastened upon him. At least some of these have to be taken with cautious reserve.

But of course far more important than these stories about More, even those that are well authenticated, is the question of his connection with the heresy trials during his Chancellorship. Here there is often bewilderment on the part of those who remember their *Utopia* and who think they see some inconsistency between the religious tolerance that is advocated there and the suppression of heresy for which, as Lord Chancellor, More had to be, to some extent, responsible.

Sometimes this is accounted for on the ground that More was suffering from the hardening of the intellectual arteries that comes over many men in middle life. The world is full of radicals turned conservatives for this reason. Sometimes also an attempt is made to exculpate More with the argument that neither he nor any judge necessarily approves of the law it is his duty to enforce.

These excuses are not needed, and even those who wish to find an excuse for More can hardly find one here. He definitely approved of the statute under which heretics were sent to the stake, and before he became Lord Chancellor, unequivocally headed the thirteenth chapter of the fourth book of his *Dialogue against Heresies*: "The author showeth his opinion concerning the burning of heretics and that it is lawful, necessary and well done." As for the alleged hardening of the intellectual arteries, no man ever lived who had less to regret and recant of his past. He was a Utopian to the end.

But as I have shown in an earlier chapter, there is a misunderstanding in this matter, due to careless reading of More's famous book. The Utopian religious tolerance existed among a people who, having only natural religion, proceeded on the live-and-let-live principle. Yet so far from their toleration being indeterminate, it dealt most severely with those who advocated their opinions in a contentious fashion—inflicting for this crime the punishment given to all misdoers, that of servitude, and for continued contumacy, death. Also those who denied Divine Providence and the immortality of the soul were absolutely excluded from all civic rights. King Utopus and More were at one in the attitude they took towards religious opinions that were in effect seditious.

It is true, however, that King Utopus "seemed to doubt whether those different forms of religion might not all come from God, who might inspire men in a different manner, and be pleased with this variety," but such a notion, though reasonable enough in his case, was of course inadmissible in the case of Christians, to whom a revelation has been given. Even so, the Utopian inference—"that the native force of truth would at last break forth and shine"[4]—is the principle upon which Catholic apologetics bases itself. There is no danger of anyone reverting to the idea, held in the sixteenth century by Catholics and Protestants alike, that heresy is an offence punishable by the law. But we must at least allow for that belief and not insist that More be, in this matter, other than a man of his time. Yet while granting this much in the question of legal procedure, I submit that there is no escape in logic from the proposition that, if religion have any importance at all, its importance must be so vast that, by comparison with it, everything else may be said to be quite unimportant. And if, as Catholics believe, the Catholic Church is the repository of truth, error (considered in the abstract) has no

[4] Here I use instead of the translation made in 1551 by Ralph Robinson, that given by Father Bridgett, as clearer and more emphatic.

absolute rights against it, whatever purely legal rights may be extended to all men to have any religion they please or none.

But More lived in a society which had been, until the very recent Lutheran revolt, a single unified structure—Christendom. He saw that heresy was a form of sedition against that society, and he regarded it, as the law regarded it, as a criminal offence to propagate opinions that were at once subversive of Christian truth and social order. His task therefore, both as a controversialist and as the chief law officer of the Crown, was to prevent, if he could, heresy from making further headway. And here Froude gives him a back-handed compliment by writing: "Sir Thomas More may be said to have lived to illustrate the necessary tendencies of Romanism, in an honest mind convinced of its truth; to show that the test of sincerity in a man who professes to regard orthodoxy as an essential of salvation is not the readiness to endure persecution, but the courage that will venture to inflict it."

The compliment is excessive. Though More certainly believed in the laws against heresy, and said so plainly, he could in 1533 write in his *Apology*: "As touching heretics I hate that vice of theirs and not their persons, and very fain would I that the one were destroyed and the other saved. And that I have toward no man any other mind than this—how loudly soever these blessed new brethren and professors and preachers of heresy belie me—if all the favour and pity I have used among them to their amendment were known, it would, I warrant you, well and plain appear; whereof, if it were requisite, I could bring forth witnesses more than men would ween." Even without that disclaimer, one might suppose that it would be impossible to believe that a man who, all his life long, showed himself so kind and gentle should have been severe, still less that a man so just as himself could have been unjust in the enforcement of the law.

Accusations of severity were made against him, as we shall see, in his own lifetime, and were met by him. But they have found their circulation mainly through the pages of Foxe's *Acts and Monuments,* the first edition of which was not published until

More had been twenty years dead. From Foxe they were taken by Burnet and others, and though Foxe has been repeatedly shown to be, to say the least, a highly unreliable writer, he is still drawn on as an authority. Gairdiner and Maitland have exposed him, and Dr. Brewer in his introduction to *Letters and Papers of the Reign of Henry VIII,* does not hesitate to declare: "Had Foxe been an honest man . . . his carelessness and credulity would have incapacitated him from being a trustworthy historian. Unfortunately he was not honest; he tampered with the documents that came into his hands." Even so, there were occasions when Foxe discovered that he had been misinformed and so removed false statements that had appeared in earlier editions of his book. This he did in the case of several of his charges against More. Unhappily the most scholarly modern edition of his work prints all these omissions, and while indicating that Foxe did omit them, shows this in so small a type in the footnotes that few people will risk their eyesight in reading them.

But first, before coming to More's denials, it might be as well to quote what Sir James Mackintosh has to say regarding them. He writes: "This statement, so minute, so easily confuted, was publicly made after his fall from power, when he was surrounded by enemies, and could have no friends but the generous. It relates circumstances of public notoriety . . . which it would have been rather a proof of insanity than of imprudence to have alleged in his defence, if they had not been indisputably true. Whenever he touches this subject, there is a quietness and circumstantiality, which are the least equivocal marks of a man who adheres to the temper most favourable to the truth, because he is conscious that the truth is favourable to him." Five pages later Mackintosh comments again: "What other controversialist can be named, who, having the power to crush antagonists whom he viewed as the disturbers of the quiet of his declining age, the destroyers of all the hopes he had cherished for mankind, contented himself with the severity of his language."

What must be borne in mind is that under the law of Henry

IV not even the Lord Chancellor, as in this case he was a layman, could sentence any heretic. That was something strictly reserved to the Ordinary of the diocese to which the accused person belonged. On the other hand, a statute of Henry V required from all secular officers of the law, including the Lord Chancellor, the taking of an oath upon admission to office to assist the Church by arresting heretics, presenting them to the proper courts for trial, and carrying out of the sentences of those courts. More also did sometimes sit on the commissions that examined heretics, and occasionally he even examined them privately in his own house, where he could hold them in temporary custody. That was the very limit of his authority.

What the Ordinary did, under the existing law, was to consign the accused, if found guilty, to the secular arm for the punishment that the law prescribed. In this the Bishop functioned in much the same way as a doctor functions when he is called upon to pronounce on a person's sanity. In that sense the doctor may be said to sentence people to the lunatic asylum; in that sense, too, a bishop of More's time might be said to have sentenced a heretic to the stake. In each case an expert opinion is given, after which the law proceeds to act. Neither expert—the doctor or the theologian—can be considered as free to indulge his private whim. And though in either case a mistake can be made, heresy trials, being held in public court, guaranteed a fair hearing for the accused.

It is not necessary to discuss the question of the Marian persecution. The only fact that concerns us at the moment is that while More was Lord Chancellor, only about a dozen burnings took place in all England, and of these only three were in the London diocese. And though a dozen such burnings may be a dozen too many, such executions are insignificant when set against the 72,000 executions by hanging for various felonies that are computed to have taken place during the reign of Henry VIII. In an age of so summary a justice it is more than clear that of all classes of criminals—for criminals heretics were in the eyes of the law—none were treated so tenderly as they. Froude is simply writing nonsense in contrasting the regimes of Wolsey and More by saying that "no sooner had the seals changed hands than the fires of Smithfield recommenced." For though it is true that Wolsey was very lenient in this matter (as we have seen from the way he handled Roper), the enforcement of the heresy laws did not become really rigorous until More had handed the seals to his successor.

But let us turn to what More says about this matter in his *Apology*. He notes that "the lies are neither few nor small that the blessed brethren have made, and daily make by me. Divers of them have said that of such as were in my house while I was Chancellor, I used to examine them with torments, causing them to be bounden to a tree in my garden, and there piteously beaten." In this connection he cites the case of "one Segar, a book-seller of Cambridge"; he was one of those More was said to have tied to a tree in the garden at Chelsea and scourged, "and beside that bounden about the head with a cord . . . that he fell down in a swoon." More continues, "and this tale of his beating did Tyndale tell to an old acquaintance of his own, and to a good lover of mine, that while this man was in beating, I spied a little purse of his hanging at his doublet, wherein the poor man had (as he said) five mark, and that caught I quickly to me and pulled it from his doublet, and put it in my bosom, and that Segar never saw it after, and therein I trow he said true, for no more did I neither, nor I trow did Segar himself in good faith." Yet a similar tale was attached in various forms at convenience to many other names—among them Tewkesbury, Frith, Petit and Bainham. And Foxe transferred some of the details—quite unaltered—he had recorded about the Tewkesbury case to that of Bainham, without any explanation or apology. The whole matter is sufficiently covered by what Professor Chambers points out, that the first three of these cases fell outside the period of More's chancellorship, adding that while the fourth case is chronologically possible, "it rests on the same basis of irresponsible gossip as the others."

More does, nevertheless, admit the beatings of two people who may be classed as heretics, though the second was more of a lunatic than anything else. The first case relates to a boy whom we know, from another passage in the *Apology,* to have been named Dick Purser, who had associated in Antwerp with an English heretic by whom he had been taught "his ungracious heresy against the Blessed Sacrament of the Altar, which heresy this child, afterwards being in service with me, began to teach another child in my house, which uttered his counsel. And upon that point perceived and known, I caused a servant of mine to stripe him like a child before my household, for amendment of himself and ensample of such other." Surely no great "cruelty" was involved in giving a boy a whipping for talk that might have led himself and others to the stake.

The other case mentioned by More was that of a man who had been confined in Bedlam, but who had been released. His specialty was that of making indecent assaults upon women in Church, when their heads were bowed low at the elevation at Mass. Then, creeping up behind them, he would throw their clothes over their heads. A beating did him a world of good, for he promised to behave afterwards, "and verily," More added, "God be thanked I hear none harm of him now."

Neither this feeble-minded man, nor the foolish boy, Dick Purser, had any formal charge of heresy brought against him; otherwise More could not have let them go. Of those who were arrested, and detained in his house while he was preparing to hand them over to the proper authorities, he could affirm that "never any of them [had] any stripe or stroke given them, so much as a fillip on the forehead."

Such heretics as he talked to during their temporary imprisonment he always tried to talk out of their heresy. Though it is just possible that Frith—a young priest with whom he had engaged in controversy—was among those arrested on a warrant signed by him, it is clear that, when he was tried, More had nothing whatever to do with the matter. Audley was by then Lord Chancellor. But it is, to say the least, very interesting to note that on the commission with Stokesley, since 1530 Bishop of London—who, as Ordinary of the diocese was officially responsible for Frith's sentence—sat Cranmer, and that the main charge against Frith was his published denial of transubstantiation—something that Cranmer himself had long denied in his heart. In spite of this, Cranmer's written report remains as to how he had personally examined Frith and had tried in vain to persuade him that there is "a very corporal presence of Christ within the Sacrament of the Altar." Really if accusations of "inconsistency" have to be bandied about, they should be fastened upon the time-serving Archbishop of Canterbury and not upon a man always inflexible in principle. Even Foxe never charged More with being otherwise, nor did it occur to any of the men with whom he had controversies even to suggest that there was any discrepancy between the *Utopia* and More's practice as Lord Chancellor. And of the three burnings that occurred at Smithfield during his tenure of office, all occurred during the last months, when his fall was imminent and when he had little power. One can only conclude that, whatever theoretical approval More gave the laws against heresy, he always stretched the law as far as he could in favor of the accused. It was during the three years of his retirement—1532-1535—that the laws were enforced with much greater vigor, precisely because the breach that had come with the papacy made the authorities (perhaps unconsciously) desire to show how very orthodox they were. During those years the number of burnings at Smithfield leaped from three to sixteen.

It is possible to do even more than prove that More was not a persecutor, for it can be shown from at least one striking episode how very kind and courteous he could be to a heretic when he was not dangerous. While he was Chancellor he entertained at Chelsea Simon Grinaeus, a German Lutheran, who was in England on a scholar's mission of gathering ancient classical texts for publication. It is probable that More, in giving Grinaeus his secretary, John Harris, as a guide when he visited Oxford University, intended to keep him under surveillance. But such was his duty, and it was not performed so officiously as to make Grinaeus conscious of it. As to this we have the scholar's own account when he gratefully dedicated one of his books to More's son. For there he writes: "Your father at that time held the highest rank, but apart from that, by his many excellent qualities, he was already marked out to be the chief man in the realm, while I was obscure and unknown. Yet for the love of learning in the midst of private and public business he found time to converse much with me: he the Chancellor of the Kingdom, made me sit at his table: going to and from the Court he took me with him and kept me ever at his side. He had no difficulty in seeing that my religious opinions were on many points different from his own, but his goodness and courtesy were unchanged. Though he differed so much from my views, yet he helped us in word and deed and carried through my business at his own expense. He gave us a young man, John Harris, to accompany us on our journey, and to the authorities of the University of Oxford he sent a letter couched in such terms that at once not only were the libraries of all the colleges thrown open to us, but the students, as if they had been touched by the rod of Mercury, showed us the greatest favour. Accordingly I searched all the libraries of the University, some twenty in number. They are all richly stocked with ancient books, and with the permission of the authorities I took away several books of the commentaries of Proclus—as many perhaps as could be set up in print within a year or two. I returned to my country overjoyed at the treasures I had discovered, laden with your father's generous gifts and almost overwhelmed by his kindness." The warmth of this good German, a theologian and a professor of Greek and Latin at Heidelberg, is apparent and no doubt accounts for the reception he received in England. But this does not in any way detract from what is revealed of the kind and generous heart of the Lord Chancellor.

CHAPTER FIFTEEN

Chancellor No More

On May 15, 1532, Sir Thomas More was permitted to resign the Chancellorship. The previous day Parliament had been prorogued, making it convenient for More to retire. He had been pleading ill health for some time, and now at last his friend, the Duke of Norfolk, persuaded the King to release More from the burdens of office.

Roper tells a story about this that is a little difficult to credit without an explanation we lack. After Mass the next day Sir Thomas, instead of sending one of his gentlemen attendants to the women's side of the church, where Dame Alice had her pew, to say with a low bow, "Madam, my lord is gone," and to escort the ladies home—himself performed this little ceremony. The inference is that this was his jocular way of breaking the news.

We can hardly believe that this could have been Dame Alice's first inkling of the matter, yet Stapleton says that Dame Alice remarked, "No doubt it pleases you, Master More, to joke in this fashion," and was in great astonishment and distress when she found that her husband was speaking the sober truth. Stapleton adds, "By this humourous way of making the announcement, More wished to soften the blow for his wife and to show what little account he made of his high honour." Cresacre More further embellishes it by telling us that More asked his daughters, "Do you not perceive that your mother's nose standeth somewhat awry?" No doubt poor Lady More's nose *was* put out of joint, yet that kind of rough banter would have been a good deal less than kind. The jest of the privileged Henry Patenson, the clown, was not so unseemly. He merely said, "Chancellor More is Chancellor no more."

More's health was not a pretext for freeing himself from disagreeable duties, for he wrote to Erasmus to tell him that he had a disorder of the chest, he did not know of what nature, except that, "I saw that I must either lay down my office or fail in the performance of its duties. . . . If I were to die I should have to give up my office as well as my life, so I determined to give up one rather than both!" He went on, "We are not all Erasmuses. Here are you, in a condition which would break the spirit of a vigorous youth, still bringing out book after book for the instruction and admiration of the world." He did, however, indicate in the same letter that resignation was an immense relief. "From the time of my boyhood, dearest Desiderius, I have longed that I might some day enjoy what I rejoice in *your* having always enjoyed—namely, that being free of public business, I might have some time to devote to God and myself. This, by the grace of a great and good God, and by the favour of an indulgent prince, I have at last obtained."

He was not, however, idle, for it is very difficult for a man active by nature to do nothing. So More devoted the years of his retirement to writing, completing that same year his *Confutation of Tyndale's Answer* (to his *Dialogue* of 1528), his *Reply* to Frith's treatise on the Sacrament and, in the following year, his *Debellation of Salem and Bizance,* a book in refuation of a nameless heretic (whom we now know to have been Tyndale[1]) who had written *The Supper of the Lord,* and finally, his *Apology.* But as More's controversial writings have been considered in an earlier chapter, there is no need to say more here, except to repeat that he continued to avoid the papal issue and to stress only those points of religion upon which Henry prided himself for being orthodox. Though perhaps not everything More said in defence of the clergy was altogether to the King's taste, there was at least nothing to which he could object. What might still be hoped for was what all the bishops (Cranmer excepted) and the vast majority of the people hoped for: that the tempest would blow

[1] More suspected Tyndale's authorship, but thought George Jay might have written the book. Certainty being lacking, he referred to the author as the "Masker".

itself out and that the ancient liberty of the English Church would be restored. Meanwhile a good deal would be effected if More could keep his fellow-countrymen faithful to the body of Catholic doctrines regarding the Mass, Purgatory and the invocation of saints. Also he might be able to allay some part of the anti-clerical spirit that was arising, for his knowledge of men told him that most of them are actuated not by abstract considerations but by personal animosities and grievances even when they believe themselves to be most strictly logical.

Of no man was this more true than of Henry VIII. On January 25, 1533, he was secretly married to Anne Boleyn, and though this fact was not publicly announced until the King had in the following May obtained the annulment of his marriage with Katherine of Aragon, it was by no means a rumor that Anne was already with child and that Henry intended to make her Queen. Five days after Cranmer pronounced the King's former marriage invalid, Anne Boleyn was solemnly crowned at Westminister, dressed in white satin as though she were a virgin bride.

To this ceremony (which was not necessary in the case of a Queen-Consort, but which Henry insisted upon) More was invited, and he was expected to be present. Yet he did not go, although his friends the Bishops of Bath and Durham (Clerk and Tunstall), who knew that his absence would be marked, wrote urging him to attend. So also did Stephen Gardiner who, as Lord Chancellor under Mary, was to play a prominent part in the restoration of Catholicism during her reign. All these men More knew to share his opinions, so they supposed he could hardly resist their appeal. To enforce it they sent him £20 for the buying of a new gown for the great occasion.

This money he kept, explaining when he next met the Bishops: "I took you for no beggars, and myself I knew to be a poor man." His non-attendance at Westminster Abbey he explained by telling them a story about a Roman emperor who made a certain offence punishable with death, unless it happened to have been committed by a virgin, because he had such deep reverence for virginity. He was put into a difficulty when the very first offender proved to be a virgin. But one of his counsellors—"a good plain man," said More ironically—made the happy suggestion "First let her be deflowered, and then after she may be devoured." More pointed his parable by telling the Bishops: "So though your Lordships have in the matter of the matrimony kept yourselves pure virgins, yet take heed, my Lords, that you keep your virginity still. For some there be that by procuring your Lordships first at the coronation to be present, and next to preach for the setting forth of it, and finally to write books to all the world in defence thereof, are desirous to deflower you; and when they have deflowered you, then they will not fail to devour you." He concluded by telling them: "Now my Lords, it lieth not within my power but that they may devour me; but God being my good Lord, I will provide that they shall never deflower me."

Lounging in his old clothes among the flower-beds at Chelsea on Coronation Day, he understood very well that Anne was now in a position to make Henry take vengeance for what she would be sure to regard as an insult. All the more was she incensed because of the sullen behavior of the London crowds on that jubilant occasion. In fact the previous August she had been waylaid by a band of men and women disguised as men, who would have lynched her could they have caught her just then. Though More had never spoken a word in public against her marriage, it was common knowledge that he disapproved of it. By staying away from her crowning, Anne considered that he had marked his disapproval before the world. More realized that she would seek her revenge.

Yet More and Henry had parted good friends and with compliments on both sides. And More was able to write to Erasmus in the late spring of 1533: "As yet no one has come forward to attack me. Either I have been so innocent or else so cautious, that my opponents must let me boast of one or other of these qualities. But as regards this business, the King has spoken to me many times privately, and twice in public. For in words that I am ashamed to repeat, when my successor (a most illustrious man) was installed, the King, by the mouth of the Duke of Norfolk, the Lord High Treasurer of England, ordained that an honourable testimony be given that with difficulty he had yielded to my request to retire. And not content with this, the King, out of his singular goodness to me, had the same thing repeated by my successor in my own presence, at the solemn assembly of the Peers and Commons, in the speech which he made at the opening of Parliament."

More knew, however, that, good as might be Henry's intentions, he was now under the influence of Anne. In a very confidential conversation with Roper, he said: "God give grace, son, that these matters within a while be not confirmed with oaths." At this Roper says that he was much offended with his father-in-law, for he saw no likelihood of an oath being exacted, yet he feared that by prophesying it, More might help to bring it to pass. These forebodings were not concealed from the family, and either then or a little later, Roper records his telling them, "If he would perceive his wife and children would encourage him to die in a good cause, it should so comfort him that, for very joy thereof, it would make him merrily run to death."

He was in straitened circumstances now. He had lost his official salary, and he had never saved much money, spending everything as it came in upon his household and his private charities. All that was left was an income from the lands—an amount given once as a hundred pounds, and another time as fifty. As he had never asked the King for anything during the years of his service, his rewards had been meagre. And from old Sir John More's estate—he was nearly eighty at the time of his death from a surfeit of grapes in 1530—nothing would come until the death of his widow. Drastic retrenchment was, therefore, necessary.

Roper describes how Sir Thomas called his children and their families together and explained that he was no longer able to pay all the expenses of the household, as he had gladly done in the past, and so asked for their suggestions. When they were silent, out of their reluctance to tell him their opinion, More went on: "Then I will show my poor mind unto you. I have been brought up at Oxford, at an Inn of Chancery, at Lincoln's Inn, and also in the King's Court, and so forth from the lowest degree to the highest, and yet have I in yearly revenues at this present left a little above an hundred pounds by the year.[2] So now must we hereafter, if we like to live together, to be contented to become contributaries together. But, by my counsel, it shall not be best for us to fall to the lowest fare first, nor to the fare of New Inn. But we will begin with the Lincoln's Inn diet, where many right worshipful and of good years do live full well; which, if we find not ourselves the first year able to maintain, then will we the next year go one step down to the New Inn fare, wherewith many an honest man is well contented. If that exceed our ability too, then will we the next year descend to Oxford fare, where many grave, learned, and ancient fathers be continually conversant; which if our power stretch not to maintain neither, then may we yet, with bags and wallets go begging together, and hoping for pity some good folks will give us their charity, at every man's doors to sing *Salve Regina,* and so keep company and be merry together."

This piece of mingled humor and good sense is just like More. And it is clear from what we hear of the whole family assembling at night before a huge fire made of ferns, instead of ordinary and better fuel, that strict economies had to be introduced. These appear to have been too strict for the Daunces and the Herons and, as they had ample means of their own, they moved into separate establishments. John Clement and his wife, Margaret Giggs, were living in More's former house, at Bucklersbury, as more suitable, presumably, for Dr. Clement's medical practice. Only the Ropers and their children remained at Chelsea, though even they took another house there, and with them went the devoted Dorothy Colley. Though Sir Thomas and Dame Alice could not have been

[2] As in his *Apology* More says that it was only £50, we must conclude that the smaller figure referred only to his income from property. For the time being he retained his salary as Councillor—£100.

in positive want, they must have been hard put to it to maintain their great house. Yet it was at that moment that More refused the four or five thousand pounds we know the English Bishops to have pressed upon him for his services as a controversialist. At the high rates of interest that prevailed, it would have brought in an income about equal to the one he had lost and have secured his family's future after his death. Yet he would have nothing to do with it, lest any mercenary taint appear to lessen the effect of what he had done for the Church. He did, however, foreseeing that it was quite possible that a charge of treason would eventually be brought against him, and knowing that this would mean the confiscation of everything he owned, prudently make over to his wife and children the legacies they would inherit, reserving only a life-interest for himself.[3] At the same time he tried to prepare his family spiritually for the misfortunes he saw ahead, Roper telling how "he would talk with his wife and children of the joys of heaven and the pains of hell, of the lives of the holy martyrs, of their grievous martyrdoms, of their marvellous patience, and of their passions and death that they suffered rather than offend God. And what a happy and blessed thing it was, for the love of God, to suffer loss of goods, imprisonment, loss of lands and life also." One day—this must have been shortly before he was actually sent for by the authorities—he even arranged that a man impersonating the King's apparitor should come into the room to give him a summons to appear the next day before the Commissioners. More observed how each person present took the dreaded news, and praised or commended as to whether it was received bravely or with tears. The characteristic practical joke had a very practical purpose. He himself, though firmly set in his resolve, many a night lay awake by Dame Alice's side, as he was later to tell Margaret Roper, sleepless with anxiety over what would happen to those dear to him.

[3] He did not, unfortunately, safeguard this arrangement carefully enough, except in the case of the Ropers, to whom he gave their share unconditionally. The result was the rest of his family got nothing, except for a small pension the Crown allowed, as an act of grace, to More's widow after his execution.

He had never had any illusions. Thus when Thomas Cromwell, who was now mounting rapidly in the King's favor, came to him one day with a message from Henry, More took it upon himself to offer some advice. "Master Cromwell," he said, "you are now entered into the service of a most noble, wise and liberal prince. If you will follow my poor advice, you shall in your counsel-giving unto his Grace, ever tell him what he ought to do, but never what he is able to do. So shall you show yourself a true faithful servant and a right worthy counsellor. For if a lion knew his own strength, hard were it for any man to rule him." The advice was of course wasted upon that unscrupulous Machiavellian. Not only was the Lion discovering his strength, and developing an appetite that grew with eating, but it was Cromwell's function to invent devices by means of which the royal rapacity might be indulged with a show of legality.

Yet Cromwell had no personal malice towards More, or perhaps towards anybody. He exercised his craft quite dispassionately for the ends he set before himself. To More he professed to the end the sincerest good will. In so far as his influence extended at this time, he seems to have used it to protect More. Similarly the Duke of Norfolk—a far more simple and honest man than Cromwell—gave him friendly warnings a little later. "By the Mass, Master More," he said to him one day, "it is perilous striving with princes. And therefore I would wish you somewhat to incline to the King's pleasure." To this More had merely smiled in answering, "Is that all, my Lord? Then in good faith there is no more difference between your Grace and me, but that I shall die today, and you tomorrow." The Duke's "tomorrow" did not, in fact, come for twenty years, but he was condemned to death for high treason in 1547 and was saved only by the King's death a few hours before the time set for his execution.

Attacks upon him, as More wrote to Erasmus, did not come at once. And at first they were veiled, for as yet the statute calling for the oath, refusing which he went to the block on Tower Hill, was not passed. His enemies, however, cast around for some charge that would at least discredit him. They thought they had found it in the case of a suit a man named Parnell had brought against another man named Vaughan, and More was accused of having accepted a gilt silver cup from Mrs. Vaughan as a bribe. Haled before the Council, More admitted that "of courtesy [he had] refused not to accept it." Immediately Lord Wiltshire, Anne Boleyn's father, a fellow notorious for his greed, rather stupidly showed his hand. "Lo, did I not tell you, my Lords," he exclaimed, "that you should find this matter true?" More was unruffled and asked that, as the Council had heard a part of the tale, they would listen to the rest. Then it was proved that, though he had accepted the cup, he had immediately made his butler fill it with wine. After he and Mrs. Vaughan had pledged one another, he returned the cup for her to give to her husband as a New Year's gift. "Thus the great mountain," comments Roper, "was turned to a little molehill."[4]

But the Boleyn gang had not done with him. They brought forward the case of a rich widow, a Mrs Crocker, for whom in a lawsuit he had decided against Lord Arundel. She had presented More with a pair of gloves as a New Year's present, and the gloves contained forty gold angels. What More was able to show was that he had kept the gloves for the sake of good manners, but had made Mrs. Crocker take her money back.

There was a third case—again of a New Year's gift. A Mr. Gresham who had a cause pending in Chancery presented More with a gilt cup, "the fashion whereof he very well liking, caused one of his own (though not in his fantasy of so good a fashion, yet better in value) to be brought out of his chamber, which he willed the messenger, in recompense, to deliver to his master; and on other condition would he in no wise received it." Though Lord Russell of Killowen, a judge of our own time, thinks More's conduct here was injudicious, adding, "I should have liked to

[4] Professor Chambers points out that the details of this case are on official record. It was heard before More as Chancellor on January 20, 1531.

have seen Mistress Crocker committed for contempt of court,"[5] More's integrity was demonstrated. All that the Boleyns got out of these spiteful proceedings were reddened faces but doubtless a fiercer anger.

The inescapable issue was approaching rapidly, but before its arrival a more serious charge than judicial malfeasance was, it was supposed, discovered. At the end of 1533 a proclamation was issued by the Council justifying the King's marriage, and in reply to this a pamphlet appeared, bearing neither the author's nor printer's name. More was accused of writing it, and William Rastell of printing it. More easily cleared himself and his nephew, and wrote to Cromwell denying that he would ever have been so foolish or so proud as to have had any hand in a matter "whereof I never was sufficiently learned in the laws, nor fully instructed in the facts." He goes on to say that, though he is always ready, should the King command him, to discharge his conscience by declaring what was in his mind, "yet surely if it should happen any book to come abroad in the name of his Grace or his honourable Council, if that book seemed such as myself would not have given mine own advice in making, yet I know my bounden duty to bear more honour to my Prince, and more reverence to his honourable Council, than that it would become me for many causes to answer such a book, or to counsel and advise any man else to do it."

After all these mare's nests, the opportunity at last came of bringing against More, and also against John Fisher, the charge of misprision of treason. It made them liable if convicted—and Fisher was so convicted, by attainder, not after open trial in court—to the confiscation of their property, though not to capital

[5] In *The Fame of Blessed Thomas More,* p. 74. Sir James Mackintosh expresses surprise that the early biographers mentioned More's conduct as extraordinary acts of virtue, but says that their doing so shows the corrupt state of public opinion at the time. "It would," he adds, "be an indignity to the memory of such a man to quote these facts as proof of his own probity; but they may be mentioned as specimens of the simple and unforced honesty of one who rejected improper offers with all the ease and pleasantry of common courtesy."

punishment. Against each man the charge was preferred as a means of exerting pressure, of making the threat of attainder "so troublous and terrible" that it would force them to say that they approved of the King's divorce and of the rejection of papal authority.

In that it failed completely, though in what follows it may be thought that More was a little too eager to disavow all connection with the affair and that he was even unduly harsh upon the poor woman concerned, Elizabeth Barton, the notorious "Nun of Kent." But it must be remembered that More was absolutely innocent, and that he deplored the indiscretion of those who had given Sister Elizabeth any sort of countenance. He can, therefore, hardly be blamed for seizing so excellent a chance for demonstrating his loyalty. No word that he could have spoken could have helped the Nun of Kent, or any have damaged her further. What More wrote to Cromwell regarding her was, "You have done in my mind to your great laud and praise a very meritorious act in bringing forth to light such detestable hypocrisy whereby other wretches may take warning and be feared to set forth their own devilish dissimulated falsehood under the name and colour of the wonderful work of God." After all, she *had* publicly confessed at Paul's Cross that she was an imposter.

Elizabeth Barton, whose name made such a stir for a while, was probably nothing worse than hysterical. She had been a maidservant and after having been cured of epilepsy—miraculously she claimed—she became a Benedictine nun. Then she had trances and visions, and took upon herself the role of prophecy. Many people were impressed, including the King and Wolsey, both of whom she saw. She kept this up until she reached the point where she was shown to be a false prophet by predicting that the King would die seven months after his marriage to Anne Boleyn. Even after that she continued to be a center of disaffection, though hardly a dangerous one. But she was made a convenient scapegoat, and she and several priests who were looked upon as her accomplices—they had certainly been her injudicious advisers

—were executed with the usual barbarities at Tyburn, though not until six months after her confession of November 23, 1533. She was probably kept alive so long in the hope of extracting from her further information that might incriminate More.

More was able to show that he had been most circumspect in his relations with her. It is true that he had been induced, rather against his will, to make her a visit, but then he had counselled her to keep to spiritual concerns and especially not to meddle with politics. He reminded her that for a chance word, spoken to a monk, the Duke of Buckingham had been beheaded in 1521. All this More set out in a long detailed letter to Cromwell, in which he enclosed a copy of the one letter he had written the nun. Investigation corroborated every word he said.

Even so, More was summoned before a commission made up of Audley and Norfolk and Cranmer and Cromwell, who received him with a show of courtesy, inviting him to sit down. Audley reminded him "how many ways the King had shown his love and favour towards him" and said that More "could ask no worldly honour nor profit at his hands that were likely to be denied him." All they wanted from him was that he should add his consent to what Parliament, the universities and the bishops had done regarding the royal divorce.

When More refused that consent, their mood suddenly changed. They told him that "by his subtle sinister sleights" he had induced the King to write his book against Luther, "to put a sword into the Pope's hands to fight against himself." To this More made the scornful answer, "My Lords, these terrors be arguments for children, not for me." As for the King's book, "None," he said, "is there that can in that point say in my excuse more than his Highness himself." He had merely helped him to arrange the material, and at that time (1521) had advised him to stress the Pope's authority more lightly. But the King had told him then, "We are so much bounden unto the See of Rome that we cannot do too much honour to it." And when More reminded Henry of the statute of praemunire, the reply that came was

"Whatsoever impediment be to the contrary, we will set forth that authority to the uttermost. For we have received from that See our crown imperial," regarding which surprising and unexplained statement More added that until "his Grace with his own mouth told it me, I never heard of it before."

Such words were very bold, as More knew that they would be carried back to the king. He also took a rather sly dig in Henry's direction when he said that it was the King's arguments that had converted him on this point, for until then he had thought of the Pope's jurisdiction as something that reposed on tradition rather than as being directly instituted by God. What More said must have carried conviction, for he was allowed to go home at the end of the examination.

On the journey there he seemed so pleased that Roper, who was in the barge with him, concluded that the trouble had blown over. "I trust, sir," he said to his father-in-law, when they were walking in the garden upon their arrival at Chelsea, "that all is well because you are so merry."

To which More answered, "It is so indeed, son Roper, I thank God."

"Are you then out of the parliament bill?"

The astonishing answer came, "By my troth, son Roper, I never remembered it."

"Never remembered it!" Roper exclaimed. "A case that toucheth yourself so near, and us all for your sake!"

Then More asked, "Wilt thou know, son Roper, why I was so merry?"

"That would I gladly, sir."

He got another astonishing answer: "In good faith, I rejoiced, son, that I had given the devil a foul fall, and that with these lords I had gone so far, as without shame I could never go back." He was so merry because he had already burned his bridges.

His name was still in the bill of attainder, and though Cromwell had in his hands evidence completely exculpating More of having in any way supported the Nun of Kent, this evidence it might have been within his power to suppress. That, however, might have been a risky thing to have attempted, so the Lord Chancellor had to tell the King quite plainly that the House of Lords was determined to hear More in his own defence, and "that if he were not put out of the bill, it would without fail be utterly overthrown of all." The Crown could not afford to chance a rebuff for the sake of attainting More.

But the King was now so offended with More that he roared that he would if necessary go to the House of Lords himself to overawe the peers. "Then the Lord Audley and the rest," writes Roper, "seeing him so vehemently set thereupon, on their knees most humbly besought his Grace to forbear the same, considering that if he should, in his own presence, receive an overthrow, it would not only encourage his subjects ever after to contemn him, but also throughout all Christendom redound to his dishonour for ever." Seeing that the King was still obstinate and ready to risk the embarrassment of a defeat in the House of Lords, Audley added, "that they mistrusted not in time against him to find some meeter matter to serve his turn better." It is clear that Henry was ragingly determined to compel More to do as was required, or to have his head. And the Council, full though it was of More's friends, was willing to ruin him. After all, every one of them had an easily detachable head.

The day after this scene Cromwell ran into Roper in the House of Commons—where Roper sat for Bramber in Sussex[6]—and had good news for him. It was that More's name had been deleted from the bill of attainder. At once Roper sent off a note to his wife, as he had a dinner engagement in London. Margaret as soon as she got it ran to her father with a radiant face to tell him what she had just heard. He received it without elation, saying in the Latin they so often used in conversation, "In faith, Meg, what is deferred is not disposed of." He understood the situation perfectly. He had,

[6] More's other two sons-in-law were also Members of Parliament, as was Sir Giles Alington, the husband of his step-daughter.

indeed, given the devil a good fall. He had already said to the members of the Council who had examined him things upon which he could not, with a good grace, go back. But now it would only be a question of time before the resourceful Cromwell found a better handle against him. Behind Cromwell and the King was the new queen, whom Chapuys always called "the Concubine" in his dispatches to the Emperor. When the "meeter matter" came to their hands, they would strike to kill.

CHAPTER SIXTEEN

The Inescapable Issue

HE DID not have very long to wait. His name was dropped from the bill of attainder on February 21, 1534. On Low Sunday, the April 12th following, he went with Roper to hear the sermon at St. Paul's, dropping in afterwards at Bucklersbury to see Dr. Clement and his wife. The officer commissioned to summon him to appear at Lambeth had noticed him among the congregation and followed him to serve the papers. This meant, as Sir Thomas knew very well, that he would be called upon to take an oath which he would be obliged to refuse. And that almost certainly would mean his death. The Nun of Kent was executed on April 21st as the government now had no use for her except to adorn Tyburn. More could be sent there without her assistance.

The issues that would be brought up by the oath he had avoided as long as possible. But he had never deceived himself with hopes that he would be left unmolested indefinitely. A year or two previously he had told Roper that he feared that the royal marriage would eventually involve an oath. The law calling for this had been passed. Now his time had come.

But before continuing with More's own story it is necessary to trace the events leading to a complete breach with the papacy. It had not come about at a single stroke, but gradually over a period of over five years, with Henry claiming a little more at each step until, as Bishop Stubbs put it, he managed to make himself for England "the pope, the whole pope, and something more than the pope." For though he was not even yet exercising doctrinal jurisdiction, that was implicit in the acts he had forced through a not too willing Parliament, packed though it was with "king's men." As Pollard sums it up, "In Henry's reign the English spirit of independence burned low in its socket, and love of freedom grew cold."

Yet it must be remembered that, though England was overwhelmingly Catholic, the central issue of the papacy was clear as yet to very few people. It had not always been clear to More himself, until as he had recently impishly told his examiners, the King had converted him by his book against Luther. He had added in the letter he wrote to Cromwell that he did not intend to meddle in the matter of the primacy of the Pope, though at the same time he made it clear that after ten years' study, he could not deny the primacy "to be provided by God."[1] He went on to say that even those who could not admit this should see that "that primacy is at the leastwise instituted by the corps of Christendom, and for a great urgent cause in avoiding schisms. . . . And, therefore, since all Christendom is one corps, I cannot conceive how any member thereof may, without the common consent of the body, depart from the common head."

Here More intended to clarify his own position, which it would have been futile of him to deny. But the bit about the departure by common consent of any member of Christendom from the whole body was of course merely an impossible hypothetical case. So also was More dealing with an impossibility in wishing the King luck, or what he called "comfortable speed," in his appeal to a General Council from the Pope. Such an appeal could not be made, nor did Henry—despite all his talk—ever wish it to be made. Blandly More pointed out that it could do the King's cause no good to deny the authority of the only person competent to summon a General Council. The King's latest actions had been quite as much a rejection of the General Council as of the Pope. Recent legislation had severed England not only from the Roman obedience but from the unity of Christendom. More did not need to stress these implications to so clever a man as Cromwell. It was enough to indicate that the whole situation was full of logical impossibilities.

Yet not even to More and Fisher—and Fisher was the only one

[1] The version Rastell printed says "seven," but "ten" is in the original manuscript.

of the English bishops ready to die in defence of the Pope's supremacy—was the issue so plain as it is now. Complete crystallization did not come until the proclamation in 1870 of the dogma of the Pope's infallibility when speaking *ex cathedra* on faith or morals. More himself seems to have held a position that would not be permissible to a Catholic today, when he suggested that a General Council was superior even to the Pope. However, what he did affirm regarding the Pope's authority was perhaps sufficient for practical purposes just then. More than what he maintained would have seemed excessive to everybody. As it was, his quiet fidelity was of inestimable value to the Catholics of Elizabeth's time. For had he not stood firm and brought the issue into the open, it is quite possible that the Protestant triumph would have been so complete that England would have seen Catholicism wholly eradicated, as it was in Scandinavia.

More's firm certainty in this matter is all the more remarkable when we remember that the prestige of the papacy had been immensely damaged by the claims of rival popes and anti-popes, and that, more recently, several of the popes were hardly notable for their private virtues, even if there was only one Alexander VI. When a man like Wolsey could aspire to the keys of Peter, and lose them only because of political considerations, it looked as though the triple tiara had become very tarnished.

And other powerful forces were at work against the tradition of Christendom. The concept of nationalism was rising and with it an exaggerated notion of kingship, ideas subsequently to be transformed to work further havoc in the emergence of the omnicompetent state. And behind the King, since the virtual extermination of the old aristocracy during the Wars of the Roses, were the new nobility, men largely without principles or manners, though often of great energy and ability, almost all of them perceiving that advantage might accrue to them from the impending changes in the framework of society.

Actual and professed Protestants were very few, but all fanatically enthusiastic. Their effect would have been negligible had they not been used by cynical politicians with the connivance of weak and subservient prelates. And there was in England a widespread feeling of animosity against the clergy. In the eyes of everybody Cardinal Wolsey stood as the embodiment of an ecclesiastical system that had grown obnoxious. However sincerely the Cardinal may have tried to defend the liberties of the English Church, he had nevertheless made it extremely vulnerable by having concentrated all ecclesiastical power into his own hands as Legate and Lord Chancellor. As Pollard remarks, "The papal legate had cowed the English clergy before they submitted to Henry VIII." When Wolsey fell it became a simple matter to transfer all the power he had possessed to the King, adding to the royal supremacy what little Wolsey had lacked. In fact, there was so general a sense of relief when the Cardinal passed from the scene—and especially among the hierarchy that had been ruled by him with an iron hand—that his replacement by Henry was in many instances welcomed by those who should have disapproved of it most. The upshot was that, while England remained strongly Catholic in doctrine and practice, the assertion of the King's supremacy seemed to most people natural, inevitable and even beneficent. In any event, it appeared to few to be a matter upon which the claims of the King could be resisted.

In spite of all this the changes could be made only step by step. How far this was by design we cannot be sure, but it is certain that there would have been more opposition than there actually was had Henry asserted his supremacy in its plenitude at once. He told the imperial ambassador, Chapuys, on one occasion that he was carefully watching public sentiment, so as to learn how far he might go and at what point he had to stop. And as late as February, 1533, he got the Nuncio to go with him to the opening of Parliament, as though to show that he had not finally broken with the Pope. This in spite of the facts that he had secretly married Anne Boleyn in defiance of the Pope only the month before, and that Parliament had been summoned to make the royal supremacy statutory.

The events leading up to this should be briefly considered. When the Convocation of the Clergy of the province of Canterbury met in Westminster Abbey on January 21, 1531, they were told that the whole clerical body was guilty under the law of praemunire. Supposing that this was merely a lever to extract a larger gift of money for the King than was customary, they voted him £40,000, and when this was refused, £100,000. Similarly the Convocation of York voted £19,000 to buy their pardon from the King. Though these sums were so enormous that they could be met only by the sale of valuable Church plate, Henry would not accept their "gracious gift" unless they recognized him as "Protector and Supreme Head of the English Church and Clergy." The Nuncio tried to persuade them to resist, but they were too frightened even to permit him to remain among them. Yet they demurred to giving the King the title demanded, and when Lord Rochford, Anne Boleyn's brother, proposed as an alternative formula, "The Supreme Head after God," they quite rightly considered that as still worse. In the end old Warham, the Archbishop of Canterbury, offered at Fisher's suggestion, "We recognise his Majesty as the Singular Protector, and only Supreme Lord, and so far as the law of Christ allows, even Supreme Head." When Convocation was silent, Warham declared the resolution passed in silence. The reservation "so far as the law of Christ allows" was disliked by the King, who wished no qualifications of any kind, but was for some time permitted. It salved the consciences of those unable to agree that the King *could* be Head of the Church. Such people took the oath willingly enough because of the phrase that might be considered to have made it meaningless. Sir Thomas More was never allowed to take it in this form, but many people, including some of the members of his household, had this less drastic oath presented to them even after the more stringent one had been introduced. More was reserved for an unequivocal adhesion.

The first title remained for a couple of years, more a threat against the Pope than a formal denial of his authority. So also with the bill introduced in Parliament on January 15, 1532, abolishing the annates, the first year's revenue each newly appointed bishop paid the Pope. Henry forced its passage by going down to both Houses and making the members vote in his presence. Clement VII was given to understand that the annates would be paid, as formerly, as soon as he had annulled the King's marriage.

Later that same year Henry proceeded further. He suddenly discovered that the clergy were only half his subjects, "for all the prelates at their consecration make an oath to the Pope clean contrary to the oath they make to us, so that they seem to be his subjects and not ours." Accordingly he demanded that they renounce their right to frame any ecclesiastical laws. Convocation accepted this, though with extreme reluctance and indicating that the transference to the King of its authority was only to him personally, and because of the confidence the clergy had in his "excellent wisdom, princely goodness, and fervent zeal to the promotion of God's honour and the Christian religion." They also praised his learning, "far exceeding in our judgment the learning of all other kings and princes that we have read of." This concession, known as the Submission of the Clergy, was given statutory effect by the House of Commons but failed in the Lords, where the opposition was led by More. When that Parliament wound up its work on May 14th, More resigned the Chancellorship the following day.

As we have already seen, he was not permitted to retire into the obscure and inoffensive life of a private subject of the King. In a consistory held in the spring of 1534 the Pope at last declared the marriage of Henry and Katherine to be valid. This meant that the King had to accept the Pope's decision or to incur the penalty of excommunication. As was expected, Henry at once cut the last link that bound the English Church to Rome. The Submission of the Clergy was reintroduced into the House of Lords and this time passed, thus becoming law. The final touch was put upon the schism when, in March, 1534, the succession to the throne was secured to Anne Boleyn's children, the Act at the same time affirming that the King's previous marriage had been against the law of

God and subjecting those who should in any way deny this to the penalties of misprision of treason.

All who were of legal age might be called upon to take an oath confirming their acceptance of this, and now no qualifying clause was allowed. The precise form of the oath, however, had not been indicated by Parliament, but was drawn up by the Council in a way that exceeded Parliament's intentions. As such, its legality was, to say the least, open to question. Nevertheless, the King was now panoplied to proceed against any of his subjects who would not take the oath, thus gaining an authority in spiritual matters that was virtually unrestricted, whereas in secular affairs the Constitution limited his powers.

We can now return to More's own story.

When he was served notice on April 12th that he had to appear the next day before the Commissioners at Lambeth Palace, he immediately left Dr. Clement's house and went home to set his affairs in order and to say farewell to his wife and family.

Early the following morning he heard Mass and made his confession and received Holy Communion, as was his custom on any important occasion. As it does not appear that this privilege was granted him while he was in the Tower, even on the day of his execution, it must be supposed that this was the last time he took any part in the offices of the Church, though he still had fifteen months of life ahead of him.

Spring was in flower in his famous garden when he went down to the landing pier at its foot, where a barge was waiting for him. Roper tells us how this time More's heart was too full to allow any of the family, except himself, to accompany him, as they usually did, kissing him goodbye just before he got on board. He did not know whether he would ever see any of them again, and his house and garden he never did see. The rosemary and the orchard trees and the rose-beds were in a mist before his eyes. He hastily pulled the wicket-gate behind him, so as to avoid all lamentations. Accompanied only by Roper and by four rowers he headed downstream towards Lambeth.

On the way there he suddenly put his hand to his son-in-law's ear and whispered, "Son Roper, I thank God the field is won." Roper had no idea what he meant by this, yet as he was loth to seem ignorant he answered gravely, "Sir, I am very glad thereof." Reflecting on his father-in-law's words afterwards, he concluded that More's love of God had "wrought in him so effectually that he had conquered all his carnal affections utterly." Another way of putting this is to say that Roper knew that More was now resolved not to take the oath, whatever the consequences might be.

More landed and entered the palace of the Archbishop of Canterbury by the great brick gatehouse that had been abuilding when he was a page in Morton's household more than forty years earlier. A different sort of man was there now as Archbishop, the pliable, obsequious, adroit, but sufficiently kindly Thomas Cranmer. With him were the Lord Chancellor, Sir Thomas Audley (he was not made Baron Audley of Walden until 1538) and Cromwell and Benson, the Abbot of Westminster. The Dukes of Norfolk and Suffolk were also members of the Commission for taking the oath, but we do not hear of their being present.

More was the one layman summoned that day. The Members of Parliament had already taken the oath, and among them were Roper and More's other sons-in-law. It is clear that he had been singled out because of his well-known disapproval of the divorce and because of the part he had taken in the rejection in 1532 by the House of Lords of the statute under which the oath was later made enforceable by law.

Those waiting for him were all of them men younger than More, though he was only fifty-six. And all of them except Benson, a lickspittle Benedictine who had gained a brief preferment by acting as Cromwell's "man," were of some distinction. This is true even of Audley, though he had cunning and dexterity and good looks and pleasant manners rather than first-rate intellectual parts. Cranmer and Cromwell, however, were, in their way, quite exceptional men who have left a deep imprint on history.

The Archbishop was only forty-five. Looking at him one saw a short, thick-set man with a weak mouth and timid eyes. He was to betray his patroness, Anne Boleyn, with a terrified letter to Henry that purported to be written in her defence, and he was to do the same thing a few years later to Cromwell. He was in his position in spite of himself—for he was devoid of ambition—and only because his peculiar talents made him indispensable. His subservience was so absolute as to become a kind of unthinking but quite sincere loyalty. Ragged and rambling as was his ordinary literary style, he could, when the occasion demanded it, show himself a master of English prose. The *Book of Common Prayer* is his imperishable monument.

Unquestionably the captain of the group was Cromwell. He probably was the architect of the policy of the schism, carefully arranging for its gradual development. Certainly he was the main instrument for its being carried to success. He had been in turn a soldier of sorts, a clerk in Antwerp (under the name of Thomas Smyth), and, after his return to England, a lawyer, money-lender and a cloth-merchant, before being taken into Wolsey's service. Prompt in abandoning that master on his fall, he had made himself invaluable to Henry, and was to be his Vicar-general over the English Church he plundered so ruthlessly. At first glance one noticed only his heavy pasty face. But his little eyes were alive with intelligence, and he could be witty and affable. His thin-lipped mouth hardly moved in his quite unemphasized way of speaking. His round head was concealed by a velvet hat. He had no malice or personal animosities—at any rate not against More—but this may have made him all the more dangerous. We still have the memoranda he made when he was plundering the monasteries—things such as: "*Item.* The Abbot of Redyng [Reading] to be sent down to be tried and executed at Redyng with his accomplices. . . *Item.* To see that the evidence be well sorted and the indictments well drawn against the said abbots and their accomplices." An earlier entry of his reads: "*Item.* What the king his pleasure shall be touching the learned man in the Tower." That item refers to Sir Thomas More. As Francis Hackett has put it, Cromwell had swum up the sewer to power.

These four men were waiting for More. Indeed, he was the only man they were really interested in just then. So though the palace swarmed with priests, summoned there to take the oath, they were all told to stand aside, and More was led up at once. He asked to see a copy of the act of Parliament and the oath; after reading them over carefully, he answered that he was in conscience unable to do what was required.

Upon this Audley said they were sorry to hear him say that, and that he was the first man to refuse. The King would be angry at this. Would he not walk in the garden a while and reconsider the matter?

He accepted the suggestion, which was kindly meant, but as the day was hot he preferred to wait in what is described as an old charred chamber overlooking the grounds. He saw there, or in the corridors of the palace, a number of men with whom he was acquainted. Two of these provided him with a little entertainment and one with a little encouragement. The Vicar of Croydon, Canon Rowland Phillips, who had been so anxious nearly twenty years earlier to go out as a missionary to Utopia, came out from the Commissioners' room after taking the oath. More could not decide whether it was from gladness or because he was thirsty or only to show upon what familiar terms he was with the Archbishop, but Dr. Phillips loudly ordered a drink at the buttery-bar. Hugh Latimer was there, too. In 1532 he had been charged with heresy and had made a complete recantation. Before the next year was out he was to be created Bishop of Worcester. He emerged from his oath-taking with several other priests and, so More wrote to his daughter Margaret: "Very merry I saw him, for he laughed and took one or twain about the neck so handsomely, that if they had been women I would have weened that he was wanton."

To offset these men who, as More put it, "played their pageant," there was Dr. Nicholas Wilson, one of the royal chaplains. He had refused the oath and was being led off under guard to the Tower, the only one More saw arrested, though later in the day he heard that Fisher, the Bishop of Rochester, had also declined to yield. More's phrase about the playing of the pageant is a little strange; he can hardly have meant that the men who took the oath were consciously playing a part to impress him; what he may have implied was that he was made to witness all this oath-taking on the part of well-known priests in the hope that it would shake his resolve.

If that was the intention, it totally failed. When he was called before the Commissioners again he was reminded that since he had been in their room a large number of prominent ecclesiastics had sworn "without any sticking." To this he replied that he laid no blame on any man on that account, but that for himself he had to answer as before.

He was then asked if he would not indicate what part of the oath "grudged his conscience." He replied very shrewdly that, as the King was already displeased with him, to mention the reasons for his refusal would only exasperate his Highness still further. His letter to Margaret, from which we learn all this, continues: "Rather than that I would be accounted for obstinate, I would upon the King's license, or rather his such commandment had, as might be my sufficient warrant, that my declaration should not offend his Highness nor put me in danger of his statutes, I would be content to declare the causes in writing." The answer they gave him was that, even should the King give him license under letters patent to speak his mind, it would not protect him from the statute. So he told them that, if he could not give his reasons without danger to himself, there could be no obstinacy in leaving them undeclared.

Cranmer now offered a characteristic suggestion. Master More had said that he did not condemn any man who was willing to take the oath. From this it would appear that he did not take what he called the dictates of his conscience as very certain, but, on the contrary, a doubtful matter. "But," Cranmer went on, "you know for a certainty, and a thing without doubt, that you are bound to obey your sovereign Lord, your King. And therefore are you bound to leave off the doubts of your unsure conscience, in refusing the oath, and take the sure way in obeying your Prince, and swear it." More admits that he was for a moment shaken by this argument; but Professor Chambers thinks that More may have been ironical in saying that it "seemed to me suddenly so subtle, and namely with such authority coming out of so noble a prelate's mouth, that I could answer nothing." Is not this to attribute to More a knowledge of Cranmer's character which we possess only because we know the whole of his shifty story? The Archbishop was a plausible man and always full of ingenious ideas. When More recovered his voice it was to say that he had not made up his mind hastily or weakly, but only after long and diligent study of the question.

Now the Abbot of Westminster, who upon the dissolution of the monasteries was to be rewarded for his services with the Deanery of Westminster, had his little say. As it struck him, Master More had reason to distrust his own judgment in view of the fact that the Council of the realm had a different opinion. So flimsy an argument More brushed aside: if it was simply a question, he said, of himself on one side and the whole Parliament on the other, he might well think that he could be mistaken. But it was not that at all; "I have . . . upon my part as great a council and a greater too." Therefore he was not bound to the Council of the realm against the universal opinion of Christendom.

Now Cromwell intervened, "and sware a great oath" that he would sooner his own son lost his head than that More should refuse. It was true enough that he, like all those present, was well disposed towards More, but his statement was so exaggerated as to be absurd. As tears in his eyes were of no use, he brought up the matter of the Nun of Kent again, broadly hinting that the King would now be sure to believe that her treason had been instigated by More. More told Cromwell quietly that the contrary was known to be true. He might have added that nobody knew this better than Master Cromwell himself. What he did add was that "Whatsoever should mishap me, it lay not in my power to help it without the peril of my soul."

Audley made a last effort. More had said that he was willing to swear to the succession—that is, to acknowledge the children of Anne Boleyn as heirs to the throne. Very well, perhaps the oath could be framed in such a way as to make it acceptable to his conscience. When More replied that he would first have to see that oath before he could promise to take it, Audley broke in somewhat impatiently with, "Marry, Master Secretary, mark that too, that he will not swear that neither but under some certain manner." To which More again answered no, of course he could not undertake in advance to accept a modified oath unless he knew what it would be; otherwise he might still be forsworn. He concluded with: "Howbeit, as help me God, as touching the whole oath I never withdrew any man from it, nor never advised any to refuse it, nor never put nor will put any scruple in any man's head, but leave any man to his conscience. And methinketh in good faith that so were it good reason that every man should leave mine to me."

He was committed that night to the temporary custody of the Abbot of Westminster. There he remained four days while his fate was being decided. Cranmer had written a most ingenious letter for Cromwell to lay before the King. In it he suggested that More and Fisher, instead of being sworn to the preamble of the oath—in which the Pope's spiritual authority was denied—should merely be sworn to the succession, which they both said they were willing to uphold. This would stop the mouths of those speaking in favor of the "Princess Dowager" (Katherine of Aragon's official title now) and of the Lady Mary her daughter. If the adhesion of these two men could be obtained, "I think," Cranmer went on, "there is not one within this realm that would once reclaim against it." He advised therefore that a small concession be made. Then comes Cranmer's crafty suggestion: "And if the King's pleasure were so, their said oaths might be suppressed, but when and where his Highness might take some commodity of the same."

The King refused this compromise—perhaps because, as Roper writes, "Queen Anne by her importunate clamour" exasperated the King against More. Probably, however, the Boleyn woman was never consulted on the point. Henry was already incensed with More; to that extent Anne had already done her work. In a matter of this sort the King was far more likely to take counsel of the sagacious Cromwell than his foolish wife. The Secretary was instructed to write to Cranmer and say that if More and Fisher were allowed to swear to the succession alone, "it is to be thought that it might be taken not only as a confirmation of the Bishop of Rome's authority, but also as a reprobation of the King's second marriage."

In this Henry was, from his point of view, quite right. No doubt he appreciated the cleverness of the suggestion that it could be given out that More and Fisher had taken the oath, and the fact suppressed—unless it should in some later case be convenient to use the modified form again with a person with similar scruples—that they had not sworn to the complete oath. But he perceived that if the truth about this should afterwards come out, it might be damaging to the Crown. No, the Bishop of Rochester and Master More were setting a bad example, so, Cromwell wrote: "The Kings' Highness in no wise willeth but that they shall be sworn as well to the preamble as to the Act . . . for, as His Grace supposeth, that manner of swearing, if it shall be suffered, may be an utter destruction of his whole cause, and also to the effect of the law made for the same."

It may be that Cranmer made this suggestion at Lambeth after More had left, and that Cromwell had asked the Archbishop to put it in writing so that he could lay it before the King. More, unlike Fisher, had not been sent to the Tower at once. He was kept under guard by the Abbot of Westminster, while the question of the secret reservation was weighed. As soon as a decision had been reached, he was rowed down the river to the Tower.

CHAPTER SEVENTEEN

The Psychology of a Martyr

More entered the Tower with a jest which several of his biographers have considered not very amusing. I confess that it does not strike me as one of More's best. When the gate-keeper asked him, as was customary, for his "upper garment," More, instead of taking off his cloak, handed the man his hat. Yet Roper thought this worth recording. And as all of us have discovered that what sounds funny in one mouth splutters flatly on another, a bit of "theatre" may have given a point to the joke that it lacks in cold print. It was not a shaft of wit such as More would have used with Erasmus; but where that might have been quite lost on a man like the gate-keeper, a little clowning may have been just the thing to raise a laugh. The fact that Sir Thomas had it in his heart to attempt any sort of joke at such a time is more important than the quality of the joke itself.

It was not his only joke that day. Sir Richard Cromwell—his real name was Williams, but he had taken the patronymic of his powerful uncle, and he was to be the great-grandfather of the great Oliver—suggested that More send home for safe keeping the gold chain he wore round his neck. "Nay, sir," returned More, "that will I not; for if I were taken in the field by my enemies, I would that they should fare the better for me." Roper also considered it laughable that More's servant, John à Wood, who was allowed to attend him in the Tower, and was a man who could neither read nor write, should have been ordered by the Lieutenant of the Tower to report to him anything that his master might write against the King or the Council.

The presence of a servant is illustrative of the treatment of political prisoners. More paid ten shillings a week for himself and five for his man—a heavy drain upon the resources of one who now had an income of only £60 a year, and an exorbitant charge for the rather poor fare received. The diet, however, could be supplemented, and Bonvisi, More's wealthy Italian friend, took it upon himself to send in little delicacies and wine to More and Fisher, most of the latter being consumed for their masters by their obliging servants. When Sir Edmund Walsingham, the Lieutenant, an uncle of Queen Elizabeth's famous minister, apologised for the meals, saying that he would offer better were it not for fear of offending the King, More told him not to distress himself. "I do not mislike my cheer," he said; "but whensoever I do, then thrust me out of your doors." The food of the Tower probably suited his simple, and even ascetic tastes, better than that of the King's board.

Nor was he ill-treated in other ways, though there was always the possibility of torture being used to compel him to speak. He was allowed, at any rate occasionally at the start of his imprisonment, to walk in the garden of the fortress, when his wife or Margaret visited him. But it would seem that he was not given the privilege of attending the services in either of the two small churches within the enclosure, and that his only way of marking Sundays and the greater feasts was to dress in the better of the robes he had brought with him. He could write as much as he pleased, and did in fact produce one whole book and part of another during his incarceration. Also he corresponded fairly freely with Bishop Fisher, who was in another part of the prison, the letters usually being carried by George Golde, Walsingham's servant, though of course without Walsingham's knowledge. This was a mistake, for Golde, instead of keeping the letters, as they asked, to prove their innocence, destroyed them. At More's trial the admitted fact of the correspondence was brought up against him in an attempt to show that he and Fisher must have been discussing the question of the oath of supremacy.

Dame Alice and Margaret Roper were allowed to visit More because the authorities hoped that his affection for them would break down his resolution. Stapleton even says that when Margaret wrote urging him to take the oath she was using a clever ruse, and so got her visits encouraged, but that her letters contained things that "were far from being her real sentiments." This, however, is clearly contradicted by some of the letters he himself quotes.[1] She did several times try to persuade her father to conform to the King's will, prompted by her love for him. As for Dame Alice, though affection was by no means lacking, she was quite out of sympathy with him and her unimaginative common sense simply could not understand how he was willing to ruin them all for what was, to her, a mere scruple. In 1535 what little property they had left began to be confiscated. Henry Norris, who was to be executed little more than a year later on a charge of being one of Anne Boleyn's lovers, got some of this, and the Duke of Suffolk asked his royal brother-in-law to let him have the More house at Chelsea. Twice Lady More appealed to the King,—at the end of 1534 and the following May—to have pity upon her poverty, saying that she was being obliged to sell her clothing to pay for the board of her husband and John à Wood at the Tower. Each time the appeal went unanswered, probably as a means of bringing further pressure on More.

One is sorry for this very good woman, but she still provided her husband with some entertainment. Roper reports a frontal attack she made with: "What the good year, Master More. I marvel that you, who have been always hitherto taken for so wise a man, will now play the fool to lie here in this close, filthy prison, and thus to be content to be shut up among mice and rats, when you might be abroad at your liberty, and with the favour and good will both of the King and his Council, if you would but do as all the Bishops and best learned men of this realm have done. And seeing that you have at Chelsea a right fair house, your library, your books, your gallery, your garden, your orchard, and all other necessaries so handsome about you, where you might in the company of me your wife, your children, and household be merry, I muse what a God's name you mean here still thus fondly to tarry."

[1] See pages 162, 163 as against page 114 of Monsignor Hallett's translation of Stapleton.

More listened to her quietly and then "with a cheerful countenance" asked, "I pray thee, good Mistress Alice, tell me one thing."

"What is that?"

"Is not this house as nigh heaven as mine own?"

To this, Roper says, she "after her accustomed homely fashion," not liking such talk, answered impatiently, "Tilly vally, tilly vally!" And when her husband asked, "How say you, Mistress Alice, is it not so?" she retorted, "Bone deus, bone deus, man, will this gear never be left?"

Even while regretting the hardships he was bringing upon her, More managed to extract whatever there was of humor in the situation. Only by such means could he bear his grief. In the same style he met his daughter's appeals with light banter, calling her "Mistress Eve," his temptress. He could, however, explain to Margaret what it was useless to try and tell Dame Alice—that he was perfectly happy where he was and that he felt himself like a monk in a cell. Indeed, he assured her that if it were not for his wife and children, he would long ago have shut himself up in a still narrower place. This sentiment, along with many others that were his own, he put into the mouth of Anthony when in the *Dialogue of Comfort* he wrote almost enviously of the "holy monks of the Charterhouse order, such as never pass their cells but only to the church fast by their cells, and thence to their cells again." He could now at last be the contemplative he had always wanted to be.

He followed this passage with one in which Dame Alice may be recognized, describing as "a stout master woman" the one whom Roper, who was of course familiar with her manner of talk and catches the tone of her voice perfectly, called "a simple, ignorant woman, and somewhat worldly too." She had told her husband that "she lamented much in her mind, that he should have the chamber door upon him at night, made fast by the jailer that should shut him in. For by my troth, quoth she, if the door should be shut upon me, I ween it would stop my breath." When she said that, Anthony (who is More himself) "laughed in his mind, but he durst not laugh aloud nor say anything to her, for somewhat indeed he stood in awe of her." His amusement was because he knew how Alice always kept all the doors and windows of her room fastened tight at night. This had well prepared him to endure the close atmosphere of the Tower.

We shall see more of Margaret later in this chapter, for her relations with her father became more beautiful and tender than ever during his last days. But first it might be as well to turn to the book More wrote during his imprisonment because of what it reveals of his mind. It is the most cheerful and humorous of all his books and it gives, so it seems to me, an altogether unique picture of the psychology of a martyr.

All of us, I imagine, think of martyrs as uplifted by the thought of giving their lives in defence of what they believe to be true. And perhaps that *is* true of most martyrs, few of whom have to wait long for death and therefore can maintain themselves in a state of exaltation. But More had to wait fifteen months in the Tower—which is not to count the two years and more that he saw his fate approaching. And so far from being temperamentally a martyr (if there is such a state), he was a man prudent almost to the point of caution, sometimes it would seem of excessive caution.

Moreover he was not a man whose occupation had steeled him to the practice of courage. Never a soldier, or even a hunter, he had lived by preference a sedentary life among his books. And though he did manifest a most extraordinary courage, this was accomplished solely on the strength of his naked will and his trust in God. Very candidly he confessed in one of his letters to Margaret that he was by nature so shrinking from pain that he was "almost afraid of a fillip"—saying also that she could not have a fainter heart than that of her "frail father," and that his flesh was "much more shrinking from pain and death than methought it the part of a faithful Christian man." Having an extremely vivid imagination, he was obliged to suffer in his mind, over and over again, every conceivable torment before he came to execution. On the other hand, he could console himself, as he wrote in another letter to his daughter, "I thank Our Lord, I know no person living that

I would have one fillip for my sake; of which mind I am more glad than of all the world beside." This was the very gentlest of all heroes.

Moreover, Sir Thomas More was in almost total isolation. Fisher was in the Tower, and went to his death shortly before he did. So also a small band of Carthusians suffered martyrdom. But though he saw them start their journey to Tyburn, he was able to have no communication with them. And between Fisher and himself there passed only a few small presents and letters that always avoided the subject of the King's Supremacy over the Church.

Dr. Wilson, arrested on the same day with him, wrote sometimes asking for his advice. This More would never give; he only wrote in reply, "For Our Lord's sake, good Master Wilson, pray for me, for I pray for you daily, and sometimes when I would be sorry but if I thought you were asleep." It was evident that Wilson's resolution was failing, and when word came that he had decided to take the oath, More wrote to him: "I beseech Our Lord give you thereof good luck. . . . With God's grace I will follow my own conscience," adding most humbly, "Whether I shall have the grace to do according to my own conscience or not hangeth in God's goodness, not in mine." Not even with his dear Margaret would he discuss the matter. The furthest that he went in that direction was to write to her: "This I am sure, that of them that have sworn it, some of the best learned, before the oath was required, plainly affirmed the contrary of such things as they have now sworn." He admitted that their change of mind might be perfectly honest, and had to fall back upon the reflection that Christendom as a whole was with him, as were the faithful departed, "that are, I trust in heaven; I am sure that it is not the fewer part of them that, all the while they lived, thought in some of the things the way that I think now."

Yet never was he so cheerful, or even so gay, as may be discovered not only in his recorded conversations and his letters of this time but in his *Dialogue of Comfort*. Though that book does have some rather arid stretches, those who will read it can be promised entertainment as well as edification.

The work purports to have been written originally in Latin, by a Hungarian noble named Anthony, and translated from Latin into French and from French into English. Anthony, a prisoner, is of course More himself, and the form of the book is that of a dialogue between Anthony and his nephew Vincent, who may be regarded as standing for Roper and William Rastell and John Heywood, and the rest of More's young men—a composite picture in which the features are not particularly distinct. The scene is of set purpose removed from England, and even from the Protestant controversy. Instead the situation described is that of the persecution of Christians by Turks. All this was to prevent any offence being given to Henry VIII, should the manuscript be taken away and read for any incriminating matter it might contain; though, as to that, More would never have been other than kind to his former friend, any more than Henry would have been likely to be capable of imagining that any of the satire in the book could possibly apply to himself. On the other hand, More does have a reference to Henry's pious practice of washing the feet of beggars on Maundy Thursday, and the one passage that might be taken as aimed at the King and Anne Boleyn is innocent of any such intention. It really is, as Professor Chambers points out, merely a belated handling of a favorite subject of More's, one that was used in no less than three of his youthful epigrams.

In the *Dialogue of Comfort* it appears as follows: "St. John Baptist was, ye wot well, in prison, while Herodias sat full merry at the feast, and the daughter of Herodias delighted them with her dancing, till with her dancing she danced off St. John's head. And now sitteth he with great feast in heaven at God's board, while Herod and Herodias full heavily sit in hell, burning both twain, and to make them sport withal the devil with the damsel dance in the fire afore them." More to the end spoke of Henry not only with reverent loyalty but with affection. As for Anne, Roper tells how More once asked Margaret while he was walking with her in the

Tower garden, during the early days of his imprisonment, how the Queen was.

"In faith, father," Margaret replied, "never better."

"Never better, Meg," he returned. "Alas! Meg, alas! it pitieth me to remember into what misery, poor soul, she shall shortly come."

In this he was a much better prophet than the foolish Nun of Kent. Anne had borne her daughter Elizabeth in the September before More's arrest, and she miscarried of a son six months after More's death. But while More was in the Tower Henry was already becoming bored with her, and that shrill hysterical laugh of hers, which once seemed so amusing, was grating on his nerves, and he resented her attempts to rule him. Soon she was reduced to playing listlessly with an old wolfhound and weeping at the death of another dog. She had always known that the people hated her, and now she was despised by the King. Her enemies were teaching the court idiot to sing-song: "Nan is a ribald; her child is a bastard." Within a year of More's execution she was to follow him to the block. Sir William Kingston was to tell Cromwell that she had joy and pleasure in dying. If so it was a joy very different from that of the great man who had dared to say that he could not admit that the King was head of the Church.

Anne Boleyn was not much in More's serene meditations. And if Herod and Herodias appear in his book it was for the same reason that he reverted to the idea of all mortal life being a prison in which all were held under sentence of death: a strong antidote to worldiness. That he should have dwelt upon this prison theme in the Tower is natural enough, but he had already handled it in his *Four Last Things*. I confess that I find the later treatment overdone. It hardly seems quite fitting to represent God as man's jailor. Yet of course More was writing to warn those who had not thought enough of life's decisive moment, and to them his grim warnings were salutary. "Some," he says, "have I seen even in their last sickness set up in their death-bed underpropped with pillows, take their playfellows to them and comfort themselves with cards, and this they said did ease them well to put fantasies out of their heads; and what fantasies trow you, such as I told you right now of their own lewd life and peril of their soul, of heaven and of hell irked them to think of, and therefore cast it out with cards play as long as ever they might till the pure pangs of death pulled their hearts from their play and put them in the case they could not reckon their game. And then left they their gameners and slily slonk away, and long was it not ere they gulped up the ghost. And what game they came then to, that God knoweth and not I." Only with such considerations, and that all men are under sentence of inescapable death, is it possible to halt some minds in their evil courses. As in his earlier controversies, More was addressing himself to the good of souls.

But for him all controversy was over, and of this he was glad. Never had he possessed the polemic temper but had written his books against the heretics only as a disagreeable duty. Now that he had no more responsibilities he could write without direct reference to the "brethren;" instead he imagined the case of Christians whose faith was being threatened by an apparently irresistible Islam. Eight years before this the knights of Hungary had been routed at Mohacz and three years later Sultan Suleiman besieged Vienna, though in vain. Yet the quarrels of Christians divided Christendom, and the danger from the Turks remained until, more than a generation after More had passed from the scene, the son of his old acquaintance Charles V, Don John of Austria, routed their galleys at Lepanto.

Nevertheless More is at peace about that peril and the peril to the Church in England, and his personal peril. Though writing with an unmistakable sincerity, he also shows high spirits and a sense of fun, often in his most serious passages. And there is a note in his voice which would carry conviction, even did we not know that he was expecting execution, when he says: "The sayings of Our Saviour Jesus Christ were not a poet's fable nor a harper's song but the very holy word of Almighty God Himself." It is an absolute faith that shines in these pages.

It is strange that he should ever have been accused of inconsistency. He is still one of the Utopians of whom he had written: "They think he shall not be welcome to God, which, when he be called, runneth not to Him gladly, but is drawn by force and sore against his will. They therefore that see this kind of death do abhor it, and them that so die they bury with sorrow and silence. And when they have prayed to God to be merciful to the soul . . . they cover the dead corse with earth. Contrariwise all that depart merely [simply, purely] and full of good hope, for them no man mourneth, but followeth the hearse with joyful singing, commending the souls to God with great affection." Now in 1534 this man whose whole life is so complete a piece, writes: "He that so loveth [God] that he longeth to go to Him, my heart cannot but give me but that he shall be welcome, all were that he should come ere he were well purged."

At the end of the *Dialogue* he makes Vincent put to his uncle a notion we may suppose had tempted More himself. What, Anthony is asked, about this possible case? A man might refuse to apostatize and then be put to torture and, under torture, forsake his faith, and yet die from the torture he was enduring; would it not be better for such a man to forsake his faith right away? Then he might have the grace to repent and so obtain forgiveness.

Anthony brushes this aside as a "fantastical fear." Nearly every death, he reminds Vincent, is painful; in fact natural death is often more painful than martyrdom. For the sharp pang of martyrdom is soon over, whereas the sufferings of illness are sometimes long. The difference may only be that of a knife cutting from the inside instead of a knife cutting from the skin inwards. In this passage, as in others, More was undoubtedly indicating his expectation of dying at Tyburn, where those guilty of high treason were cut down while still alive and disembowelled and made to endure indignities too horrible to mention. "Is it wisdom then," he asks, "to think so much upon the Turk that we forget the devil?" And what is it of which Vincent's hypothetical man will most repent when he comes to die in bed except that he had not been willing to suffer death for his faith? And should he save his life by apostasy, all his life after he would mourn it, for, says More, "I ween almost every good Christian man would very fain this day that he had been for Christ's faith cruelly killed yesterday, even for the desire of heaven, though there were none hell." To Margaret he wrote that to be loth to die showed lack of wit. In another letter he told her, "It were great folly for me to be sorry to come to that death, which I would after wish that I had died." Long before More laid his head on the block he had given himself to God. Though he most movingly told his examiners, when they urged him to declare himself, that he had not been a man of such good life as to dare rush upon his fate, though he believed it his duty to hold it off as long as possible, and to avoid a single word that might hasten it, he had fully accepted death.

Sir Thomas More, however, made his consideration of human tribulation much wider than the single point of death. All prosperity—especially that of material wealth—was, if continuous, a real danger to the soul and might even be a sign that it would be lost. Nevertheless the man of wealth could hold what he had as though from God and to be used for God. Moreover, such a man might have "many tribulations that every man marketh not," for "the temptations of the devil, the world, and the flesh, soliciting the mind of a good man unto sin, is . . . a great inward trouble and grief unto his heart." On the same page he adds: "I dare be bold to warrant him that the pain in resisting, and the great fear of falling that many a good man hath in his temptation, is an anguish and a grief."

And More, the ascetic, says a surprisingly "modern" thing, when he writes: "Let no man think strange, that I would advise a man to take counsel with a physician of the body" when his temptations come from the flesh, though he hardly foresaw that many psychiatrists would suggest in effect that the easiest way of getting rid of such temptations is to yield to them. He continues: "Since the soul and the body be so knit and joined together, that they both between them make one person, the distemperance of the other, engendreth sometimes the distemperance of both twain." In the same key are some wise remarks on the spiritual disease of scrupulosity that indicate that More would have made an excellent director of souls.

The essence of his book is that we should be glad of all our tribulations, as sent us in God's mercy, and even of temptation, as an opportunity for the exercise of virtue. As for the devil, whose roaring is heard in many of these pages, when resisted, he flees, "for that proud spirit cannot endure to be mocked." His greatest deceit of all is to persuade men that he does not exist—until too late they encounter in hell "such black bugs indeed as folk call devils, whose torments [they] were wont to take for poets' tales."

But More's purpose is to give comfort against tribulation. And the first stage of comfort he says is "the desire and longing to be by God comforted," and its last stage too. This is because "surely the greatest comfort that any man may have in his tribulation is to hide his heart in heaven." Therefore what men regard as a shameful death has "therein no piece of very [real] shame at all. For how can that death be shameful that is glorious? Or how can it be but glorious to die for the faith of Christ?" At that kind of a death "God with His whole heavenly company beholdeth the whole passion and verily looketh on." So far from ever being depressed, More felt, as he told his daughter, that "God by this imprisonment maketh me one of His wantons and setteth me on His lap and dandleth me."

There has been attempted here hardly more than a brief summary of the book's serious substance. This is, however, frequently shot with humor, grim or gay, and with a number of amusing anecdotes which have, in several instances, been already drawn upon. Yet they should not be separated from the rest of the *Dialogue of Comfort,* as they are part of its smiling piety and give it a special charm. The whole book is immensely moving as the work of a man who, if he did not die in prison as his failing health often led him to expect (and to desire),[2] was sure that he would come at last to execution. It is all the more touching because it has so few "exalted" moments but glows with a simple sincerity, the quiet reflections of a happy man who had never been happier than he was in the Tower.

Yet before leaving this book it might be pointed out that, though one is naturally most keenly interested in the recognisable portraits of the resplendent and vainglorious Wolsey and the sharp-tongued Dame Alice, it has scattered throughout vignettes that are, in their way, almost as good, as when More describes "all the lust of an old fool's life, to sit well and warm with a cup and a roasted crab, and drivel and drink and talk." More even reverted to the pastime of his youth, the production of such little portraits (now in English verse, each complete in a stanza of rime-royal) as those of Lewis the Lost Lover and Davy the Dicer.

An account of his examinations while in prison will be deferred to the next chapter, that on his trial, as they were preparatory to it. All that needs be said at the moment is that he steadily refused to discuss the question of the oath with anybody. Even to Margaret he said nothing, not because he did not trust her discretion but because he wished to be able to swear that he had observed an absolute silence. When Dr. Wilson asked his advice, More refused it, saying, "As touching the oath, the causes for which I refused it, no man knoweth what they be."

When Margaret tried to get him to change his mind before it was too late—Cromwell had sent word "as your very friend" that it would be as well for him to remember that Parliament was still sitting and that even more stringent legislation could be passed—he merely told his daughter, "Too late! I beseech Our Lord that if ever I make such a change it will be too late indeed; for well I wot that such a change cannot be good for my soul." That she made her appeals at a time when she was with child made them

2 Thus he wrote to Margaret: "I have since I came in the Tower, looked once or twice to have given up the ghost ere this; and in good faith mine heart waxed the lighter with hope thereof."

all the more harrowing. Yet he stood firm, even while gently jesting with her. She turned from pleading to jest with him, saying one day that one of the servants had encountered Henry Patenson, the Mores' former fool. He laughed when she related how Master Harry had said, "Why, what aileth him that he will not swear? Wherefore should he stick to swear? I have sworn the oath myself!"

These last meetings with the dearest of his children were among the sweetest incidents of More's whole life. Always they began with their reciting the seven penitential psalms together; afterwards they would have a long tender talk festooned with raillery. And under everything was a gravity that gave an exquisite edge to the gayety. The father kept telling the daughter: "Nothing can come but that God will. . . . And if anything should hap to me that you would be loth, pray to God for me, but trouble not yourself: as I shall full heartily pray for us all, that we may meet together in heaven, where we shall make merry for ever, and never have trouble after."

There was little that the family could do. But when Lady More's appeals to the King were disregarded, Lady Alington, More's stepdaughter, who was married to the Sir Giles Alington who had been first cup-bearer at Anne Boleyn's coronation, took the opportunity of speaking to Audley one day when the Lord Chancellor had chased a buck in her husband's park. But Audley was, or professed to be, powerless. He probably saw no reason why he should try to help a man who could so easily get himself released from prison if only he would utter the few words that nearly everybody else in England had uttered without any evident qualms. So he dismissed the matter by telling Lady Alington some animal fables, which she might apply to More's case. When Margaret carried these to the Tower More was able to utilize them in a more pointed way in the book upon which he was engaged.

Even with the strong possibility of torture before him he wrote to Margaret: "If it so were that I wist well now, that I should faint and fall, and for fear swear hereafter, yet would I wish to take harm by the refusing first: for so should I have the better grace to rise again." More openly he spoke of torture to a priest named Leder who wrote to him to congratulate him when a rumor got out that he had taken the oath. The tale, so More assures Leder, was "a very vanity." He says further, "If ever I should mishap to receive the oath (which I trust Our Lord shall never suffer me) ye may reckon sure that it were expressed and extorted by duress and hard handling." In advance he discounts anything he might do in his weakness if put to the rack. It should go on record that this was the reverse of a free act.

Why was he not put to the rack? Henry VIII did not hesitate to subject his former friend, Sebastian Newdigate, once a courtier and a famous rider in the tilting-yard but now a Carthusian, to abominable tortures. If he spared More it could hardly have been out of compunction. The supposition must be that from More he would accept nothing less than what could be proclaimed to the world as a voluntary change of mind. Anything extracted by torture would be tarnished. More and Fisher were in a special category, and accordingly were spared as a matter of policy.

Margaret must always have dreaded that her father would be subjected to torments. Yet harrowing as were her meetings with her father, she was full of pride in his constancy. Dame Alice had scant patience with what she considered obstinate folly, but Margaret understood. And though her daughter's heart made her attempt to persuade him, still deeper in her heart was her approval of his refusal of the oath. Had he not told her, did she not fully believe what he told her? "Never trouble thy mind for anything that shall happen to me in this world. Nothing can come but what God wills." She would leave the Tower with a radiant face, even though she had arrived sorrowful. In one of her last letters to him, she could therefore write: "Father, what think you hath been our comfort since your departing from us? Surely the experience we have of your life past, and godly conversation and wholesome counsel and virtuous example, and a surety not only of the continuance of that same but also a great increase by the goodness of Our Lord, to the great rest and gladness of your heart, devoid of all earthly dregs and garnished with the noble vesture of heavenly virtues, a pleasant palace for the Holy Spirit of God to rest in, who defend you (as I doubt not, good father, but of His goodness He will) from all trouble of mind and of body and give your most loving obedient daughter and handmaid and all us, your children and friends, to follow that that we praise in you and to our comfort remember and commune together of you, that we may in conclusion meet with you, mine own dear father, in the bliss of heaven, to which our most merciful Lord hath brought us with His precious blood." He could read between the lines there. She dared not say more, nor would he have permitted any avowal of sympathy with the position he had taken that was more open than this.

More had in the beginning been permitted to write as much as he pleased, but afterwards his confinement grew progressively more rigorous. Yet so long as he had pen and ink he kept at his manuscript. The *Dialogue of Comfort* had fortunately been completed before this; so also was a *Godly Meditation,* though that was brief enough for charcoal to have sufficed. Several biographers quote from it; Miss Routh at the end of her book gives it in full. It is a kind of free-verse poem.

His last manuscript written in ink was his *Treatise on the Passion,* which was composed partly in English and partly in Latin, the Latin part being translated by his grand-daughter, Mary Bassett, who was a lady-in-waiting to Queen Mary. It stopped short with the words, "They laid hands on Jesus." William Rastell, the editor of the folio of 1557, noted: "Sir Thomas More wrote no more of this work, for, when he had written thus far he was kept in prison so straight that all his books and pen and ink and paper were taken from him. And soon after he was put to death." There is also a little Latin tract found among his papers that contains the sentence, "If you save your life today by offending God, you will hate it tomorrow, and lament that you did not undergo death yesterday." It is not certain that that was written by him, but it has an idea elaborated in the *Dialogue of Comfort*.

With the end put to his literary labors, More closed the shutters of his cell and sat in darkness. Walsingham was surprised to find him like this and wondered why it could be. The explanation no doubt is that in darkness—it must really have been half-light—he could meditate best. "Overmuch light," he had written nearly twenty years earlier in the *Utopia,* "disperses men's cogitations." Though the books composed in the Tower were themselves meditations, they involved some distraction. Now at last he could give himself to pure contemplation.

Even so, he did write little scraps now and then. Among these charcoal manuscripts of his are the following lines, written, Harpsfield says, just after Cromwell had left him on the occasion of his last examination.

By flattering fortune, look thou never so fair,
Nor never so pleasantly begin to smile,
As though thou wouldst my ruin all repair,
During my life thou shalt not me beguile.
Trust shall I God, to enter, in a while,
His haven of heaven, sure and uniform;
Ever after this calm look I for a storm.

In his last letters, which were necessarily brief, he said farewell again to his family,[3] sending special affectionate messages to each, but concluding in a note that had its humorous touch: "Written with a coal by your tender loving father, who in his poor prayers forgetteth none of you, nor your babes, nor your nurses, nor your good husbands nor your good husbands' shrewd wives, nor your father's shrewd wife neither, nor our other friends. And thus fare ye heartily well for lack of paper."

Well might Margaret Roper say in reply to such a letter, "Though it were written with a coal, [it is yet] worthy in mine opinion to be written in letters of gold."

[3] These included, Cresacre More says, a letter in charcoal to Dame Alice which his father, More's grandson, had inked in. This was in his possession and accounted by him "as a precious jewel." Unfortunately it no longer exists.

CHAPTER EIGHTEEN

Mummery Before Murder

MACAULAY'S phrase applies to almost all the treason trials of the sixteenth century, but to none of them with such force as to the trial of Sir Thomas More. In this case there was glaring illegality in his being detained in the Tower at all. It was only *after* his arrest that an act of parliament was passed (on February 1, 1535) which made it high treason by speaking or writing maliciously to deprive the King or his heirs of the "dignity, title or name of their royal estates."

Yet because of this Act the forms of law could be preserved, though as "Ro.Ba." remarks acidly, "Sir Thomas More was condemned with pretended justice, which aggravates the iniquity of the fact." Henry VIII was no Duke of Gloucester, the Protector who made himself King Richard III, suddenly ordering with a roaring oath that the head of the unsuspecting Lord Hastings must be struck off before he would have his own dinner. The new Act, though pushed through Parliament only after much "sticking," with the word "maliciously" twice introduced specifically to protect men like Fisher and More, could nevertheless be given an interpretation by the judges, under which the saving clause was made of no effect. Therefore it wore the appearance of legality; Henry VIII was always most punctilious in such matters.

As he was punctilious, he found himself unable to go further—even when armed with the later Act—than imprison Fisher and More until they had said something. This at last Fisher was tricked into doing when Sir Richard Rich, the Solicitor General, gave him a solemn promise of immunity from the King who, so Fisher was assured, was seeking merely a confidential opinion on a point of theology from one of his bishops. On this Fisher was convicted. As More was too wary to say anything at all, he could be convicted only by Rich's perjury, before a bench of judges and a jury every man of which knew that Rich was lying. Lord Campbell does not hesitate to describe the whole trial as "the blackest crime that has ever been perpetrated in England under the form of law."

A glance at Rich might be advisable at this point. As he became Lord Chancellor under Edward VI, he had to be included in Campbell's *Lives of the Lord Chancellors*. When he obtained during Henry VIII's time the Priory of Lighes in Essex for his valuable services, it was expected, upon his being raised to the peerage in 1548, that he would take Lighes as his territorial title. He feared, however, Campbell remarks, that "some scurvy jests" might be passed if he were known as the Lord of Lighes, and so avoided them by choosing to be titled Baron Rich. Before Henry died Rich had racked Anne Askew, the Protestant martyr, when the Lieutenant of the Tower flinched from stretching her out further; and again in Mary's time he was conspicuous for his zeal in persecution. Nevertheless between the two reigns he had promoted Protestantism vigorously, though not so vigorously as he promoted his political advantage by betraying, in turn, his patrons Somerset and Northumberland. Campbell might well describe him as "one who has brought a greater stain upon the bar of England than any member of the profession to which I am proud to belong . . . and never before or since so far degraded as to have its honours won by palpable fraud, chicanery, and perjury."

Campbell, because of his expert knowledge of such matters, is specially good on the malpractices of the prosecution during More's trial. He does, indeed, seem to think that More, on one or two points, might have made a better defence than he did. This may be so, though to a lay mind it seems wonderful how well More conducted his own case. Like all those accused of treason, he was not shown his indictment until he stood before his judges. This, however, must have been much less of a handicap to him than it was to any other person ever accused of treason. He had a good idea as to what that indictment was likely to contain, and to him the rule that permitted no legal counsel was no hardship at all, as he was easily the ablest lawyer in the court, and as such dominated the proceedings from start to finish. But he was well aware, of course, that his condemnation had been decided upon in advance and that nothing he could urge would save him—nothing but a last-minute expression of willingness to take the oath.

His indictment still exists. We have also in More's letters to Margaret a rather full account of the preliminary examinations. Finally we have an account of the trial from Roper who, though not present, was a lawyer and who obtained detailed reports from those who *were* there. Of few trials of this period do we have a more complete or circumstantial record. All the lawyers who have since written on the subject are one in their indignation and horror.

Yet before we come to the trial itself, we had better see what led up to it during the fifteen months of More's incarceration. For nearly a year nothing could be done but to hold him, hoping that he would say something to incriminate himself. But after the Act of Treasons of 1535, a test case was made of a group of Carthusian Priors. They had gone, a little naively, to Cromwell, asking how a layman *could* be Head of the Church, a question which provided the evidence needed for their conviction. They pleaded that they were not refusing the oath "maliciously," and the plea was rejected. One could not refuse it except maliciously, so the judges ruled. Even so, the jury would not bring in a verdict of guilty until Cromwell, after sending them a message threatening them with death, went to them in person, when they remained stubborn. By this trial the precedent was established that one could not be protected by the word "maliciously."

They were taken out to die on May 4th, a day when Margaret Roper was visiting her father. From the window of More's cell they watched while the three Priors—Houghton, Webster and Lawrence—and with them Reynolds, the Bridgettine, and John

Hale, a secular priest, the Vicar of Isleworth,[1] were tied to their hurdles and started on the journey to Tyburn. Possibly this was staged for More's benefit, in the hope of shaking him. Instead he turned enviously from them to Margaret Roper and said, "Lo! dost thou not see, Meg, that these blessed fathers be now as cheerfully going to their deaths as bridegrooms to their marriage?" He went on to contrast their lives, spent in so strict, hard, penitential and painful a way with his own, which he called one of pleasure and licentious ease. "Thy silly father, Meg," he said, "like a most wicked caitiff hath passed the whole of his miserable life sinfully." Therefore he thought that God, "thinking him not worthy so soon to come to that eternal felicity, leaveth him here still in the world, further to be plunged and turmoiled with misery."

Just after these executions—so a story runs—Cromwell came to More and told him that the King "minded not with any matter wherein he should have cause of scruple to trouble his conscience." If this was so, Henry must have been supposing that a few kind words might be effective where harshness had failed. More likely this was a device of Cromwell's for getting More to relax his guard. For it was on May 7th that Rich extracted from Fisher the opinion on the Supremacy that Fisher had until then refused to give. It is possible that both Rich and Cromwell were acting on their own responsibility and that Henry had no share in the treachery. Let us hope, as Henry's name is sufficiently tarnished without this, that such is the case.

A new group of Carthusians were now arrested. These were imprisoned, not in the Tower but at Newgate, where, as Rastell writes: "They remained seventeen days, standing bolt upright, tied with iron collars fast by the neck to the posts of the prison, and great fetters rived on their legs with great iron bolts; so straitly tied that they could neither lie nor sit, nor otherwise ease themselves, but stand upright, and in all that space they were never loosened for any natural necessity." This information Rastell ob-

[1] All of these men were beatified as martyrs.

tained from Margaret Clement,[2] More's adopted daughter and the wife of the royal physician, who used to go to these men in disguise, having bribed the jailors, with food and to remove their ordure from their stinking cell. When her visits were forbidden she still contrived to feed them by food let down from a hole in the roof. The treatment of prisoners in those days, though often cruel, was sometimes also very casual. And a few tips could work wonders.

On June 19th these men were executed at Tyburn, those of them who had survived the horrors of such an imprisonment. And three days later Fisher was sent to the block, though he had just been designated a cardinal by Clement VII's successor, Paul III. It would seem that the only reason the old Bishop was not dragged to Tyburn was that he was in such a weakened condition that he might die on the road. He was perfectly calm on being awakened at five in the morning, and when told that his execution was to be at ten, he asked to be allowed to sleep another couple of hours as he had had a rather bad night. At nine the Lieutenant of the Tower found him putting on his fur tippet against the chilly air, and when he was asked why he was so careful of his health when he was to die so soon, he answered that he meant to take care of it until the very last minute. Rastell, who was present at his execution, wrote that he looked "a very image of death, and, as one might say, Death in a man's shape and using a man's voice." In spite of all the courage he had shown, he feared that

[2] This is in a life of a daughter of Margaret Clement, a nun in the Low Countries where her parents, like others of More's circle, went into exile after Elizabeth's accession. It relates that Mrs. Clement died at Mechlin in 1570, on the thirty-fifth anniversary of More's execution. One would suppose that if anyone appeared to her while she was dying it would be (on that of all days) the man who had brought her up in his household and whose gentle reprimands she used to seek as a child by committing some tiny naughtiness. But no. Instead, to quote the manuscript life of her daughter which is still preserved at the English convent at Bruges: "Calling her husband therefore she told him that the time of her departing was now come, for that there were standing about her bed the reverend monks of the Charterhouse, whom she had relieved in prison in England, and did call upon her to go away with them, and that therefore she could no longer stay, because they did expect her."

even on the scaffold he might declare himself willing to take the oath, and so asked for the prayers of the crowd that at the very instant of death's stroke he might not faint in any point of the Catholic faith out of fear. As he spoke, the sun caught his head, and there seemed a halo round it.

By now More, though he had never doubted what his end would be, was quite sure that they were about to kill him.

He had been examined several times in the Tower, but most closely on three occasions about this time. After the last examination he wrote to Margaret, "As far as I can see, the whole purpose is, either to drive me to say precisely one way, or else precisely the other." Steadily he refused to admit the King's Supremacy over the Church or to deny it.

His examiners were Archbishop Cranmer, Audley the Lord Chancellor, the Duke of Suffolk, Anne Boleyn's father Lord Wiltshire, and Cromwell. They were getting impatient with him, and urged him, if he would not take the oath, plainly to utter his "malignity." To this he could return but one answer, that he had no malignity and therefore could utter none. In a letter to Margaret he said: "I thanked God that my case was here such in this matter, through the clearness of my own conscience, that though I might have pain I could not have harm. For a man might in such a case lose his head and have none harm. . . . I had always from the beginning truly used myself, looking first upon God, and next upon the King, according to the lesson that his Highness taught me at my first coming into his noble service." When Audley and Cromwell told him that the King might compel him to make an answer one way or the other, More replied that he did not dispute the King's authority but that it seemed to him hard to have to decide in this way; for on the supposition that his conscience was against the statute—though as to that he had made no declaration—he could swear only to the danger of his soul, and they were making his refusal to swear a danger to his body. As Fisher had said something along the same lines at his trial, More's answer was noted down to be used against him later, as proving collusion, or what, at his own trial, was called "conspiracy."

Cromwell pressed him further, saying that he believed he was right in saying that when More was Chancellor he had examined heretics and obliged them to say whether or not the Pope was head of the Church. At least, as Cromwell amended himself, the Bishops used to do so. Why should the King not have the right to demand an answer from More to a similar question? More did not trouble to declare that this was not true of his own practice, though all his controversial writings suggest that he never brought up a matter, when examining heretics, that he had avoided when writing against them. What he did say in answer to Cromwell was that the two cases were very different, as at the time he was Chancellor, "here as elsewhere through the corps of Christendom, the Pope's power was recognised for an undoubted thing," whereas now it was denied only in England but taken for granted in all other realms. When Cromwell gave him one of those sidelong looks of his, the small cold eyes glinting with an unpleasant light in his large heavy face, and commented with pleasant cynicism that men could be beheaded for denying the King's supremacy as they had been burned for denying the Pope's, More retorted that a man could not be so strictly bound by the law of one kingdom—as that was a local law—as he was by the universal law of Christendom, and that the real difference was not between beheading and burning but rather between beheading and hell.

In conclusion, More told Margaret, they asked him to swear an oath that he would make true answers "to such things as would be asked me on the King's behalf." This More refused, and when they said that this was done every day in the Star Chamber, his own court, and in every other court of law, he replied: "True, but I can well conjecture what should be part of my interrogatories, so that it is as well to decline now as later." No, Audley told him, they had only two questions to ask: Had he read the statute? Was the statute lawful? To the first More answered, yes; to the second he would give no answer.

During the examination the men there told him that they marvelled that he made such an ado about his conscience, about which "at the uttermost" he could not be perfectly sure. To this More said that he *was* perfectly sure, that his conscience "so informed as it is by such diligence as I have so long taken therein, may stand with my own salvation."

The shrewd gray eyes looked these men through and through. He did not know to what infamy some of them would yet descend, but he was too good a judge of men, and knew this group well enough, not to be sure that every one of them would willingly adapt his beliefs to his profit. He had said over and over again that he meddled with no other man's conscience. And when they came back to the old question—why did he not speak out unequivocally against the statute, as it seemed that he was determined to die?—he, the saint standing before judges much worse than Pilate, had just one thing to say: "I have not been a man of such holy living as I might be bold to offer myself to death, lest God, for my presumption, might suffer me to fall."

As they got nothing out of him, on June 12th Sir Richard Rich arrived for an interview. He brought with him two men, one named Palmer and the other Sir Richard Southwell, who were there ostensibly to pack up his books, which were to be taken away, but, as the trial was to show, actually to be corroborative witnesses. That two days after this interview the examiners went back to see More makes it clear that what Rich had obtained was not regarded as of much weight, as it stood, and that they would prefer not to use perjury. It is, however, possible that Rich kept to himself the use he intended to make of the "evidence" he now possessed. Yet this seems hardly likely, for to do so would have been to risk astounding the Court upon which several of the examiners sat with the panel of judges. We must conclude that they were prepared to fall back upon perjury as a last resource, but that they hoped to lure More into employing some phrase, such as Fisher had trapped himself with, and convicting him upon that. As they failed in this, Rich's story had to be produced.

What actually happened on June 12th was this. Rich began, "Foreasmuch as it is well known, Master More, that you are a man both wise and well learned, as well in the laws of the realm as otherwise, I pray you therefore, sir, let me be so bold as of good will to put unto you this case. Admit that there were, sir, an act of Parliament and that all the realm should take me for King, would not you, Master More, take me for King?"

Without hesitation More returned, "Yes, sir, that would I."

"I put the case further," Rich went on, "that there were an act of Parliament that all the realm should take me for Pope, would you not then, Master More, take me for Pope?"

More now distinguished: "To your first case: the Parliament may well, Master Rich, meddle with the affairs of temporal princes. But to make answer to your other case, I will put you this case: suppose the Parliament would make a law that God should not be God. Would you then, Master Rich, say that God were not God?" To which of course Rich replied that Parliament did not have the power to make any such law.

So far so good; though one suspects that some of this may have been a bit touched up by Rich afterwards, it is no doubt substantially accurate and was accepted as such by Roper. But when Rich reported this conversation at the trial he added that More had gone on to say, "No more could Parliament make the King Supreme Head of the Church." It was what Rich had hoped to trick More into saying. It was what More did *not* say.

That is the only real scrap of evidence brought out at the trial on July 1st. Upon it Sir Thomas More was condemned to the death of a traitor.

The trial took place in Westminster Hall, where More had often sat as judge, where he had often been with King Henry VIII, and where he had sat covered with confusion hearing himself praised to his face by the Duke of Norfolk at the King's command on the day he took his oath as Lord Chancellor of England. Now for refusing another oath he was brought there as a prisoner, and among his judges was his friend the Duke of Norfolk. Previously

More had always insisted on standing before his examiners, though they had always asked him to be seated. This time he took the chair they offered, for he had become ill during his imprisonment. His hair was gray and he had grown a beard. Obviously he was now a sick old man. Sitting down, he studied the long indictment, unseen by him until then.

In his defence he made at the outset the point that the statute did not apply to him. He had never "maliciously" resisted the King's second marriage, and he contended that this word had precisely the same weight as the word "forcible" had in a charge of forcible entry. But he admitted that he had never concealed his opinion regarding the marriage from the King; indeed, had he done so, he would have been an unfaithful counsellor and subject. But as for having incurred any penalty under the act passed during his imprisonment, he had kept absolute silence. He added, "For this my silence neither your law nor any law in the world is able justly and rightly to punish me." When the prosecution answered that his silence was a demonstration of his malice, there came from More the reminder that a maxim of the Civil Law is that silence gives consent. His silence ought to be taken in that sense. He affirmed once more that he had never disclosed what was in his conscience "to any person living in all the world."

Now came Rich's chance. Lord Campbell writes that it was to the eternal disgrace of Rich, who as Solicitor General was conducting the prosecution, and to the eternal disgrace of the Court that permitted such an outrage on decency, that he left the bar and presented himself as a witness for the Crown. It would have been a disgraceful proceeding in any event; it was made a thousand times worse by the fact that Rich's testimony was perjured.

More made what was perhaps the most crushing answer ever given by a man accused of a crime. He turned to his judges—Audley the Chancellor, the Dukes of Norfolk and Suffolk, Lords Huntington, Cumberland, Wiltshire, Montague, Rochford and Windsor, with Cromwell, the real manager of the performance, and Fitzjames the Chief Justice of King's Bench, Baldwin, Chief

Justice of the Court of Common Pleas, Lister, Chief Baron of the Exchequer, and seven other Justices, Paulet, Porte, Spelman, Luke, Fitzwilliam and Fitzherbert. It was virtually the entire justiciary and the leading members of the Council. Addressing them he said: "If I were a man, my Lords, that did not regard an oath, I need not, as is well known, in this place, at this time, nor in this case, to stand here as an accused person. And if this oath of yours, Master Rich, be true, then pray I that I never see God in the face; which I would not say, were it otherwise, to win the world." After telling the Court what had really happened, he continued: "In good faith, Master Rich, I am [more] sorry for your perjury than for my own peril. And you shall understand that neither I, nor no man to my knowledge, ever took you to be a man of such credit as in any matter of importance, I, or any other, would at any time vouchsafe to communicate with you. And I, as you know, of no small while have been acquainted with you and your conversation, who have known you from your youth hitherto. For we long dwelled in one parish together, where, as yourself can tell (I am sorry to say) you were esteemed very light of your tongue, a great dicer, and of no commendable fame. And so in your house at the Temple, where hath been your chief bringing up, were you likewise accompted."

Such words could not have been used in this public fashion had their truth not been well known to those present. More asked his judges a single scornful question: "Can it seem likely unto your honourable Lordships that I would, in so weighty a cause, so inadvisedly overshoot myself as to trust Master Rich, a man by me always reputed for one of so little truth, as your Lordships have heard, so far above my sovereign Lord the King, or any of his noble councillors, that I would unto him utter the secrets of my conscience touching the King's supremacy . . . a thing I never did, nor never would, after the statute thereof made, reveal either to the King's Highness himself, or to any of his honourable Council. as is not unknown to your Honours, at sundry times sent from his

Grace unto the Tower unto me for none other purpose? Can this in your judgment, my Lords, seem likely to be true?"

Rich had to do something to try and establish his discredited testimony. He therefore put Southwell and Palmer into the box, counting upon them to bear out his perjury with their own. But though neither man was of good reputation—Southwell[3] had only with difficulty been cleared of a charge of murder—they quailed before the prisoner's candid eyes and muttered something about having been too busy trussing up Master More's books to have paid any attention to the conversation. They dared not back up More; but neither would they corroborate Rich's evidence.

The Court should never have allowed Rich, the prosecutor for the Crown, to go into the witness-box. But even supposing what he said had been true, the law required two witnesses in treason trials. As there was only one, on that ground alone Rich's evidence should have been thrown out. More had to be content with having scored a devastating point; he realised that it would be of no practical service to him.

Yet there was another attempt to show that More had discussed the question of the oath of supremacy. More admitted having corresponded with Fisher but insisted that the letters never bore on this issue. Regarding this, Fisher's servant, Wilson, and More's attendant John à Wood had already been examined, along with George Golde, a man employed by Walsingham. All that really came out was that small presents had been exchanged—a custard and some greensauce and the like. As for the letters, Golde had been asked to keep them to prove their innocence, but fearing Walsingham, he had decided that "there was no keeper better than fire." But though the letters were no longer there to be used as evidence by either side, it was argued that they must have contained matter of "conspiracy." Both Fisher and More had stressed the word "maliciously"; and each of them had made a similar

[3] Chambers points out in one of his historical notes to Dr. Hitchcock's edition of Harpsfield (p. 348) that as Southwell was still alive when Roper's *Life* and Harpsfield's *Life* were being written and circulated, the inclusion of his name is an additional guarantee, if one is needed, of the biographers' good faith.

point about having to choose between peril to the soul or peril to the body. It was the weakest kind of evidence, mere inference. More met it at his trial by remarking that any similarity in the arguments they had used "must have been from the agreement between us in opinion, but not because we ever arranged it between us." He insisted that he had always taken the position with Fisher "that I had informed my conscience, and so he also ought to do the same."

Nevertheless, on the basis of Rich's perjury and arbitrary deductions completely at variance with known facts, the jury found Sir Thomas More guilty. A quarter of an hour's deliberation sufficed for men who knew that only a verdict of guilty would satisfy the King.

The Lord Chancellor immediately started to give sentence. More, however, held up his hand and stopped him. "My Lord," he said, "when I was toward the law, the manner in such case was to ask the prisoner before judgment why judgment should not be given against him." Audley accepted the correction of his legal manners; he probably only wished to get an unpleasant duty finished as quickly as possible and had never supposed that More now intended to open his mind to the world.

To say what Sir Thomas More proceeded to say called for immense courage. He was well aware that his best chance for getting the merciful death of beheading instead of the hideous indignities of Tyburn was to accept his sentence gracefully. Cromwell five years later purchased the more honorable and far less painful death of decapitation by abjectly signing every question put to him, and then whining in a postscript, "Most gracious prince, I cry for mercy, mercy, mercy!" More's calm speech after condemnation was likely, as he knew, so to infuriate Henry as to get him not only Tyburn but Tyburn with specially protracted pangs. Yet he spoke out.

It was very plain speaking. He said, "It is not for this Supremacy so much that ye seek my blood, as that I would not condescend to the marriage." As to this the King had always known his views, but it could not be treason for one of his advisers to give him, upon request, honest advice. He told his judges that the indictment was based upon an act of Parliament repugnant to the laws of God and of His holy Church, of which no temporal prince could be the governor, even of a part. Its government belonged to the See of Rome, and was derived from Christ Himself when on earth. It was given "only to St. Peter and his successors."

He went on to affirm that the realm of England, "being but one member and small part of the Church, might not make a particular law disagreeable with the general law of Christ's universal Catholic Church, no more than the city of London, being but one poor member in respect to the whole realm, might make an act of Parliament to bind the whole realm." He quoted Magna Carta's declaration: *Quod ecclesia Anglicana libera sit, et habeat omnia jura sua integra et libertates suas illæsas,* reminding them that anything else was contrary to the oath every king took at his coronation. He reminded them also: "You, my Lords, the Peers of the realm, explicitly promised, and confirmed your promise with an oath, that you would maintain the rights of the Church inviolate." He added that "no more might this realm of England refuse obedience to the See of Rome than might the child refuse obedience to his own natural father."

When More had finished Audley curtly said that all the bishops—it *was* all by then, for Fisher had been executed—had agreed, along with the Universities and the "best learned" men of the realm, to the statute. Therefore he marvelled that More should so stiffly stick against it and argue so vehemently.

To this More replied that this was no reason why he should "change his conscience." His appeal was to Christendom as a whole, where "they be not the fewer part that be of my mind therein." And beyond the living he appealed to the dead, "of whom many now be holy saints in heaven." Therefore, he concluded, "I am not bound, my Lords, to conform my conscience to the Council of one realm against the general council of Christendom."

Audley attempted no rejoiner. Instead he turned to the Lord

Chief Justice, Sir John Fitzjames, to ask whether the indictment was sufficient or not. To which Fitzjames, "like a wise man," says Roper sarcastically, swore his customary oath by St. Julian and made the sagacious decision that if the act of Parliament was not unlawful then the indictment was good. Which of course begged the whole question.

After this the Lord Chancellor asked More whether he had anything else to say. Yes, he had just one more thing, and it was said with the most extraordinary courtesy. St. Paul, he told his judges, had consented to the stoning of St. Stephen, "and yet be they both twain holy saints in heaven. . . . So I verily trust, and shall therefore right heartily pray, that though your Lordships have now on earth been my judges to my condemnation, we may yet hereafter in Heaven merrily all meet together, to our everlasting salvation."[4]

There was an uneasy silence after More had done. His judges must all have been conscious of having done a monstrous wrong to the greatest and noblest man in England, and the most loyal of all the King's servants. He bowed to them, and they watched him go slowly down Westminster Hall, among the halberdiers and with the edge of the axe turned towards him. Then there was a shuffling of papers and some forced talk and laughter by which they tried to call themselves back to ordinary concerns.

Sir William Kingston, the Constable of the Tower, a tall and handsome man and a close friend of More's, had him in charge. Kingston was so overcome that the tears were running down his cheeks. Afterwards he told Roper, "I was ashamed of myself that, at my departing from your father, I found my heart so feeble, and his so strong, that he was fain to comfort me, which should rather have comforted him." Within twelve months it was he who had to assure the hysterically laughing Anne Boleyn that she would not feel the stroke of the swordsman brought over from Calais.

[4] Most of the above comes from Roper who, though he was not himself present at the trial, was furnished full reports by those who were, among whom he mentions Sir Anthony Saint Leger, Richard Heywood and John Webbe. A few other details are taken from the other contemporary lives.

"It is so subtle," he told her. In all his life he was never so deeply moved as when he led Sir Thomas More away.

The Constable said farewell to his prisoner at the Old Swan, from which point More could see St. Anthony's, where fifty years before he had begun his schooling. There More said to him, "Good Master Kingston, trouble not yourself, but be of good cheer, for I will pray for you and my good lady your wife, that we may meet in heaven together, where we shall be merry for ever and ever."

At the Tower wharf Margaret Roper was waiting for her father. One may suppose that her husband was with her, though as to this Roper is silent. It would account for his not having been present at Westminster Hall. Nothing could be more vivid than his account of the last meeting between Sir Thomas More and Margaret. "As soon as she saw him," he writes, "after his blessing on her knees reverently received, she hasting towards him, and without consideration or care of herself [she was with child], pressing in among the middest of the throng and company of the guard that with halberds and bills went round about him, hastily ran to him, and there openly, in the sight of them all, embraced him, took him about the neck, and kissed him. Who, well liking her dear daughterly affection toward him, gave her his fatherly blessing and many goodly words of comfort besides. From whom after she was departed, she, not satisfied with the former sight of him, and like one that had forgotten herself, being all ravished with the entire love of her dear father, having respect neither to herself, nor the press of the people and multitude that were about him, suddenly turned back again, ran to him as before, took him about the neck, and divers times together most lovingly kissed him; and at last, with a full heavy heart, was fain to depart from him: the beholding thereof was to many of them that were present thereat so lamentable that it made them for very sorrow thereof mourn and weep."

CHAPTER NINETEEN

The Scaffold

As was customary at that time, no date for the execution was set when sentence was passed; this was something left to the discretion of the King, and it could be deferred almost indefinitely. Then the condemned man was told, usually on the morning when he was to meet death, to get ready. But More, in a letter that he wrote to Margaret on July 5th, said that he expected to be executed the following day. With this letter he sent her his hair-shirt and his scourge.

He told Margaret that July 6th was a day "very meet and convenient" to him, as it was the eve of the feast of St. Thomas of Canterbury. It was also the octave day of St. Peter. As Sir Thomas More was laying down his life to affirm his belief in the Supremacy of the Pope, no day could have been more appropriate than this—especially as it coincided with the commemoration of the great Thomas à Becket who was murdered for having dared to oppose an earlier English King who sought to tyrannize over the English Church.

More had come to his clear conviction regarding the authority of the Holy See relatively late in life—some time after 1521, when Henry VIII's book against Luther was published. The reading of that book had made him study a question which until then he had not thought much about. His friend Bonvisi, the rich Italian merchant, reported to Cardinal Pole a conversation he had had with More. "Alas, Mr. Bonvisi," More had said, "whither was I falling. . . . *That* holdeth all up." Once More had reached conviction on this point, he was unfaltering.

His attitude had so enraged the King because to Henry it seemed a bit of mere obstinacy that could only be interpreted as personal illwill. It involved not only a refusal to recognize the lawfulness of his marriage to Anne Boleyn but appeared to cast a reflection upon his orthodoxy. This was something upon which he specially prided himself. When the Pilgrimage of Grace occurred the following year, provoked by the looting of the monasteries, Henry was genuinely hurt, not only by the rebellion itself but because the rebels had failed to see, as he told the deputies who presented their grievances, that it was far better "to relieve the head of the Church in his [financial] necessities, than to support the sloth and wickedness of the monks." Henry Tudor's egotism was so immense as to give him a kind of innocence.

The King did, however, mitigate the sentence that Audley had imposed that of hanging, drawing and quartering, with the bowels and heart ripped out of the victim while he was still alive—to one of simple beheading. This was customary in the case of very great nobles, though only to them; and More was merely a knight, in spite of having been the Lord Chancellor. He had not counted upon this mercy, and he was grateful for it.

Sir Thomas Pope, who came with this message from Henry, said, when More asked him to convey to his Grace a request that Margaret might be present at his burial, that the King had already granted this privilege to More's kindred and friends. This presumably indicates that there was some admiration in Henry's mind for the constancy of his victim. There would even seem to have been some affection, for Stapleton says that when the King was told that the execution had taken place, he turned on Anne Boleyn and said bitterly. "You are the cause of that man's death." Henry was already very tired of her.

At parting with More Sir Thomas Pope could not hold back his tears. But if he conveyed a favor from the King, he had also a favor to ask. The King wished that Master More should not make a long speech on the scaffold. Henry knew of his eloquence, and no doubt he had heard of the impression More had made at his trial. He could not risk a repetition of this.

More asked Pope to thank the King and said that he was glad of the warning about the speech, as he had prepared one, though it contained nothing "wherewith his Grace, or any other, should be offended." Especially, he said, he was grateful to the King for all the honors and benefits bestowed upon him in the past, but most of all "bounden am I to his Grace for putting me into this place, where I have had convenient time and space to have remembrance of mine end." Also because "it pleaseth him so shortly to rid me of the miseries of this wretched world, and therefore I will not fail earnestly to pray for his Grace, both here, and also in another world." The King, however, apparently did not allow a priest to attend him. The last time More had heard Mass or made his confession or received Holy Communion was on April 13, 1534, the day of his arrest.

He dressed for the occasion in a fine silk camlet gown Bonvisi had sent him. But when Sir Edmund Walsingham arrived soon after eight, he suggested that More take it off, as this would be one of the perquisites of the headsman, and he, said Walsingham, was only a "javill" or no-account fellow. More protested that nobody should be considered a javill who would that day do him so great a service; nevertheless, with his usual good-humored reasonableness, he put on old clothes and contented himself with sending the executioner a gold coin.

When he went out to Tower Hill, passing under the gateway of the Middle Tower, he could see the little church of St. Peter's ad Vincula in which his headless body was to lie beside Fisher's, with those of Anne Boleyn and her brother to join them the following year, and Cromwell's a little later.[1] People noticed how old he looked, though he was only fifty-seven, and how frail. The long beard he had grown in his imprisonment was quite gray. In his hand he was carrying a red cross.

On that short walk a compassionate woman offered him a drink of wine. Chambers thinks that this may have been Mrs. Clement, whom we know to have been present. If so, surely we would have

[1] His head, after being exposed on London Bridge, was obtained by Margaret Roper, who embalmed it and kept it until she died in 1544. It is supposed to have been buried at the Roper vault in St. Dunstan's, Canterbury.

heard her name. In any event, More refused the cup, saying, "My Master had easell and gall, not wine, given Him to drink." Another woman screamed at him, "Do you remember, Master More, that when you were Chancellor, you were my hard friend, and did me great injury in giving wrong judgment against me?" He stopped a moment and said with gentle sternness, "Woman, I am now going to my death. I remember well the whole matter; if I were to give sentence again, I assure thee I would not alter it. Thou hast no injury, so content thee, and trouble me not."

Another little incident occurred. It is mentioned by both Stapleton and the unsympathetic chronicler, Edward Hall; and it was used in the Elizabethan play, *Sir Thomas More.* But where the prose account tells only of a rough demand by a woman for some papers of hers that More had had, in the poetry of the play it becomes a quiet request answered with quiet regret:

"What, my old client, art thou hither too?
Poor silly wretch, I must confess indeed,
I had such writings as concern thee near,
But the King has ta'en the matter into his own hand,
He has all I had. Then, woman, sue to him."

To which she returns:

"Ah, gentle heart, my soul for thee is sad,
Farewell, the best friend that the poor e'er had."

Stapleton tells another story, which may be found also in the writer known only as "Ro.Ba." It is of an unnamed Winchester man who, when More was still at liberty, had confided to him his temptation to despair. More had given him good counsel and promised to pray for him, but after the imprisonment his temptation returned stronger than ever. As soon as he heard that Sir Thomas had been condemned he hastened to London, and that morning of July 6th thrust through the throng and said, "Master More, do you know me? I pray you, for Our Lord's sake, help me: I am as ill troubled as ever I was." To this Sir Thomas answered: "I remember thee full well. Go thy ways in peace, and pray for me: and I will not fail to pray for thee." Never again was the Winchester man assailed by despair.

This man and Margaret Clement were among those who saw Sir Thomas More mount the scaffold. As it was so flimsily built that it looked as though it might fall, More turned to Walsingham and said, "I pray you, Master Lieutenant, see me safe up, and for my coming down let me shift for myself."

Then he stood as erect as he could and, as the very circumstantial Paris News Letter gives the report of his brief speech, "asked the bystanders to pray for him in this world, and he would pray for them elsewhere." (This was probably said for the benefit of the Winchester man of whom More caught sight in the crowd.) "He then begged them earnestly to pray for the King, that it might please God to give him good counsel, protesting that he died the King's good servant but God's first." Neither Roper nor Stapleton quote that last phrase,[2] but it rings true. It was also extremely witty, for it contained an allusion (of which the writer of the News Letter would have been ignorant) to King Henry's admonition to More when he first took office under the Crown, which Roper cites as "the most virtuous lesson that ever prince taught his servant, willing him first to look unto God, and after God to him." Roper and Stapleton—who here shows that he is using Roper's notes—tell of More's asking those present "to bear witness with him that he died in and for the faith of the holy Catholic Church."

He then knelt down and said some prayers. After this he kissed the executioner, who had knelt and made the customary request for forgiveness. The headsman must have been shaking with nervousness, because More told him, "Pluck up thy spirits man, and be not afraid to do thy office; my neck is very short; take heed therefore that thou strike not awry, for saving of thy honesty." There was good reason for the remark; executioners did sometimes badly bungle their job. Cromwell, of whose counsel to the King More had cause for fear, was frightfully mangled when he died at that spot five years later.

[2] Stapleton comes very close to it, though.

When the executioner offered to blindfold him, More said that he would do this himself. But after he had stretched his head over the low block—it was merely a log of wood—he made a signal to the man to wait a moment. Then he made his last joke: his beard was lying on the block; he would like to remove it. At least *that* had committed no treason.

The heavy axe went slowly up, hung a moment in the air, and fell.

Index